# What's Happening To Labor

## by Gil Green

**INTERNATIONAL PUBLISHERS New York**

© 1976 by International Publishers Co., Inc.
All rights reserved
Second Printing, 1977    209
Printed in the United States of America

Library of Congress Cataloging in Publication Data

Green , Gilbert.
    What's happening to labor.

    Includes bibliographical references and index.
    1. Trade-unions—United States.  2. Labor and
laboring classes—United States. I. Title.
HD6508.G74      301.44'42'0973     76-14861
ISBN 0-7178-0465-8
ISBN 0-7178-0464-X pbk.

# CONTENTS

# ACKNOWLEDGMENTS

I AM greatly indebted to the many individuals who made this book possible. More than two score labor activists, most of them men and women employed in diverse industries and occupations across the land, gave generously of their time to read the lengthy manuscript and to send me their impressions and criticisms.

I am particularly grateful to David Englestein with whom I discussed—by mail—each section of the book as it evolved. Other friends whose judgment I value, also submitted the draft to careful critical scrutiny. While each of these left his or her mark on the final product, none may agree with the final text in its entirety. Only I, therefore, bear responsibility for whatever errors and shortcomings the book may contain.

I am further indebted to friends who helped in the research, in checking the numerous references, or in making suggestions relating to structure, content, style and grammar. I am likewise grateful to the Louis M. Rabinowitz Foundation for a grant when the work on this book first began more than three years ago.

Above all, this book would not have been possible without the loving patience, understanding and concern of my wife, Helen, and without her active participation as relentless critic. Every page bears evidence of her solicitous intervention.

*H*

*To*

# INTRODUCTION

THE YEARS since World War II have been far from tranquil. They were marked by worldwide turbulence and revolutionary change. A score of new countries took the path of socialist revolution, and the old colonial system crumbled under the blows of oppressed peoples.

In the United States, too, crisis followed crisis. Cold-war tensions led to hot-war involvement in Korea and later to the longest war in U.S. history, in Vietnam and Indochina. The oppression of racial minorities at home gave rise to powerful movements for equality and rights, while increasing poverty and police brutality induced waves of ghetto and barrio upheavals. It was a time, too, when a young generation rebelled against the war in Indochina and the hypocrisy and deception in American society.

But the post-World War II period was also one of relative economic growth and prosperity for U.S. capitalism. Depressions were generally milder and of shorter duration than in pre-war years. Strikes were numerous, but not the do-or-die battles of earlier times. Nor was organized labor the militant force it had been in the thirties. Hence, by the mid-fifties the illusion took hold that American capitalism had succeeded in subduing the boom-bust cycle, and that the class struggle, although still with us, was tamed, anemic and safely institutionalized. It seemed that Marx had been proven wrong about modern capitalism and that government intervention in the economy and large-scale deficit spending—particularly for armaments and war*—had ironed out the kinks in the capitalist economic system.

The phrase "end of ideology," coined by the Columbia University sociologist Daniel Bell, in a book by that name which appeared in 1960, epitomized the moment.[2] Bell did not mean an end to all ideology, only the ideology which challenged the capitalist status quo and pointed to the need for a radical reconstruction of society. After all, who needed the revolutionary ideology of Marxism when capitalism had learned to square the economic circle?

Not all agreed with Bell, but a surprising number of intelligent people accepted his view that the class struggle was ebbing; the ancient war between capital and labor was ending. Some intellectuals discovered Karl Marx's early writings on alienation and latched on to these as the "true Marxism" they were seeking. The young Marx, "the philosopher," was pitted against the older Marx, "the economist."

The psychoanalyst Erich Fromm reprinted sections of Marx's *Economic and Philosophical Manuscripts of 1844* with an introduction by Fromm himself.[3] But there was an omission. The sections dealing with alienation were reproduced, but those stressing the class struggle were eliminated. In this way an incomplete version of the *Manuscripts* was used against the Marx who wrote *Capital* two decades later. Marx's theory of surplus value, with its concomitant exploitation and class struggle, was thus replaced as the rock upon which his fully developed economic analysis of capitalist society rested. Alienation was substituted in its place.

There are valid reasons, of course, for serious concern about alienation. Never have people been more estranged from the objects of their labor and the society which produces them. Craftworkers of the past took great pride in their skill and its finished product. It was creative, part of them. But most workers today have little to say about the jobs they do. They work to earn a living, not to create. The tools they once deftly manipulated are now monstrous machines manipulating them. The stress on alienation is therefore understandable.

But its substitution for exploitation cannot be separated from the fact that exploitation presupposes the existence of exploiters, while alienation

---

* From 1948 to 1956, so-called defense spending increased by 22.4 percent per annum, compared with a yearly increase of only 3.1 percent in private domestic investment.[1]

does not. "Alienation" is a far vaguer, less easily defined concept—a feeling of estrangement from one's work or other aspects of social existence. "Alienation has supplanted exploitation as a key criticism of industrial society," notes one writer, but, he adds, "Unfortunately, the concept of alienation is murky and spongy, frequently employed to embrace any attitude and behavior that a critic dislikes."[4]

In the *New York Times* of June 3, 1973, an article under the heading, "The Failure of the Successful," reported the results of a survey of 2,800 "business and corporation executives." It showed that job alienation "has not merely spread to, but may even thrive in, the managerial suites of American business." "The executive," it claims, "may be as dissatisfied as the men who work for him." The writer notes that while giant corporations are experimenting with methods to alleviate worker alienation, "The symptoms and possible cures for executive malaise are more elusive."[5] Thus, Wall Street, too, suffers from alienation—and in even more acute forms!

How one undertakes to cope with alienation depends, therefore, on the perception of the cause. If it is seen as a product of class society and class exploitation, it is a powerful inducement to struggle for social change. But if it is seen as arising from some inherent antagonism between the individual and society, or the individual and industrial society, then it leads to a blind alley—to individualistic attempts at "escape" by means of idyllic pastoral communes, religious mysticism, or drug culture.

DANIEL BELL did not agree with those who used the concept of alienation as a means "to cling to the symbol of Marx." He wanted no part of Marx, young or old, symbol or otherwise. According to him, the early Marx was "not the *historical* Marx. The historical Marx had, in effect, repudiated the idea of alienation." [emphasis in original—GG][6] One need but read *Capital,* Vol. 1 (1867), to see that Marx never abandoned his views on alienation. What he did was to ground them more firmly into his theory of exploitation. For Marx, the appropriation of a person's mental and physical capacities to create, as well as the fruits of this labor, by someone else, is the root cause of alienation as it is of exploitation.

C. Wright Mills, the radical sociologist, rejected the view that ideology had come to an end. Nor did he make the error of pitting the young Marx against the mature one. Yet he, too, was influenced by the atmosphere of the time. In the very book in which he came to terms with Marxism, declaring it to be the only solid foundation for the science of human society, Mills expressed doubts about Marx's theory of exploitation and class struggle. Marx, he believed, had become the victim of his own dialectics; he was guilty of what Mills termed "a labor metaphysics." Marx's conclusion that exploitation is built into the capitalist system, Mills characterized as a "moral judgment, disguised as an economic statement."[7]

Thus, even this most seminal of American sociologists, a man who made impressive contributions to postwar radical thought, who took his place at the side of socialism and embraced the Cuban revolution as his very own, could not transcend the limitations of personal experience and the state of things at the time.

Mills placed his hope for change on intellectuals and the university community. These, he urged, should take bold issue with the cold war and its know-nothing intellectual climate and should challenge head-on the notion of an end to ideology. The New Left he called for did come into being, although he did not live to see it reach fruition.

Within the limitation of the time and its own class origins, the New Left played a noteworthy role. It rekindled the flames of radicalism by attacking the system on its vulnerable moral side, enlisted in the battle for civil rights in the South, and participated significantly in the fight against the Vietnam War.

The New Left accepted Mills' assessment of the working class. To think otherwise seemed to fly in the face of reality as they experienced it. Coming largely from well-to-do families, or at least those somewhat better off, the New Left readily succumbed to Herbert Marcuse's view that advanced capitalism had transformed the working class into a conservative force. It agreed with him that capitalism was now capable of providing material well-being for workers "in a way which generates submission and weakens the rationality of protest."[8] It, too, believed that the only hope for change—although at times Marcuse was not too sure there was any hope—lay with non-working class sections of the population.

Hence the view arose that Marx was right about the working class of his day, but wrong about the modern working class. Just as present-day workers were seen as all conservative, those of a century ago were seen as all revolutionary. But had they read Marx more carefully they would have come to quite other conclusions.

Marx was not a notebook-in-hand sociologist who recorded the thinking of the moment and from this drew straightline projections into the future. To the contrary, he stressed that it was not a matter of what workers thought at any given moment, but what historical circumstances would compel them to do. In their book *The Holy Family,* Karl Marx and Frederick Engels stated:

> It is not a question of what this or that proletarian, or even the proletariat as a whole, may imagine for the moment to be the aim. It is a question of what the proletariat actually is and what it will be compelled to do historically as the result of this being.[9]

Marx distinguished between what he called "a class in itself" and "a class for itself," that is, between a class existing in a historically defined system of social production but not yet fully conscious of its place in history and its own class interests and goals, and a class that has already achieved such consciousness.

On numerous occasions Marx and Engels found it necessary to criticize the workers of one or another country, and their movements, for succumbing to the ideology of the bourgeoisie. They were most critical of the working class of their own adopted land, England. They accused it of "becoming more and more bourgeois" and, in 1890, Engels referred to the forty years' "long winter sleep" of the British working class.[10]

Yet during this long stretch of time, and despite innumerable disappointments, Marx and Engels never departed from their basic analysis. The working class remained for them the most revolutionary class in modern society. This estimate had nothing to do with mythology or labor metaphysics. It had everything to do with a scientific analysis of the inner dynamics of capitalist society. Capitalist production, they noted, was becoming ever more social in character, but ownership and accumulation were concentrated in ever fewer hands. This was a contradiction that capitalism could not resolve. It would necessarily lead to a growing antagonism between the many and the few, between those who owned the productive wealth of society and those who labored for them. The ensuing protracted and deepening crisis could only be overcome when society itself took possession of the productive forces and made them serve the interests of the great majority instead of the enrichment of the few. The crisis would endure until the workers, the great producing class of society, became the conscious revolutionary gravediggers of capitalism.

The radical, Left-minded young people of the thirties had no difficulty grasping this analysis and accepting its premise and conclusions. True, the workers of that day were neither revolutionary nor socialist-minded in their mass. Yet the depths of the crisis were so obvious that no one could possibly believe in an end to ideology. And there was little doubt that the working class was the battering ram for social change.

This consciousness was reinforced daily by the tumultuous struggles of the time—the pitched battles of the jobless; the dramatic Hunger Marches; the militant strike waves and general strikes; the General Motors sit-ins that broke the corporate empire's resistance to industrial unionism; the scores of working-class martyrs; the fiery class rhetoric—all reinforced the conviction that the workers were in the lead and would remain there.

What happened after World War II rapidly tarnished this image. The Congress of Industrial Organizations (CIO), born out of the pain and agony of the thirties as a fighting rejoinder to the sclerosis-ridden American Federation of Labor (AFL), also yielded to the blandishments and allurements of class-partnership policies. It joined the cold-war and anti-Communist witch hunt and purged its ranks of those who had contributed the most to making the CIO a militant, fighting organization. "Much of the effective and democratic leadership in the labor movement was either ousted or muzzled."[11]

## A Reactionary Labor Leadership

The CIO lost its sense of mission and *esprit de corps*. By 1955, the difference between it and the old AFL had become so minimal that a reunited federation became possible. It was a marriage of convenience that proved barren. Instead of the promised growth, bureaucratic stagnation became the normal and permanent order of things. On critical issues of policy, particularly those related to foreign affairs, the official position of organized labor was not too different from that of the ruling establishment. On the issue of cold war, the Korean and Vietnam hot wars, as on the question of military expenditures, the top officialdom was on the right of the political spectrum. It was not conservative but outright reactionary.

In this way labor leaders, too, joined the chorus of those crooning an end to ideology. Philip Murray, then president of the CIO, declared "We have no classes in this country. We are all workers here."[12] Somewhat later, George Meany reiterated the same profound observation. Neither bothered to explain, however, why, if this was so, they were still collecting dues from workers in the labor movement.

Murray and Meany were always defenders of what those who find it hard to pronounce the word capitalism euphemistically call "the free enterprise system." But Walter Reuther, the president of the United Auto Workers, knew better. He was born and raised in an old socialist family, for years had been an active member of the Socialist Party, and on many occasions had publicly advocated socialism. What he said during the cold-war fifties is a barometer of the conservative change that had occurred.

Addressing a conference on "The Challenge of Automation" in 1955, Reuther took the occasion to give the Communists their lumps. Referring to the Communist view of an on-going class struggle in the United States, Reuther said, "I believe the Communists are wrong. We can prove it, not by pious declarations, but by working together, free labor and free management, free people, free government and free society, finding the answers to our basic problems."[13]

This was Reuther's pious declaration to end pious declarations. It was as if his repetition of the word "free" would really make things so. He could have added, and with equal justification, "free poverty," "free racism," and "free monopoly."

The glue that made all this stick, that made it plausible, was the relative prosperity of the time. For many this was more fictitious than real, yet for the majority the system seemed to be working. The generally expected postwar economic plunge had not taken place. Unemployment, high compared with other developed capitalist countries, was nonetheless kept within bounds. Its effects were felt mainly by the racial minorities, the young, the women, and the unskilled on marginal and seasonal jobs. The effects were felt less by skilled workers and those on steady jobs with long seniority. Most workers objected to the superrich hogging most of the gravy for themselves, but were ready to accept such gluttony if they, too, shared in "some part of the action."* Especially when there was hope and promise of still more to come.

It appeared to many of those who were "making it" that those who were not had only themselves to blame. They were too lazy, did not work hard enough, left school too soon, were not smart enough, or what have you. Even those who did not really believe such nonsense still *wanted* to believe it. It provided self-justification. The racial prejudice which pervades American society made it easier to shift responsibility from the

---

* It is estimated that from 1948 to 1965 real take-home pay for factory workers rose by 2.1 percent a year.[14]

social system to the racial minorities; to blame the poor for their poverty. The governing ideology of individualism also made it easier to believe that those who were better off were the more deserving of it.

It is in this setting that the viewpoint took root that the workers were now "part of the establishment," and that the organized labor movement was and would remain hopelessly conservative. But change is ever constant. To think it has come to an end is to forget that every end is but a new beginning. Just as changing conditions had influenced the thinking of workers and the policies and leadership of the labor movement up to now, newer changes under way, and still others to come, will likewise leave their mark.

Beneath the superficial surface of things, change continues—in the size and make-up of the working class, in racial, sex, ethnic, and age relations among workers, in the newer forms of capital concentration and exploitation and their new kinds of resultant problems; in the organizational structure and internal dynamics of the labor movement; and in the rise of new militant forces within it.

Above all, the entire world capitalist system is in a deepening crisis of general decline, and this is particularly true of U.S. capitalism. It is bound to affect class relations and the class struggle profoundly.

From World War II to the present, U.S. capitalism has been engaged in a futile attempt to halt the tide of world revolutionary change—to prevent peoples from breaking their oppressive imperialist chains. This was the meaning of the long, costly, barbarous Vietnam War. In the name of "national security" and anticommunism, the United States has supported military-fascist puppet regimes abroad; spent over $1.5 trillion dollars since World War II on the military; built hundreds of military bases on foreign soil; enabled the CIA and FBI to grow into monstrous police-state agencies; participated in plots to subvert foreign governments and assassinate their leaders; and enabled the Presidency to usurp autocratic powers.

By means of special tax inducements, the government has encouraged the export of vast sums of private capital, instead of compelling this capital—produced by the labor of American workers—to be reinvested in needed, even if less profitable, enterprises at home. Gargantuan multinational corporations were thus spawned, and hundreds of thousands of jobs lost to American workers.

In addition to huge military spending, government expenditures in the national economy also went to serve corporate interests, not the people. About 20 percent of federal, state and local government spending went into highway and road construction, to the direct benefit of the auto and oil monopolies. Even federal aid for depressed Appalachia went 80 percent for highway construction.[15]

The immense wastage of the nation's human and material resources has now come home to roost. It has resulted in growing inflation and unemployment; in urban squalor and decay, in a growing crisis in housing, health, public transit, education, air and water pollution, and in public services generally.

## End of an Era

In many ways we have come to the end of one postwar era and to the beginning of another, quite different one. The conditions of general economic expansion that characterized much of capitalist postwar development are now largely over. Problems of growing unemployment and inflation confront all countries. Only the socialist bloc of nations is exempt from these, with unemployment nonexistent, prices stable, and living and cultural standards steadily advancing.

No one knows exactly what lies ahead; much depends on human action. But the general contours are discernible. A period of relative "good times" for many is giving way to one of hard times for most. Even when the production curve is upward again, things will not return to "normal." Stagnation and inflation will still be with us. Keynes' great cure-all for depression—government deficit spending—is a remedy which has produced its own perilous side effects. To increase the public debt further is to give another whirl to the inflation spiral. Thus, many branches of government are cutting back expenditures despite the need for increased public services.

Other factors that fed the long period of economic expansion are also largely spent. The revolution in science and technology stimulated investment in new industries and in the modernization of old ones. This enabled more to be produced with ever fewer workers. The great increase in government and service employment helped absorb many workers no longer needed in goods-producing industries. But now this, too, is being cut back. In fact, the Establishment's leading economists look upon continued mass unemployment as a necessary evil—a desirable antidote to uncontrolled inflation. Hence, the general trend in living standards is now down, and the percentage of people living in poverty increasing.*

The huge migration of U.S. capital abroad greatly spurred the export of American technology. But this, too, is now a negative force, since plants in other countries successfully compete with their counterparts here. The emergence of nearly 100 newly independent states at varying levels of economic development was a stimulant to world trade. But wild inflation, especially for industrial goods, has hit these countries the hardest, with the exception of a few major oil producing nations. The underdeveloped countries have all they can do to maintain their present level of purchases in capitalist markets, let alone increase them.

Nor is the United States the dominant economic power in the capitalist world that it was when World War II ended. It is being pressed hard by capitalist competitors, holding its edge primarily in military and agricultural exports. And, as Cuba and Vietnam showed, the United States is no longer able to prevent smaller nations from winning their freedom, where they are determined to do so and are united around firm revolutionary leadership.

Faced with this situation, U.S. capital seeks to shift the burden of crisis to the backs of the American people. There is a deliberate effort to lower living standards through greatly intensifying labor productivity, holding down wages, and slashing government expenditures for welfare and social benefits. The corporations see increased unemployment as giving them the upper hand in the labor market, believing that this will reduce workers' resistance to increased speed-up on the job. Even the rhetoric about ending work alienation—so fashionable a few years ago—is now largely disappearing. Workers are being told that if they are dissatisfied there are others waiting to take their places.

All this adds up to a sharpening of class struggle on a scale not witnessed since the thirties. As most economic issues are also linked to governmental policies, the struggle is bound to spill over into the political arena. World labor history has shown that whenever the demand for labor is greater than the supply, or approximately even, workers will resort to economic trade union action as their prime weapon. But when the demand for jobs is vastly greater than the supply, workers are compelled to augment their economic leverage by greater concerted political action.

---

*According to the Bureau of the Census, 1.3 million Americans were added to the nation's poor people in 1974, and real income for American families fell 4 percent below 1973 levels.

IN THIS situation it is extremely important to know more about the changes that have occurred in the working-class and labor movement since the big war, their meaning, and the dynamics of change at work now. A new labor upsurge is inevitable. But that this will bring with it a labor movement greatly different from the present one is not inevitable. Much depends upon a clearer perception of what went wrong, why, and what labor should do to avoid similar pitfalls in the future

Organized labor is the strongest movement of common people in this country. Although a somewhat smaller proportion of wage- and salaried-workers are in unions, as compared with the forties and fifties, a large percentage of workers in the basic production industries, and in transport, communication, construction and mining, are in unions. The existence of a stable movement of more than 20 million organized workers is a potentially powerful force. What it does, how it perceives its role, what kind of leadership it has, will greatly determine the period ahead, whether progressive or reactionary.

As often occurs in history, opportunity and danger appear in the arena together, invariably engaged in mortal combat. The country can either move in harmony with the needs of its people and with the great progressive and revolutionary developments in the rest of the world, or move in conflict with them—thus opening the door to the danger of fascism and new wars, and crushing the democratic hopes and aspirations of the American people.

What happens to this country depends greatly upon what happens to organized labor.

# part
# ONE

---

## 1 : THE CHANGING CLASS

---

IT IS generally acknowledged that the working class of the thirties was extremely militant, but that this militancy ebbed in later years. The CIO, born as a new kind of labor movement, retrogressed into a virtual industrial-union replica of the old and stodgy AFL.

One factor influencing this metamorphosis was the change that occurred in the size and make-up of the working class. In 1938, a year before World War II, the total number of gainfully employed persons was 43 million. By 1944, the last full year of the war, it had expanded to 63 million,[1] with a 62 percent rise in manufacturing employment.[2] Many of these additional workers came from the ranks of the unemployed, but many came also from farms or small towns, women came from their homes, youth from schools, and Black and Spanish-speaking people from the cotton fields of the South and the peasantry of Mexico and Puerto Rico.

Some unemployment persisted, especially in nonindustrial areas and in the ghettos and barrios, but was so reduced that it actually disappeared as a statistical entry in Department of Labor figures. In 1938 there were still close to 10 million listed as jobless; by 1944 there were 7 million more on jobs than the Department of Labor listed as in the total labor force.[3] Two facts explain this. When work is scarce, government labor force estimates shrink and many get listed instead as "housewives," "students," or "unemployables." But when work opportunities increase, many enter the labor market who were not there before. In 1944, for example, 35 percent of the female population was listed as in the labor force. In 1947, with the war over, it had fallen to 28.9 percent.[4] Also, when employment is high more jobs are filled than the actual number of workers employed, as millions "moonlight" on more than one job.

A radical shift also took place within the employed labor force. The 11 million in the armed forces in 1944 did not come from the unemployed or the new entrants into the labor force alone. Many came from industry, and a majority from the working class. Young workers in nondefense plants, or on less than critical jobs in defense industries, were drafted in large numbers. Then, numerous anti-fascist and class-conscious workers enlisted. Their places were taken in union ranks by workers without the same backgrounds of militant struggle. A considerable internal migration also took place—from agriculture to industry, from regions of light industry, lower pay and labor surplus, to centers of heavy industry, higher pay and labor shortage.

Hence, by the end of the war the working class had been greatly altered in size, composition and geographic location. The same was true of the labor movement. It was during the war that the CIO completed the unionization of the auto and steel industries, as Ford and "Little Steel" complied with the rest. Thus, in the course of the war some six million new members were added to union rolls, a million more than in the period of intense labor turmoil from 1934 to 1939.[5]

These changes were accompanied by a certain alteration in outlook. Although a number of bitter industrial battles were fought during the war, the majority of the newly organized came into the unions under somewhat different conditions. With the law of supply and demand favoring the workers in the sale of their labor power, and with the war effort demanding maximum production, the die-hard corporation opposition to unionism tended to soften. In addition, the war brought steady employment and relative prosperity. The insatiable appetite of the war machine was seen by many workers as an economic blessing in disguise. The wholesale death and destruction wrought by the war was a tragedy happening elsewhere, not here.

All this left its mark on the working class and labor movements, by now no longer what they had been during the bitter thirties.

THE process of change did not halt with the ending of the war. A heightened process of capital concentration (monopolization), and the revolution in science and technology, became the main stimulants toward further change. In 1947, according to the Department of Labor, 19 percent of the total labor force was self-employed. By 1974, this had dropped to less than 9 percent.[6] Black, brown and native Indian people had the lowest percentage of all—only 2½ percent were self-employed.[7]

In other words, roughly 90 percent of those who work or seek work, whether in agriculture, industry or services, are wage or salary employees. This is a fact of enormous significance. The American people have long since ceased to be small independent producers, merchants or professionals. They now work for somebody else, whether corporation, individual employer, private institution, or government. The doctor's shingle and the small family-run neighborhood store are still with us, yet they make up a tiny and dwindling minority; the overwhelming majority work for someone else.

The most dramatic change of all took place in agriculture. In 1940, 23 percent of the population was still on the farm. By 1970, it was less than 4 percent, representing a great internal migration.[8] More than 22 million human beings were uprooted from the soil from 1945 to 1972, compelled to move to urban areas.[9]

Black people were affected by this migration even more than white. The 1930 census showed a majority of Black people still living on the land.[10] The 1970 census showed 81 percent of Black people living in urban communities, with 78 percent in central cities. The white popula-

---

* In all likelihood the urban percentage of Black people is even higher. The Census Bureau has admitted that as many as five million people were "missed" in its 1970 tabulation, many of them Black. Most of these were in overcrowded, teeming ghettos where an accurate count is more difficult than in rural communities.

tion, in comparison, was 73 percent urban, with only 64 percent living in central cities.[11]

The technological revolution in agriculture was the main factor forcing people off the land. By 1972, technological advances made it possible for an average farm worker—whether self-employed or working for wages—to produce enough food to feed more than 50 people.[12] There are gigantic factory farms covering thousands of acres where an average worker can produce enough to feed as many as 100 people. Mechanization being expensive, the trend is toward the huge agro-corporation. More than half the farmland in 1970 was occupied by farms of over 1,000 acres.[13]

Agricultural mechanization is thus responsible for important demographic changes in both geographic location and class composition. Those who left the farm did not do so to become bankers, industrialists, professors, doctors, or even small business people. In overwhelming numbers they left the land because they could no longer make a living. They flocked to the cities in search of work and in the hope of sinking new roots for themselves and their children. This mass migration from the farm resulted in a further augmentation of the working class and its proportion of the total population.

Many people will agree that an increasing majority work for wages or salary, yet disagree that the country is becoming more and more working class in its make-up. They believe it is becoming more middle class. For them, the terms "worker" and "working class" refer primarily to income status. Those in low wage brackets are considered to be working class; those with somewhat higher incomes are thought to be middle class; or they apply the term working class only to those who work with their hands or wear a blue collar.

Each person is entitled, of course, to his or her system of social classification. We believe the Marxist method to be the most scientific and meaningful. According to this, a worker is one who is compelled to sell his or her laboring power—work ability—to an employer in order to live. Whether wages are high or low is important, but has no direct bearing on working-class status.

Not all salaried employees are workers in the Marxist sense. The president of General Motors is also listed in government statistics as a salaried employee. But his check of close to a million dollars a year is really a fee for expertise in the most efficient extraction of surplus value from the workers.* Should the corporation show a declining profit curve, he could be replaced by someone else more adept at making profits. He is part of corporate management, not the working class. His salary is so large that most of it goes back into gilt-edged stocks and bonds.

In nature there are intermediary forms of life that combine characteristics of more than one generic type. The whale and penguin come to mind. In human society, too, there are individuals who possess traits of more than one socio-economic category or are in passage from one to another.

Workers who earn a wage or salary sufficient to enable them to invest a surplus in order to earn additional increment from other than their own labor, cease to that extent, small though it may be, to remain only workers. And should they leave their jobs to open their own filling station or tavern, they change thereby into self-employed small business people. Even should their earnings fall as a consequence, they are petty-capitalists notwithstanding. Conversely, should a small proprietor begin to work part-time as a wageworker—as do many small farmers and trades-people, or their wives or children—he thereby becomes something of a semiproletarian, a human penguin that still carries the wings of a merchant but walks like a worker. And should he finally give up his private business for the life of a wageworker, he becomes thereby a full-fledged member of the working class, even if his aspirations still remain largely middle class.

THE revolution in science and technology has also altered the internal structure and composition of the working class. It has induced a changed ratio and relationship between production and nonproduction workers, between those with blue collars and those with white, between skilled and unskilled, between men and women and Black, Latin, native American Indian and Asian workers.

Within a total working class that is greatly enlarged, the proportion of white-collar workers has increased steadily. Between 1950 and 1970 white-collar employment rose by 70 percent and blue-collar employment by 19 percent. In the white-collar category, clerical workers increased by 80 percent, sales personnel by 27 percent, and professional and technical

---

* In 1973, GM chairman Richard C. Gerstenberg received a total compensation of $923,000. The company's president, Edward N. Cole, received $833,000. Thomas A. Murphy, the GM vice-chairman, got $832,997, and three vice-presidents received $758,976 each.[14]

employees by 148 percent.[15] Scientists, engineers and technicians in private industry increased most swiftly of all—from 553,800 in 1953 to 1,860,000 in 1969—a more than three-fold increase.[16]

The great expansion of this last group is largely accounted for by the new role of science as a more direct productive force. Research and development is now something of a separate knowledge branch of industry, in which brain power takes its place alongside of other forms of labor as a commodity for sale on the labor market. Another factor is the increasing use of engineers and technicians in the direct supervision of the new technology on a plant-wide level.

In the blue-collar category, skilled workers (listed in government statistics as "craftsmen and kindred workers") grew fastest of all—by 32 percent. Semiskilled workers ("operatives") increased by 14 percent, while unskilled workers ("nonfarm laborers") barely increased at all—by but one-half of a percent.

These figures indicate that society needs a labor force with somewhat greater overall scientific knowledge and with a larger percentage trained in specialized fields and disciplines. It also requires more workers with the educational facility and flexibility to adjust to productive forces in a constant state of technological excitation.*

The need for higher educational requirements plus the lack of jobs for young people explain the unprecedented expansion in school enrollment in postwar years. In 1950, less than 7 million were enrolled in high schools. In 1974, there were over 15 million. In 1950, 2.5 million youth were in colleges and universities; in 1975, there were more than 11 million.[17] Higher education is itself a big business now, operating in close partnership with government and industry. "Service workers," listed separately by the Bureau of Labor Statistics, grew by 49 percent, while "farm workers," also listed separately, fell by 56 percent.

There is good reason, however, to question some of the government's white- blue-collar designations. In the first place, managers and administrators are also listed as "white-collar workers," but these are either private owners or managerial and executive personnel in corporations.

The separate listings for service and farm workers are also deceptive, as if these workers wore no collars, neither white nor blue. But agricultural wage laborers are blue-collar manual workers whether they drive a

---

* At the same time there is another tendency at work not yet reflected in government census statistics. The simplification of production processes is eliminating the need for many former skills, enabling semiskilled and unskilled workers to replace highly skilled ones.

tractor in Illinois, pick oranges in Florida, or follow the crops in California. (Traditionally, Marxists have characterized such workers as the "rural proletariat.")

Service employees are a more mixed grouping. Yet an extremely high percentage of these consist of blue-collar workers—household and building maintanance, auto, television and other types of repair, filling station employees, bus drivers, waitresses, telephone operators, cooks and bartenders, and hundreds of other service occupations. Facts, however, do point to a constant diminution in the *proportion* of blue-collar employment and production workers.

But a few more facts should be considered before rushing to conclude, as do some, that the blue-collar worker is now the vanishing American.* In 1974, production workers still constituted 82 percent of all those in private nonagricultural employment.[19] "Production and related workers," as defined by the Bureau of Labor Statistics (BLS), include all nonsupervisory workers "engaged in fabricating, processing, assembling, inspection, receiving, storage, handling, packing, warehousing, shipping, maintenance, repair, janitorial, watchman services, product development, auxiliary production for plant's own use (e.g. power plant) and record keeping and other services closely associated with the above production operations." Those excluded are "supervisory employees (above the working foreman level) and other clerical staffs."[20]

On the whole, this is an accurate listing of occupations that make up the category of "production workers." Most of these are manual jobs, but by no means all of them. No artificial wall exists between certain types of service and clerical functions and the process of production itself. The BLS also correctly includes those employed in "product development" as necessary to production, avoiding the tendency to isolate research and development into an ivory tower separate from the mundane world of production. Karl Marx, a century ago, pointed out that mental and manual labor may be separated "among different people," yet this "does not prevent the material product from being the common product of these

---

* Andrew Levison, in his book *The Working Class Majority*,[18] makes an important contribution in exposing misleading government statistics that place many service workers into the white-collar category when they actually do what is traditionally considered blue-collar work. We do not agree with him, however, when he places clerical and sales people in the middle class, treating the working class as composed exclusively of blue-collar workers. (A saleswoman at Woolworth's is certainly not middle class!) Nor do we agree with him when he confines his statistics to male workers. Were he to recognize that most white-collar jobs are also working class this would not be necessary.

persons." All of them, he added, are "*directly* engaged in the production of material wealth" [emphasis in original].[21]

In many occupations the old distinctions between blue- and white-collar workers are now fading. The blue collar is becoming gray and the white collar frayed. The large modern office is now filled with machines, and the modern automated or semi-automated factory may resemble an office. New types of office machines are making a great deal of office work similar to factory labor. The work of a telephone operator, it has been aptly suggested, or of a secretary in a typing pool, is not too different from that of a machine operator in a textile plant.[22] Only habit and prejudice would hold that the woman who operates a keyboard on an office billing machine is less a manual worker than the man who operates a keyboard on a print shop typesetting machine. It is estimated that two-thirds of the labor force operate some kind of machine and that 42 percent operate machines almost constantly. "Fifty or even 25 years ago the image of the machine operator as typically a person of low income and educational attainment may have been correct; it is no longer correct today."[23] The office has become "a paper processing factory, with worker tied to the machine."[24]

## Machines Need No Coffee Breaks

There is still another factor to be considered. If machines are eliminating the need for manual labor, on what basis can it be assumed that they will not do the same for nonmanual work? The fact is that they are doing the same, even if not yet at the same speed.

Technological change has already greatly reduced industrial employment in the meat-packing, oil-refining, electronics, coal, shipping, steel, paper and other industries. In some of them the reduction has been by more than 50 percent. But the computer in the front office is beginning to do its share of head-chopping too. It is making the bookkeeper and file clerk "as obsolete as the goose quill."[25] Files are now automated; the mere press of a button retrieves the required file. In one Internal Revenue district office as many as 80 percent of the bookkeepers were eliminated by the computer.[26]

The post office, too, is being automated. Machines stack and cancel 30,000 letters an hour. Reading devices scan coded addresses and sort and direct mail at the rate of 43,000 items an hour.[27] In banks, the auditing of accounts that once required 1,100 hours of labor is now done by a computer in 10 hours. One corporation president has said, "You'd be amazed at how many useless white-collar workers there are. We're getting rid of them.''[28] The result is ''an increasing 'proletarianization' of the office force and an imposition of work standards not unlike those in the factory.''[29] The machine, after all, does not require coffee breaks.

In the service branches of industry, as well, the machine is replacing the worker. Long distance telephone calls no longer require the aid of operators. More and more gas stations are self-service. It is estimated that by 1980, 30 to 50 percent of retail gasoline sales will be served in this way. Since 1967 more gas stations have been closing down than opening up.[30] Increasingly now, coin-vending machines, not people, dispense coffee, sandwiches, hot soup, cigarettes, subway tokens and commuter train tickets.

The reaper is also beginning to mow down many in the professions. One of the largest postwar employment expansions has been in the field of education. This is over. More teachers are needed, but government funds have become scarce. Bachelors, Masters and Doctors degrees that yesterday opened doors to well-paid, prestigious jobs, no longer do.

THE MORE rapid increase in white-collar and professional workers creates contradictory trends. On the one hand, salaried employees can no longer live in self-enclosed enclaves, smugly content with their white collars and the right to use the boss's john. They cannot ignore the fact that wages of skilled blue-collar workers are sometimes higher than white-collar and professional salaries. It was estimated that the average annual wage of a nurse in a private hospital in 1967 was $3,900, while that of an average factory worker was $4,730.[31] Since then salaries of nurses and teachers have risen because they tore a page out of the book of blue-collar experiences: they organized and participated in strikes. In this respect, at least, there has been a white-collar identification with manual workers and a rise in their trade union consciousness.

But there is another side to this development. The increase in white-collar and professional employment has led many sons and daughters of manual workers to become engineers, teachers, research workers, doctors, social workers, computer operators and programmers, and so forth. Hence, it is less true than it once was that a miner's son will also dig coal, a steelworker's son toil in a hot fume-filled mill, or a dressmaker's daughter work at a sewing machine. More coal, steel and clothing are being produced with ever fewer hands.

This has introduced a new sense of fluidity and upward movement in many white, blue-collar families. The older manual worker may be resigned to his life of factory drudgery, but he dreams that his children will escape this.

Surveys made of factory workers' thinking on this matter all found that when asked whether they wanted their children to work where they did, the response was invariably, "no." John Edward, an employee at a Swift meatpacking plant in the Midwest, answered, "I would come out of here if I had it to do over again, but I wouldn't like for my children to follow in my footsteps." A Mrs. Larson in the same plant was more emphatic. "Dear God, no! I believe I'd break both legs. No, sir, I couldn't even want them to smell Swifts as they went by. . . .'Cause if they get here they'd never leave. . . . If he goes into the factory, I'll beat hell out of him."[32] Mrs. Larson was a white union steward.*

Thus, the very same process that is bringing white-collar and professional employees into an enlarged working class, and thereby encouraging trade union organization among them, is also creating new illusions. Referring to the historic factors that held back class consciousness in the United States, J.B.S. Hardman, labor editor and commentator, observed that "there could be no genuine class consciousness where men did not stay put in permanent, stratified classes, or at least were not convinced that they would for long; certainly they were sure that their children would not be proletarians forever."[33]

Under entirely new conditions, this old historic factor of class fluidity—or illusions of it—was resurrected in the postwar period. Manual workers believed that if their sons and daughters changed blue collars for white that they would be escaping from the working class.

This illusion is by no means limited to parents. Something also happens to the sons and daughters who give manual labor the slip. Cesar Chavez, militant leader of the United Farm Workers, put his finger on the problem. "You know how we make enemies? A guy gets out of high school, and his parents have been farm workers, so he gets a job, say, as a clerk in the Bank of America. This way, you know, he gets into the climate, into the atmosphere and I'll be damned if in two years they haven't done a terrific job on him, not by telling him, but just by . . . immersion, and before you know it the guy is actually saying that there's no discrimination! 'Hell, there's no proverty!' See? He knows his place. Or he gets a job at a retail store and then feels threatened because our

---

*A major exception to the above rule is the white, skilled craftsman in construction. He brings his own sons into the union and craft on the aristocratic assumption that the job is his private property and his male progeny the legitimate heirs.

people are making more than he does. 'Look,' he says, 'I went to high
school for four years, so how come these farm workers are making more
than I do?' That really hurts.''[34]

If this happens to the son of a Chicano farm hand with only a high
school diploma and a job as a bank or store clerk, it occurs even more
frequently and in more virulent form to sons and daughters with college
degrees and higher paid professional jobs. The very system of higher
education frequently breeds an air of superiority and a snobbishness
toward those who labor with their hands.

## Dual Labor Market

There is still another aspect to the effects of the technological changes
since World War II. The increased demand for workers with higher
educational qualifications has been particularly detrimental to racial
minorities and to women and youth. The painters' and plumbers' unions
in many cities, for example, require high school certificates of their
apprentices. But the cutting and fitting of pipes, or the plying of a brush or
roller, can be mastered without four years of high school.

Black youth with high school diplomas find it extremely difficult to get
jobs. Those without diplomas cannot find them at all.[35] Or when they do
get them, they are in seasonal industries, in smaller production units, in
dangerous occupations, or in the extremely low-paid service and retail
lines. Even before the economic crisis which began in 1974, it was
estimated that 43 percent of Harlem's employed workers were in unskilled, "dead end" occupations.[36]

This has led manpower experts to speak of a "dual labor market," of
"primary" and "secondary" entrants. The "primary" force is made up
of workers with relatively high pay, more stable jobs, and better working
conditions. The "secondary" force is composed of the urban poor, "the
minority, undereducated, unskilled potential worker, the adult woman
reentering the world of work, the youth requiring a special lift into
employment, the employable welfare mother, the potentially employable
physically and mentally handicapped, and special groups such as pro-
bationers and prison releasees."[37] These are condemned to accept the job
leftovers.

The gap, therefore, between workers who are relatively well off and
those living in acute poverty has been greatly widened. While many
white workers are also on the deprived side of this divide, its effects upon
Black, Chicano, Puerto Rican, native American Indian and Asian

peoples are devastating. Racial oppression is not new in this country. But the technological storm has given it a new twist.

THE changes that occurred in the size and make-up of the working class affected different people in different ways, influencing mass consciousness and the level of movement and struggle. Most significant of all postwar trends, and a harbinger of what's to come, is the irreversible process of proletarianization, in which an ever increasing majority of the American people make a living by the sale of their laboring power.

## 2 : A GLANCE BACKWARD

AT THE height of the CIO organizing drive in 1937, John L. Lewis asked a mass rally of Akron rubber workers the rhetorical question, "What have Goodyear workers gotten out of the growth of the company?" Then, curling his lips, he contemptuously spat out the word: "Partnership! Well," he boomed, "labor and capital may be partners in theory but they are enemies in fact."

Ten years later, testifying before a congressional committee in 1947, the same Lewis was asked whether he favored government operation of the mines. "No, perish the thought," he replied, "I favor free enterprise."

In 1936, Lewis likened the workers' upsurge for industrial unionism to a mighty "river of human sentiment." A decade later his simile was far less dramatic and of another quality. He compared unions with "business organizations."

The difference between these observations spans the distance between the late thirties and the late forties.

Lewis always believed in capitalism and in class harmony. In the twenties, too, he compared unions with corporations. His greater militancy and fiery oratory in the mid-thirties was not a conversion to radicalism. It was a bitter protest at the refusal of the giant industrial

corporations to permit their workers to organize, and the canny perception, based upon the new mood of working-class struggle, that this time
the goal of unionization would be won.

EVEN before the war, in 1937, a number of the largest monopoly corporations began to modify their previously die-hard opposition to industrial
unions. The wave of sit-down strikes in which, from September 1936
through May 1937, some 485,000 workers participated, finally convinced General Motors and United States Steel that concessions were
necessary if they were to avoid an even more intense industrial conflict.

Managements' experiences during World War II reinforced this tendency to compromise. The corporations learned that they could live with
industrial unions and reap greater profits than ever. John T. Dunlop,
former Secretary of Labor in the Ford Administration, discussed the
effects of the war in a book published in 1960:

> . . . four years of preoccupation with a common wartime effort under
> maintenance of membership and other policies determined by the government
> agencies were to assist in firmly establishing collective bargaining beyond
> serious possibility of disruption and for long enough to permit changes in basic
> attitude among many parties. *The war produced transformations in attitudes
> and policies which otherwise might have taken many years,* . . . Except for a
> minority and for unorganized companies, large managements had shed much
> of their anti-unionism. Opposition was more subtle (emphasis added—GG).[1]

Thus, the corporations were ready to forego a frontal assault on labor
such as took place after World War I, if the relatively harmonious
wartime relationship could be continued after the war. They also realized
that giving the unions their lumps would not be as easy as before. It could
even prove impossible. Furthermore, such a head-on collision might
hamper plans for a great postwar expansion of U.S. capitalism.

## Vision of an "American Century"

Already in 1940 the vision of an "American Century" was being
discussed openly. This foresaw a Pax Americana in which Uncle Sam
would determine the shape of the peace and become the world's god-
father, banker, policeman and boss. Dr. Virgil Jordan, president of the
National Industrial Conference Board, placed this prospect before a
convention of the Investment Bankers Association of America, on December 10, 1940:

> Whatever the outcome of the war, America has embarked upon a career of imperialism, both in world affairs and in every aspect of her life, with all the opportunities, responsibilities and perils which that implies. . . . Even though, by our aid, England should emerge from this struggle without defeat, she will be so impoverished economically and crippled in prestige that it is improbable she will be able to resume or maintain the dominant position in world affairs which she has occupied so long. At best, England will become a junior partner in a new Anglo-Saxon imperialism, in which the economic resources and the military and naval strength of the United States will be the center of gravity. Southward in our hemisphere and westward in the Pacific the path of empire takes its way, and in modern terms of economic power as well as political prestige, the sceptre passes to the United States.
>
> We have no alternative, in truth, than to move along the road we have been travelling in the past quarter century, in the direction which we took with the conquest of Cuba and the Philippines and our participation in the last World War.[2]

As the end of the war came into sight, the practical implications of this perspective were set forth by Charles E. Wilson of General Electric, at that time the Executive Vice-President of the War Production Board. Speaking before a meeting of the Army Ordnance Association in January 1944, Wilson urged an alliance of the military, the executive branch of the government, and the large corporations. He proposed that each large company establish its own direct liaison with the military by placing a colonel of the reserve on the firm's roster. He warned, however, that if industry was to fulfill its part of the arrangement, it must not be hampered by "political witch-hunts" or be "tagged with a 'merchants of death' label."[3]

Wilson was referring to the antimilitarist traditions of the country and the pre-war attacks on the "economic royalists" and the arms profiteers. Thus was projected the plan for what later became known as the "military-industrial complex"—in reality a triad of industry, government and military.*

One more component was essential to this grand imperial plan. A postwar domestic labor peace had to be assured. This, in turn, required the cooperation of organized labor, especially the unions in the mass-production industries.

---

* It is no coincidence that this same C.E. Wilson was appointed by President Truman in 1950 to head the new Defense Mobilization Office.

Once the war was over, the Truman Administration rushed to mitigate the danger of a grand labor-capital confrontation. In November 1945, it convened a National Labor-Management Conference in Washington. The conference was a dud. It agreed on some general platitudes, both sides promised to behave, and all present were in accord that strikes be postponed "until all peaceful procedures had been exhausted."[4] But when union representatives touched on the sensitive issue of wage increases, the corporation spokesmen turned deaf ears. They warned labor not to become obstreperous and made clear their determination to repeal the Wagner Labor Act. The issue of wage increases was turned over by Truman to a newly created Wage Stabilization Board.[5]

It was a foregone conclusion, however, that wages would go up. The workers were determined to make up for the war years in which they had not used the strike weapon. Wages had risen only 15 percent above the 1941 scale, while prices had jumped by 45 percent and profits by 250 percent.[6] The workers also feared another major depression; they were already feeling the dislocating effects of reconversion, and sought increased purchasing power to make up for the wartime strides in labor productivity.

The corporations were not unalterably opposed to wage increases as long as these were kept "within bounds" and paid for by a boost in prices rather than from company profits. They were adamant in their contention that "wage increases could not be given without price increases."[7] The Office of War Mobilization and Reconversion refused to grant permission for such price rises. It held that "industry in general could maintain its pre-war profit level and raise wages 24 percent without affecting prices."[8] This was also the initial position of Truman, who, on October 15, 1945, declared that "there is room in the existing price structure for business as a whole to grant increases in wage rates." He even held that this was imperative to cushion the shock of reconversion and sustain adequate purchasing power.[9]

### Postwar Strike Wave

This issue became the nub of the dispute in the great 1945-46 strike wave. In November 1945, the workers of General Motors struck and 180,000 of them stayed out for 113 days. In January their ranks were joined by the workers of meat packing, electrical and steel unions. In 1946, more days were lost in strikes than in any year of American history; more than four times as many as in the turbulent strike year of 1937.[10]

But the 1945-46 strike wave was different. One labor historian referred to is as "unique." He noted that, "For all its size there was little violence; plants were closed in orderly fashion and remained closed throughout the course of the strike."[11] The corporations made no attempts to challenge the picket lines nor to resume operations with scabs.

It was the GM strike that set the tone. U.A.W. President Walter Reuther asked for a 30 percent increase in wages to come from corporation profits. Only in this way, he argued, could mass purchasing power be maintained and prices kept from rising. Truman appointed a special board to investigate the facts and to make recommendations. It found that GM could afford to raise wages without a rise in prices, and on this basis proposed a 19½ ¢ hourly wage increase. GM curtly turned this down.

The impasse was broken in February when the Wage Stabilization Board granted the steel workers 18½ ¢ an hour and gave the U.S. Steel Corporation the right to boost steel prices five dollars a ton. On February 14, 1946, Truman issued an executive order permitting industry to raise prices to compensate for wage increases.[12] Thus Truman gave way to corporation demands. Rather than force the corporations to pay the wage increases from their profits, he permitted them to pass on the wage increases in the form of higher prices. Indeed, as a consequence, the corporations raised their profit ratios considerably above previous levels.

THE first postwar strike wave represented a gain for the workers. In this new major test of strength their ranks remained so solid that the corporations made no frontal assault to break them. The workers also won a much-needed and substantial wage hike.

But, in a deeper sense, and in retrospect, the employers also gained something of great magnitude. They got the Administration—and labor—to back down on the principal issue at stake: whether the wage increase would come from increased prices paid by the consumer or from the bulging coffers of the corporations. In fact, the corporations used the strike wave to get the Administration to eliminate price controls.

The pattern set by this first postwar retreat before capital has been with us since. In many mass-production industries it has often taken the form of outright collusion between management, government and union leaders to permit moderate wage rises to be written off with wild price increases. The gains won have not been at the expense of labor's antagonists, but often squeezed out of increased speed-up on the job and the worker as consumer.

Obviously workers in one enterprise or industry cannot effectively demand that wage increases from their employers preclude a rise in prices, when prices are rising for everything else. Yet had the workers been more conscious of how they were being paid with one hand and robbed with the other, and had they been united in both political and economic action, they could have built a powerful movement to curb and control monopoly profiteering.

THE postwar labor surrender to big business opened a Pandora's box of inflation spirals. Within two weeks of the dumping of controls, the prices on a number of basic commodities shot up as much as 25 percent. Between June and December 1946, consumer prices rose 15 percent and food prices 28 percent. The 1946 wage gains evaporated almost immediately, but "corporation net profits soared to the highest point in history . . . 20 percent higher than the best war year."[13]

Not all sections of the working class gained equally from the wage increases, nor suffered proportionally from the price boosts. The workers in the monopoly-dominated industries and in the stronger unions got larger-than-average wage increases and, therefore, were hurt less by higher prices than those employed in generally low-paying industries or occupations.

From 1947 to 1969, for instance, wages in primary metals (basic steel) rose by something less than 8 percent a year. But in the apparel industry, where there is less monopolistic control, greater competition and weaker unions, in this same period wages rose by less than 3 percent a year. Bearing in mind that the starting base of apparel wages was already lower than in steel, one notes a growing differential between wage rates in the two industries. In 1950, for example, a worker in basic steel was earning on an average 33 percent per hour more than a worker in apparel. By 1973 the average steel worker's hourly earning was 89 percent more.*[14]

The scandalous way in which the monopoly corporations arbitrarily fixed prices can be seen by still another example from the steel industry. In the fifties, the steel magnates made a major policy decision to modernize and expand steel capacity. They decided to raise the funds for this expansion without touching their profit reserves — by raising prices still

* The word "average" is a bulldozer that flattens peaks and raises valleys to one common plain. Also, work in the apparel industry is far more seasonal than in steel. The gap between the highest and lowest wages paid in these industries, therefore, is even greater. Nor is it irrelevant that most steel workers are men and most apparel workers, women.

higher.[15] Hence, the overall consumer price index from 1946 to 1960 rose some 40 percent, but the price of steel shot up by 120 percent![16]

"It is somewhat anomalous," writes Professor James R. Schlesinger, "that such price trends should be manifested in those industries of high and advancing productivity in which we might normally anticipate a fall in relative prices."[17] But what was normal in the competitive youth of capitalism is no longer normal in its monopolistic old age, even though the corporations blame high prices on the workers instead of their own insatiable greed.

When the large corporations were in a tooth-and-claw vendetta to prevent or destroy unions in basic industry, it was because they feared, among other things, that every wage demand would threaten profit returns. But where outright monopoly or oligopoly control over productive facilities and market prevails, and price competition is eliminated, "no reduction in profits may be required from yielding to the union," says John Kenneth Galbraith. "The mature firm can maintain income by increasing its prices."[18] Unions, he believes, even assist price stability in a given industry by standardizing wage costs.[19]

There is a grain of truth here but Galbraith must know that corporations raise prices through monopoly price-fixing practices irrespective of union demands. In 1973, for example, wage increases were exceedingly modest but price increases broke all previous records.

## The Taft-Hartley Act

Shortly after the gains of the first postwar strikes were largely washed away in the inflation flood, the cry arose in labor's ranks for a second round of wage increases. The corporations and the government became increasingly apprehensive of endless labor turmoil and work stoppages. When the miners went on strike in November 1946, and when some months later the railroad unions rejected a fact-finding board's proposed 16¢ an hour settlement and began a nationwide shutdown, the time to clip labor's wings had come.[20]

Truman rushed to Congress, asked for and received emergency powers to break the railroad strike, "including the induction of strikers into the army and the imprisonment of officers of striking unions."[21] The stage was set for the passage of the Taft-Hartley Act in June 1947.

Its central objective was threefold—first, to curb labor's right to strike. This was done by imposing a ban on strikes "for the 60-day notice period before termination or modification of a contract," and a further 80-day "cooling-off" period in strikes affecting the so-called national welfare.[22]

Second, the law established a network of legal impediments to prevent the spread of unionism to still unorganized industries and regions. It forbade the closed shop, the secondary boycott and mass picketing; reestablished the use of injunctions in labor disputes; enabled employers to sue unions for "unfair labor practices"; and gave employers rights to combat unionism they did not have under the Wagner Labor Act. The independent powers of the National Labor Relations Board (NLRB) were weakened by giving the President the authority to appoint a General Council to supervise NLRB affairs and to "have final authority" to investigate charges and issue complaints.[23]

The Act's third objective was the purging of the labor movement of its radical, class-conscious and, in the first place, Communist influence. In many respects this objective was the most important of all, for on it hinged the ability of the employers, government and right-wing labor officialdom to enforce the first two objectives.

The law demanded that each and every union official from international union president to local executive board member, file a sworn affidavit "disclaiming Communist membership or proscribed beliefs." The falsification of an affidavit subjected one "to severe penalties of fines up to $10,000 or ten years imprisonment." But if even one official of a union failed to file the required non-Communist affidavit, the entire union lost its right to represent workers in collective bargaining.[24] In case of new elections, or where challenged by employer or competing union, its name could not appear on the election ballot. Where workers were determined to keep their union, nonetheless, they faced the impossible procedure of first voting "no union" to block another union from winning representation rights, and then resorting to economic muscle, mainly strike action, to compel recognition from the given employer. Hence, any officer who decided not to sign an affidavit appeared to be jeopardizing the very existence of his union. Even where noncomplying unions won elections before the new law went into effect, "the Board felt it necessary to 'close the investigation' without certification."[25]

In this way trade union democracy was impaired by law, and workers were denied the right to elect Communists to office. The cold war against communism abroad became linked with the cold war against communism at home. But more than communism was the target. Once again C.E. Wilson of General Electric bluntly put into words what was being put into deeds. More than a half year before the Taft-Hartley Act became law, on October 14, 1946, Wilson set the record straight in these words: "The problem of the United States can be captiously summed up in two words: 'Russia abroad, Labor at home.' "[26]

Official labor leadership did not agree, of course, with such a linkage. If anything, it sought to prove the opposite. But the connection was quite "logical" once the logic of the cold war was accepted. If it was true that the United States was menaced by a Soviet military threat; if it was true that everything had to be done to prepare the nation for a new, possibly atomic, war, then every labor strike, every shutdown of production, was ipso facto aid to the "enemy."*

On another score as well, the labor movement boxed itself in. Once it accepted the unequal exchange of higher wages for even higher prices and profits, it became more difficult to combat the employers' charge that it was higher wages that had caused the inflation. Thus labor gradually lost the good will it had won during the CIO's formative years when it fought the corporations and defended the best interests of the great majority of the people. In this way, and by supporting the cold war, labor lost the ability to muster the kind of massive public support needed to block the passage of the Taft-Hartley Act.

Even after the Act itself became law, the labor movement still had the means with which to make it inoperative and compel its repeal. This required the simple refusal to sign the non-Communist affidavits even if this meant foregoing NLRB "favors" for a more determined reliance on labor's own economic muscle and potential political clout. Had this course been followed by a number of the key industrial unions, the government and employers would have beat a hasty retreat.**

But this was farthest from the minds of most labor leaders. They were loud in their condemnation of the Taft-Hartley Law and eloquent in their promise to mount an all-out fight for its repeal. But when it came to complying, the AFL bureaucracy did so at once; Reuther and the UAW leadership were not far behind; and Murray and the steel union first refused to sign and then also capitulated. Only the Left-led and progressive unions of the CIO, and the United Mine Workers and Typographical Union conducted a serious fight to make the law inoperative.

* The *Wall Street Journal* of April 9, 1952, berated "piously anti-Communist [labor] leaders" for "actually playing, unintentionally, we hope, Russia's game by striking or threatening to strike."

** As workers in England showed by opposing the Industrial Relations Act imposed by the Tory government in 1972.

In truth, many right-wing labor leaders were ready to accept the new law's restrictions in exchange for its promise to purge the Left from organized labor's ranks. With World War II over, the top labor official-dom rapidly lost the militancy it had acquired in the hard times of the thirties. It was now prepared to take it easy, to give up the difficult task of organizing the great mass still outside unions, and to climb into a soft bed with management. The Communists and other left-wing and progressive workers were the main obstacles to the harmonious consummation of this marriage. They had to be gotten rid of; they were gotten rid of.

Using the Left's refusal to support the cold war, the Marshall Plan for Europe, and the Truman candidacy for reelection in 1948 (it supported instead the independent Progressive Party candidacy of Henry Wallace), the CIO leadership expelled eleven Left- and progressive-led unions representing a combined membership of about 700,000 workers.

In unions under right-wing leadership, a purge began of those who refused to comply with the Taft-Hartley affidavit provision, although in many instances left-wing workers resigned their posts voluntarily to avoid endangering the bargaining position of their unions.

Matters did not stop there. Taking advantage of the anti-Communist hysteria of the time, conservative-led unions amended their constitutions to bar Communists from the right to membership, and a few of them rushed to raid the expelled progressive unions. The largest and most important of these unions was the United Electrical Workers (U.E.). The CIO leadership was intent upon destroying this union by first splitting it and then setting up a counter-union in the industry. This undertaking was considered so important by the Washington Administration and the CIO leadership that President Truman's message to the 1949 CIO Convention alluded to it and urged support for the splitting effort.*

*Two months later, James Carey, the handpicked leader of the new rump union, reciprocated. "In the last war we joined with Communists to fight the fascists," he said, "in another war we will join the fascists to defeat the Communists."* [28]

### The Witch Hunt

Thus was eliminated from labor's councils nearly a whole generation of its most militant and dedicated fighters. The history of the labor movement demonstrates that every forward advance is linked with the

* One labor historian has characterized this action as "rare in the history of the presidency." [27] And in the labor movement as well, let us add.

pioneering efforts, the foresight and self-sacrifice of class-conscious workers. These see the daily skirmishes on the broader social canvas of a larger class conflict, recognizing that gains are won only through combat, and that militant organization, unity, and class awareness are decisive ingredients of victory.

In the turbulent thirties many Communists rose as natural leaders of workers. Long before the CIO was born, they proved by example that industrial unionism was an idea whose day had finally come. The first nationwide strike of steel workers in 1919 was led by William Z. Foster, who later became a Communist and the leader of the Communist Party. In the twenties, in the face of dormancy, corruption, and open hostility to the idea of industrial unionism in the AFL leadership, the Communists helped form the Trade Union Educational League and then the Trade Union Unity League, seeking to unite militant rank-and-file workers for the change that had to come.

While it has become stylish in recent times to belittle the role of the Communists in the thirties, those who wrote about that period before the cold war ice age had fully hardened, even though they themselves were opposed to communism, had something quite different to say. In a book published in 1954, *Six Upon the World*, Paul F. Douglass discusses the great role of William Z. Foster. In his opinion, Foster was one of six men who were shaped by and left a lasting imprint on American experience. The author points out that even before there was a CIO, the Communists in the labor movement "pressed along theoretical and practical lines for the advancement of the industrial unions." He relates that within the Ford plant "a small group of militant Communists had organized the Auto, Aircraft and Vehicle Workers of America. As an underground operation among Ford employees,* it was closely related to William Z. Foster, the militant advocate of industrial unionism. The *Ford Worker*, a spicy little one-penny sheet issued by this group, was first distributed at the Ford plant gate and then found its way by subterranean channels to the rank and file."[29]

The Communists helped initiate and lead the movements for unemployment insurance, old age pensions, aid to poor farmers, and other progressive social legislation. They were in the forefront of the struggle for full Black equality, at a time when this issue was far less popular than today. The Public Relations Director of the National Association for the

---

* It had to be underground, for unions were prohibited.

Advancement of Colored People, writing in the later forties, paid grudging tribute to the role of the Communists in this fight:

> It is a matter of record that the Communists have generally fought for full recognition of Negro rights. They have carried on this fight through their own organizations and through those organizations in which they exert influence. They have pushed the Negro to the forefront in party work. They have consistently nominated him for office on the party ticket. They have dramatized his problem. They have risked social ostracism and physical violence in his behalf. They have challenged American hypocrisy with the zeal, if not the high principle, of the Abolitionists. In all this they have performed a vital function as an irritant to the American conscience.[30]

Another book written in the same period gave the Communists credit for the CIO's ability to attract Black workers. The author states, "it is not likely that union leaders would have given as much attention to the matter or developed the specific programs they did in the absence of prodding from the Communist elements . . . the Communists served as a hair shirt."[31]

Likewise in the fight against fascism, the Communists were second to none. American Communists helped form the Abraham Lincoln Brigade that fought in defense of Republican Spain. Among the 1,500 young Americans who gave their lives and lie buried in Spanish soil there is a large percentage of Communists.

It is now recognized by many, including some who participated in the purges of the McCarthy era, that the ousting of the Communists and their Left and progressive allies maimed the labor movement. A former UAW official, still strongly anti-Communist, pointed this out a few years ago:

> I submit we made a great mistake when we kicked the Communists out of the CIO—and, as you know, I was one of those who fought most belligerently to throw them out. . . . And when we did it, we really threw out the baby with the bath, because we set up a pattern of conformity; we set up a pattern of refusing to break with the traditional ways of thinking. . . .
> That is why you can't dignify what goes on at a UAW convention today by calling it "debate." Policy questions are not debated at UAW conventions. What is being argued about is administrative jazz and union legislative problems. There are no arguments about foreign policy questions or even most domestic policy questions.[32]

This is certainly true, and the UAW is by no means the worst example of this. The ousting of the Left from the CIO led to its castration, to the disappearance of exactly those features of militancy and vitality that distinguished it from the decrepit business unionism of the AFL high command.

# 3 : THE CIO EXPULSIONS

EVER since the Left was expelled from the CIO in the fifties, there has been divided opinion over whether that particular episode in labor history could have been avoided. Some believe it could, and that the Left bears responsibility for its own later dismemberment and near annihilation. Two opposite views have been expressed.

The first holds that the Left should not have joined battle over issues doomed to defeat. It could not stop the cold war, prevent the Korean hot war, change the enveloping climate of McCarthyite repression and conformity, or make a meaningful difference in the final outcome of the 1948 Henry Wallace third party candidacy. By picking up the gauntlet on these issues, it is contended, the Left only got what it asked for; it should have held its fire and kept its powder dry for another and better day.

A second line of criticism comes from those who believe the Left was defeated because it was not militant enough in defense of workers' needs. They point to the Left's support of the wartime no-strike pledge, claiming that it was this that resulted in its subsequent defeats. Other voices go so far as to say that the Left should never have joined in the building of the CIO, but should rather have opted for its own "revolutionary" unions.

THE argument that the Left should not have fought for its views really says that the Left could have saved itself by ceasing to be Left. A number of trade union officials did resort to this safer course. But in the cold-war atmosphere of the time, neutrality was also treated as "subversion"—

and of an even more sinister kind. The unrelenting pressure was for full conformity. Most of those who thought they could just sit out the battle ended up on the other side.

Who can say that those who braved the current did so in vain? What would have happened had there been no opposition to the rabid drive for "preventative" nuclear war against the Soviet Union? Some say the Left, particularly the Communists, exaggerated the war danger. Possibly. But Korea and Vietnam would seem to validate that "exaggeration." At one point during the Korean War, American military forces were a hair's-breadth from crossing the Yalu River into China. Had General Douglas MacArthur, the commander of U.S. troops in Korea, had his way, that crossing would have been made, inviting a larger, possibly nuclear, confrontation with the socialist countries. If President Truman stayed MacArthur's orders, even relieved him of his command, it can be attributed in part to the growing opposition to the Korean military adventure and the mounting fears of a nuclear showdown. The Henry Wallace presidential campaign of 1948 had the great merit, therefore, of forcing the issue of war or peace into the public debate. It compelled Truman to modify his position on some questions in the course of the election campaign itself, demagogically seeking thereby to keep millions of voters from bolting toward the Henry Wallace third party ticket.

Those who believe that the split in the CIO could have been avoided by the Left "pulling in its horns," forget the atmosphere at the time and the central objectives of the ruling class. These were: to reverse the democratic trend set in motion by the popular upsurge of the thirties and the defeat of the fascist powers in the war; to put the labor movement "in its place," especially the militant industrial unions; to get the nation to accept the cold war and the inevitability of a hot war with the Soviet Union; to win acceptance for an ever escalating military budget; and to sell the idea of an "American way of life" supposedly superior to all others, giving United States imperialism the moral justification to intervene against peoples abroad whenever it deemed this necessary.*

*"I remember how within three, four weeks the atmosphere changed. A delegation of CIO leaders led by James Carey came back from a trip to the Soviet Union for the CIO, and put out a report. They didn't say it was a workers' paradise but presented it as a country that was doing something for its people. They had some good words for the unions there. We distributed the report in our local union meetings. And then, about a month later, we had a banquet and Van Bittner from the Steelworkers Union got up and attacked the Soviet Union and everyone gave him a big hand. The climate changed overnight. This was in 1948, when [Henry] Wallace ran for president."—Mario Manzardo, in *Rank and File*, Edited by Alice and Staughton Lynd, Beacon Press, 1973, pp. 145-5.

The split in the CIO was part of a wider strategy to divide the world labor movement along cold-war lines. It is hardly an accident that only a few weeks separated the expulsion of the progressive unions from the CIO and the split that was engineered in the World Federation of Trade Unions (WFTU). This federation had been formed in 1945, with the active and enthusiastic cooperation of the CIO, to unite the trade unions of 52 countries with 64 million members. Unable to expel the Left from the WFTU, the right-wing unions, with the AFL and CIO leaderships playing a leading role, formed a counterfederation, the International Confederation of Free Trade Unions. Similar splits were engineered in Italy and France.

In face of these facts, it is hard to believe that a split could have been avoided in the CIO, short of complete surrender to the cold-war hysteria. The split in the CIO was not provoked by Communists or other Left-progressives. If anything, they bent over backwards to prevent it. When a resolution was introduced at the 1946 Atlantic City convention of the CIO to "resent and reject" so-called Communist Party interference in the affairs of the CIO, the Left, including Communists, voted for it in the interests of unity. This was a serious mistake; it only fed right-wing arrogance.

Writing about this period in his important autobiography, *Labor Radical*, Len De Caux, the editor of the *CIO News*, until he, too, became a victim of the anti-Communist purge, states:

> There was some method to the meekness of the lefts. They had to retreat under conditions that threatened a rout. To preserve unity of a still relatively progressive CIO, they continued to make concessions as they had done since CIO began. They valued their CIO status for themselves and for their unions. One thing was certain. The lefts didn't start anything! All aggression came from the right. The left conceded, compromised, even turned around. To break up unity, the right had to do it.[1]

## Cold War Repression

Anti-communism within the labor movement did not succeed by its own efforts alone. All means at the disposal of the ruling class were thrown into the breach. The Taft-Hartley Law, as we have seen, made it a crime for a Communist—or one suspected of being a Communist—to hold union office. On top of this, the McCarran Act of 1950—further amended in 1954 as the Butler "Communist Control Act"—called for the registration of all Communists. It provided that unions accused of aiding so-called Communist fronts be hauled before the Subversive Activities Control Board and, if found to be "Communist infiltrated," lose all rights to be represented before the National Labor Relations Board.

In addition, the House Committee on Un-American Activities got paid informers to read long lists of names into its records, thereby instigating the persecution of thousands. Ten well-known screen writers and directors, and other prominent citizens associated with the movement for aid to Spanish anti-fascist refugees, were sent to prison for refusing to cooperate with the witch-hunt. The FBI worked closely with employers to dismiss militant workers; many were discharged for pleading the 5th Amendment when asked about Communist Party membership, and the courts upheld the firings; strong-arm thugs drove militant workers out of plants and union halls; eleven top Communist Party leaders served long prison terms, and 140 Communists went to trial during the repression. Most shameful of all, Julius and Ethel Rosenberg paid with their lives, and Morton Sobell with more than 18 years in prison, only because the government needed a spy case, fraudulent though it was, to fuel the anti-Communist hysteria.[2]

The conscious motive behind all this is reflected in a comment that appeared in the *U.S. News and World Report* of Feb. 17, 1950. "War scares are easy to create," it wrote, "and are nearly sure-fire producers of money for more arms. . . ." And just prior to the outbreak of the Korean War, it elucidated this theme further:

> Government planners figure that they have found the magic formula for almost endless good times. They are now beginning to wonder if there may not be something to perpetual motion after all. . . . Cold war is the catalyst. Cold war is an automatic pump-primer. Turn the spigot, and the public clamors for more arms spending. . . . Cold war demands, if fully exploited, are almost limitless.[3]

This thinking also found its reflection inside the labor movement. Workers remembered that the Great Depression had ended only when the world war began. With the demand for more arms many saw an assurance of continued employment and prosperity. And a labor bureaucracy that had been bought off by capital went out of its way to drum up support for the military and to outdo others in blatant chauvinism and anti-communism.

Thus the expulsion of the progressive unions from the CIO did not arise from normal differences over ideology or tactics where one side wins or loses without rupturing the movement's organic unity. It was the product of a campaign of repression in which government, employers, labor officials and all the media were involved. "Against this background of government, business and union hostility," notes one labor historian, "it is not surprising that the expelled unions experienced difficulties and that several quickly passed from the scene." What is to him more surprising, is that a few survived "and that of these, two have remained strong and impervious to outside attack."[4]

## The Wartime No-Strike Pledge

Those who claim that the Communists and other Left and progressive forces lost the battle in the CIO because they ceased to be militant, usually start their criticism with the World War II no-strike pledge. They believe that this pledge proved to be the undoing of the Left.

They are mistaken. The winning of the war was in the interests of the American people just as it was in the interests of the people of the rest of the world. Many countries had already been ground down under the fascist heel. Had the fascist powers succeeded in destroying the Soviet Union and winning the war, all of Europe, Asia and Africa would have been subjugated. In time, the fascist wave would have engulfed this hemisphere as well. Winning the war was of decisive importance, therefore. The worldwide democratic and revolutionary sweep which followed the war, and which continues to this very day, would not have been possible had German and Japanese fascism emerged the victors.

THE war created a complicated political situation in the United States. For its own imperialist interests, the ruling class sought the defeat of its fascist rivals. To accomplish this it was compelled to enter into a wartime alliance with the Soviet Union, hoping at the same time that the war would somehow end without a strengthening of Soviet influence or a triumph of its arms.* It was therefore important for U.S. workers to throw their full weight behind the war effort to crush the fascist powers. The outcome of the war was by no means certain.

---

*Harry Truman expressed this viewpoint quite clearly. A day after the Nazi invasion of the Soviet Union, and five months prior to the Japanese attack on Pearl Harbor, Truman declared: "If we see that Germany is winning we ought to help Russia and if Russia is winning, we ought to help Germany."[5]

This was not the first time in U.S. history that a temporary identity of interests occurred between otherwise antagonistic social classes. In the American War of Independence, mechanics and poor farmers joined with sections of the gentry and men of property to overthrow the British yoke. Even more analogous was the situation during the Civil War. The workers of that day found themselves in a dilemma—to defeat the Southern slave-owners' insurrection required fighting on the side of their own exploiters, the Northern industrialists. Yet most workers understood that a victory for the Southern Confederacy would extend the system of unpaid slave labor, thereby drastically lowering the price for wage labor.

The British workers were in an even more difficult situation. The Civil War in the United States meant mass joblessness and hunger for them. Textile mills had to close because cotton from the South could not reach English shores. But the British workers did not join the cry of their mill owners for military intervention against the North. They remained steadfast in their opposition to the slave states and slavery. They knew how to distinguish between fundamental long-time interests and shallow momentary ones.

The expulsion of the Left from the CIO was not motivated by their support for the wartime no-strike pledge. Most labor unions supported the pledge, as did the whole CIO. As one active participant in the struggle inside the National Maritime Union pointed out, "the anti-communist campaign was conducted during a period when the Communists supported militant strike actions and independent politics. Naturally, this made many enemies both in and out of the labor movement."[6] It was because of this militancy that they were expelled.

Mistakes, of course, were made. These are inevitable in any major undertaking, yet many of them could, and should, have been avoided. Sometimes the no-strike pledge was applied mechanically, without regard to specific circumstances and to whether sufficient countermeasures had succeeded in halting employer abuse of the pledge. These were errors committed in carrying out a generally correct policy. But quite different was the error made at one stage of the war effort, when the Communists began to believe that the no-strike pledge would be applicable in the postwar period as well. This erroneous assumption came from a revisionist estimate of U.S. capitalism as somehow having lost its predatory nature by participating in the war against the fascist powers. This was a harmful and costly error. It helped feed illusions about the progressiveness of U.S. capitalism and failed to prepare workers in advance for the inevitable change that would come in both class and labor movement relations with the end of the war.

## Left Support for the CIO

A current view holds that the Communists and other left-wing forces were mistaken in lending aid to the building of the CIO. This is the estimate of a number of New Left historians, who believe that support for the CIO was aid really for the designs of what they call "corporate liberalism." These historians believe that the big breakthrough of industrial unionism in the thirties was due less to the mass upsurge of the workers than to the conscious objectives of a "sophisticated corporate leadership," which recognized the need for industrial unions as the best way to integrate workers into their system.[7] From this estimate flows the conclusion that the Communists and other radicals, who played so important a part in helping to organize the new unions, "unwittingly became the allies of those whose concern was to fit labor into the corporate structure."[8] In other words, they were doing what the corporations wanted.

But if winning the right to industrial organization was just a matter of pushing on a door already ajar, it is hard to explain the decades of bloody struggle and sacrifice, the scores of lives lost on picket lines, the efforts of the General Motors Corporation to break the Flint sit-in strike of 1937, or the need for that strike in the first place.

It is true, of course, that when the corporations finally acceded to the movement for industrial unionism, they did so for their own class interests; certainly not because they had become suddenly softhearted or softheaded. They sought to integrate the workers more firmly into their system by making concessions. But this is a danger inherent in the winning of every important reform.

Some of those who hold that it was a mistake for the Left to help build the CIO unions argue that "revolutionary unions" should have been built instead. There is something wrong with this logic. If the workers were unable to win industrial unions by their own efforts, and had to wait for these until the "corporate liberals" granted them, by what stretch of the imagination could they have succeeded in building so-called revolutionary unions?

There is an important reason why the Left united with men such as John L. Lewis, Philip Murray, Sidney Hillman and others, even though these men believed in capitalism and often practiced class-collaboration policies in their own unions. This unity was essential because these Center forces in the labor movement also saw the need for organizing the unorganized into industrial unions, were ready to join with Communists in accomplishing this objective, and because the Left could not do the job all by itself. The results of this unity produced the greatest and most successful organizing drive in labor history.

True, the hopes that the new industrial unions would become bastions of radical, class-conscious trade unionism did not materialize. Yet something very important was gained. From a bare three million organized workers in 1932, the labor movement has grown to embrace well over 20 million workers today. An extremely large proportion of these are workers in the mass production industries. This is unprecedented. When a new upsurge comes—as it will—it will start where the old one left off.

## Problems of Left-Center Unity

Without the unity of the Left and Center forces, the organization of the mass production industries could not have been accomplished. But the marriage was one of convenience and necessity, not of long-range ideological or political accord. The dictatorial way Lewis ran the Miners' union was not the way the Left sought to build the unions it influenced. The Hillman policy of close collaboration with the employers in the mens' clothing industry was far from the Left's militant class-struggle policies and practices. And the differences on longer-range perspectives were just as basic.

Under such circumstances it was essential for the Left to maintain its own identity, to pursue and argue for its own policies and take issue forthrightly and openly with those with which it disagreed, while at the same time maintaining the unity of the alliance for the agreed-upon objectives. There developed, however, a tendency on the part of Communists and other left-wingers to overlook the points of disagreement and to highlight only those of agreement. In the name of unity, the Left often gave up its own independent positions without even making them publicly known. Yet only by raising the class understanding of the workers, and showing them the difference between class struggle and class-collaboration approaches, could sufficient mass pressure be exerted to sustain unity in the face of changing objective conditions.

Discussing Communist errors made in the building of the steel workers' union, Gus Hall, one of the founders of that union, later to become the General Secretary of the Communist Party, wrote in September 1949:

Our weakness was not that we collaborated with the present union leadership, but that while doing so we did not expose and criticize the treacherous, class-collaborationist policies of that leadership. Our main effort should have been directed toward organizing and mobilizing a militant rank-and-file movement, activating and uniting the membership around a progressive program of action. Unfortunately, this was not at all times the case.[9]

Attempts to correct such errors sometimes resulted in swings in an opposite direction, especially at critical turning points. Thus Communists sometimes pressured labor leaders to take public positions that their membership did not understand and were not prepared to support. Often it was easy to get a good resolution adopted at a union meeting, especially when the leadership proposed it, but the content did not always correspond to the level of understanding of the membership. As a consequence, there were at times exaggerated estimates of what was possible and not enough effort to really educate the rank and file on the substantive issues involved.

Another error was the failure of more Communists to come out proudly and openly as such. Fewer Communists might have been elected to union office, at least temporarily, but the air would have been cleared of the lies, slanders, suspicions and misconceptions spread assiduously by enemies. Such a course was not possible everywhere, for Communists were still being fired from jobs, and the whole CIO was being charged with being "Communistic." Thus one had to be careful not to play into the hands of CIO enemies by bringing grist to their mill. Yet, in retrospect, the failure to fight more vigorously for the full rights of Communists to function openly on all levels of the labor movement, on the same basis as all others, was an error. Later, in the cold-war years, the witch-hunters made it appear as if the Communists, who were on the ground floor of the building of the new unions, were some kind of trespassers and "infiltrators" within them.

The Left's uncritical acceptance of the dues "check-off" system seems also to have been another mistake. Dues "check-offs" originated in the mine fields when miners were paid in company scrip because the homes they lived in and the stores they patronized were company-owned. When John L. Lewis brought this method into the CIO, it seemed an ideal way to consolidate the new unions by guaranteeing regular and full dues payments without going through the difficulty of collecting dues, worker by worker, month after month. And it certainly did help release union forces to go out and organize new plants and territories.

But in our opinion—and we know many good people on the Left disagree with this—a heavy price was paid for this "service." It enabled leaders to take the rank and file for granted, and workers lost one way of exercising leverage on officials. As most corporations were asked to send the dues checks directly to the international office of the union, it also helped entrench a top bureaucracy with a financial whip over regional and local officials. Using the corporations to bring about a rapid consolidation of the new unions brought with it a rapid consolidation of new bureaucracies.

The lack of a dues "check-off" system does not automatically make a union more democratic. Building-trades unions, in which workers change work sites frequently, do not employ the company "check-off" method. They collect dues from each worker directly every month. This has not made these unions more democratic, although in many instances the locals have more autonomous rights than the industrial union locals. In the building-trades unions, however, it took generations for bureaucracies to consolidate; in the industrial unions the dues "check-off" helped to do this relatively overnight.

We are not suggesting that unions which have dues "check-offs" now be urged to give them up. It is an efficient method of collecting dues from all workers. But this efficiency can be positive only where its negative side is recognized and measures are taken to establish direct and more intimate contact with the members.

One example should suffice to show how employers consciously recognize that the "check-off" can be used to strengthen a top bureaucracy against lower bodies of a union. In the 1956 contract negotiations between the International Longshoremen's Association and the East Coast shipowners, the employers offered the "check-off" as a means of strengthening the International's control of the locals. A book by Vernon H. Jensen, *Strife on the Waterfront–the Port of New York*, describes this incident:

> Because the latter [the locals] sent in per capita tax irregularly and for only part of the actual membership, the International office was always short of funds. If the four-dollar monthly dues went to the International through a "check-off," the International would feed money back to the locals and so gain more control. So the employers reasoned. They did not count on the astuteness of local leaders, who concocted a unique arrangement. Instead of checking off the $4.00 monthly dues, they left the old system intact, wherein the local collected the dues, and provided for an additional "check-off" of one cent an hour, amending the ILA constitution to permit it.[10]

In this particular union, local bosses, some of them no less crooked than those of the International, wanted their own hands in the dues till. But it is worth noting that in a union in which rank-and-file turbulence and wildcat strikes were endemic, the employers saw the "check-off" as a way to strengthen the control of the top bureaucracy.

## Historical Assessment

Notwithstanding the errors that were made these were not responsible for the split that occurred in the CIO and for the general weakening of the Left in the labor movement. The avoidance of errors would have prevented some losses, but not reversed the trend. Communists and other left-wing forces were not strong enough to overcome the united efforts of the most powerful capitalist ruling class and its labor lackeys at a time when economic and political conditions had changed vastly and confusion and illusions were rife among the workers. It was impossible for the Left to wish upon the working class a class consciousness that was not yet there. Even in France and Italy, where workers were class-conscious and where the Communist parties had immense influence and following, it was impossible to prevent the labor-movement splits that took place. Only now are these splits gradually being healed.

The Communists and Left generally can well be proud of the role they played in the historic struggles of the thirties and forties, and in their refusal to bend their knees before the witch-hunt of the fifties. In the building of the industrial unions; in the struggles of the unemployed, the employed, farmers and youth; in the fight for Black equality and the rights of all minority peoples, they advanced the class interests and economic conditions of the workers in a way unmatched in American radical and socialist history. By so doing they left an indelible mark on a historic period, helped bring into being the many progressive reforms of the New Deal, helped create a powerful social movement that changed the climate of its time and the lives of millions, enriching them, enabling them to see themselves not only as the objects and victims of history, but also as its makers.

To the extent that patterns of the past have bearing on the future, this will repeat itself. The movement of the workers is never a steady and consistent forward progression. At times it slows down to a snail's pace, even halts or retreats, only to plunge forward again. Sometimes there are long intervals between working-class insurgencies, for these are related to cyclical economic, social and political developments, and to the character of leadership at hand. Periods of giant forward leaps and exhilarating thrusts in depth alternate with longer stretches of relative stagnation or of a wider consolidation in breadth.

This peculiarity was noted by Marx. The working class, he pointed out, criticizes and interrupts itself repeatedly, returns to tasks seemingly accomplished only to begin them anew, throws its adversary to the ground periodically only to see him rise again stronger than before, and "recoils ever and anon" from accepting the logical consequences of its own historic position and movement, "until the situation has been created which makes all turning back impossible."[11]

Yes, the Left suffered a serious setback, but only for a time.

# 4 : EXPLOITATION U.S. STYLE

MOST PEOPLE readily agree that a worker who is compelled to work excessively long hours for less than a living wage is cruelly exploited. But many would not agree that a worker earning a relatively high wage for a 40-hour week, who owns an auto, a television, and sometimes a home, is also exploited.

Yet if "the making of profit from the labor of others" is an acceptable definition of economic exploitation, then we must agree that employers often make more profit from the labor of people earning relatively high wages than from those earning low ones. It all depends on the intensity and productivity of labor.

At the time Marx was writing his epic work *Capital*, wages in England were higher than on the European continent. For the English manufacturer, however, wages represented a relatively smaller part of production costs. Marx explained this as due to the greater development of capitalism in England and the consequent higher intensity and productivity of labor. "It is self-evident," he wrote, "that in proportion as the use of machinery spreads and the experience of a special class of workmen habituated to machinery accumulates, the rapidity and intensity of labor increases as a natural consequence."[1]

Without a doubt a worker who receives below what is needed to sustain himself and his family is bitterly exploited. But the intensity of his exploitation or, in Marx's words, the "*rate* of exploitation," that is, the difference between what he produces in new values and what he earns as wages, may be considerably less than it is in the case of the worker with a higher wage.

In primitive times the productivity of labor was so low that a man could produce barely enough to cover his own sustenance. As there was no surplus being produced there could be no profit. In those days war captives were put to death. Nothing was to be gained by keeping them alive. But once productivity increased to the point where a surplus became possible, even a small one, it became "immoral" to slaughter one's foes. The "moral" thing was to put them to work as slaves. Ancient slavery was abhorrent, and many preferred death in its stead, yet the rate of economic exploitation was relatively low.

Capitalist production changed this. The ever greater use of machinery and more sophisticated technology raised the rate of exploitation enormously. According to official government statistics, the average production worker in the United States earned $7,800 for the year 1972. But the value added per production worker after costs, excluding wages, are deducted was estimated to be $26,200. In other words, for each dollar spent on production-worker's wages, employers netted $2.26 in added value (surplus value).[2] When all those listed as employees are considered—including corporation executives and personnel in management and advertising—the value added per dollar spent on wages and salaries was $1.99. Even assuming that the exorbitant salaries paid corporation executives and those paid to administrative and research personnel can be considered as workers' wages, which they cannot, it would still leave a rate of exploitation of 100 percent. Thus the high productivity of U.S. labor has a great deal to do with the relatively higher wages and standard of living. But productivity is not the only element involved.

Wages in the United States were generally higher than in England even when productivity here was generally lower. Historic factors explain this. From the very inception of capitalist social relations in this hemisphere, the vast North American wilderness stood in stark contrast to the sparsity of population. Millions of hands were needed if capitalism was to develop, expand, conquer the hinterland and emerge as a world power. In this kind of a situation, Marx explained, "the law of supply and demand favors the workingman. Hence the relatively high standard of wages in the United States."

Try as it may, continued Marx, the United States "cannot prevent the labor market from becoming continuously drained by the continuous conversion of wage laborers into independent self-sustaining peasants. The function of wages laborer is for a large part of the American people but a probational state. . . ."[3]

This historically unique situation, in which an absolute labor shortage was coupled with a sieve-like frontier through which many wage earners could pour to become independent farmers or merchants, is now long past. It had a great deal to do with the traditionally higher standard of living in this country as well as with the historical roots of the deeply imbedded petty-bourgeois ideas and aspirations.*

## The Changing Standard of Living

The standard of living is not something fixed and frozen. It is socially and historically conditioned and varies from country to country and generation to generation.

Obviously, a worker who owns a car is "rich" compared with workers in countries where such a possession is completely out of reach. Yet in the United States today a car is not necessarily a luxury; it is often a dire necessity. For many, there is no other way to get to work or to periodically escape from the foul air and tensions of the city. This is doubly true where there is no public system of rapid, efficient transportation.

The age for leaving school has also risen greatly. This has placed an additional burden on parents. Formerly, young people contributed to the family income before leaving home. Today, those who do not continue their education find it increasingly difficult to find jobs, while those who go to college often leave home before finishing school, but expect their parents to continue supporting them.

This change too must be weighed on the measuring scale of living standards. For while the standard of living can rise and fall, it cannot fall beneath the needs of maintaining a family as workers and the rearing of a new generation prepared to meet the more complex conditions of its own time. Where it falls beneath this the working class ceases to reproduce itself.

---

* This did not hold for all labor and not at all for Black labor. Brought here in chains as slaves, Black labor was completely unpaid. The greater surplus extracted from its toil provided a form of primitive accumulation for burgeoning U.S. capitalism, which Marx compared with the pillage of Africa, Asia and the Americas by European capitalist powers.

Therefore, the great increase in college enrollment since World War II has had an adverse effect on the living standards of many working-class families. In Japan, for example, a worker's wages tends to increase with his years of employment. In the United States this is true only of professional workers. "Blue collar workers inevitably reach a plateau in their capacity to earn, yet their expenses continue to rise as their family matures."[4]

An economist for the Bureau of Labor Statistics estimates that the increased education of children would not have been possible to the same degree "if working mothers had not added to family income."[5] This is also a factor in the number of workers eager to obtain overtime work. In 1970 more than 14 million workers were on extended work weeks.

A survey conducted in 1973 showed more than four million workers holding two or more jobs. The percentage was highest for married men with increased family responsibilities. There were 500,000 more "moonlighters" than a decade earlier.[6] Significantly, the proportion working at second jobs the year around was greatest among those earning $150 or more a week on a primary job. About 10 percent of government employees held second jobs. Among men, the rate of moonlighting for teachers below the college level was about 17 percent — more than double the rate for all men. These are precisely the groups in the labor force greatly concerned with sending their children to college.*[7]

The standard of living must keep abreast, therefore, of ever new needs if it is to be kept from falling. With a majority of wives now breadwinners, at least part of the time, and the many new real and artificially created needs, it is questionable whether the much vaunted "high" living standard in this country has kept pace with the times.

THE standard of living is socially conditioned in other ways as well. A hut is a palace for a family with no roof at all. It is a degrading, humiliating hovel, however, if spacious mansions and luxury apartments rise nearby, and if new technology makes possible higher standards of housing for all.

No one felt deprived without running water, flush toilets, electricity, or washing machines before these conveniences became current. Once they did, and as they became commonplace, to live without them seemed an imposition — not only the denial of a right but of a necessity. And for many it was a necessity because the new technology made the employ-

* "Moonlighters" often work as "extras" below the prevailing wage rate and exert a downward pull on wages generally.

ment of the old more difficult. As one-time luxuries became necessities, some old necessities became luxuries. They came to be invested with the charm of being rare, antique and more expensive. To eat under soft candlelight, to own an old shack in the woods, to ride a horse and buggy, became hallmarks of cultured wealth. Thus it is impossible to compare the living standards of different countries without careful regard for history, culture, level of economic development and psychology. The poor of Bombay live under conditions far worse than the poor of Harlem. But poverty in the United States is ever more humiliating and degrading in face of the vastness of national wealth, the gluttony of the upper class, and the ever mocking refrain of slick advertising to buy, buy, buy.

## Quality of Life

The standard of life cannot be separated from the quality of life. A new car, large color TV and other modern gadgets provide little comfort to the worker who comes home from work limp as a rag, and is a worn-out shell at 50 years of age. True, workers no longer toil a 12-hour day, or do it only infrequently. More tension builds up today in eight or nine hours of machine-paced labor than did previously in the ten or twelve. Physically, work may no longer be as demanding of a strong back, but frayed nerves can be more debilitating than weary muscles.

Antonio Gramsci, the Italian Marxist, noted that the "humanity and spirituality" of a worker, is realized in creative production. "They existed most in the artisan when the worker's personality was reflected whole in the object created and when the link between art and labor was still very strong."[8] That link is now shattered for the great majority.

The rapid increase in work absenteeism, especially on the assembly line, is one expression of the alienation from the job and the inability of workers to stand the inhuman grind of contemporary industrial production. From 1957 to 1961, production-worker absenteeism at Ford's averaged 2.6 percent a day. "Each year since then the figure rose until it reached 5.8 percent in 1968. On Mondays and Fridays though, the figure often goes almost to 15 percent." And at GM, "These absences are occurring in every geographical area — and all races and types of workers are involved. They often take one or even two days off every week."[9]

This rebellion on the job makes clear that the length of the work week in industry, especially for those working at great speed and intensity, is now highly destructive of workers' health and contributes to the mounting toll of industrial accidents and illness.

Ralph Nader, in an address to the American Association for the Advancement of Science, pungently noted that "crime in the streets" results in only half the fatalities of the unpublicized and hard-to-find facts of "crime in the factories." He estimated that in 1970 there were eight to nine million injuries on the job, resulting in 2.5 million temporary, and 250,000 permanent, disabilities.[10] Some 14,000 deaths occur annually from industrial accidents.

No reliable statistics exist on occupational diseases, yet it is known that more than 40,000 different chemicals are used in industry and that neither the government nor private industry has troubled to ascertain the long-term effects of most of these. Many "have not even been tested on animals."[11] Exposure to dangerous pollutants caused one million new cases of occupational disease in 1969. Among these were "over 800,000 cases of burns, lung and eye disease, dermatitis and brain disease."[12]

Industry has become a huge and bloody battlefield, with the workers as the casualties. Most people are aware, of course, that construction workers' hourly wages are relatively high. But how many are also aware that the percentage of fatalities caused by work injuries in contract construction is considerably higher than it is for policemen?[13] When a policeman is killed in action it makes headlines. When a construction worker is killed on the job it does not even make the obituary column. Government statistics indicate that the accident rate in construction is twice that in primary metals, and the injury severity rate is 2.5 times greater. Although it constitutes only 5 percent of nonfarm employment, construction accounts for 11 percent of all industrial accidents.[14]

It is hard to believe that in this day and age workers in auto foundries — mainly Black — face "almost daily explosions" and that the "smell of burning flesh is commonplace." Yet this was the charge made by union leadership at the supposedly safe Michigan casting center of the Ford Motor Company.[15]

The question of on-the-job safety, therefore, is one of paramount importance for blue-collar workers. The nation has learned about "black-lung" disease in coal mining; it has still to learn about "brown-lung" disease in textile and about the smell of burning flesh in auto foundries. Only an aroused working class can enforce safety regulations on corporations, who consider profits everything and human lives nothing.

The length of the work day and week also has a bearing on job safety.

Accidents are inevitable under conditions of speed-up and tension. These increase geometrically with every additional hour of the working day. Thus the issue of a shorter work week is on the order of business once again.

It is now nearly four decades since the forty hour week became law. Yet according to the Bureau of Labor Statistics, total hours worked by full-time workers in May 1970, averaged 45 hours a week. And this was no exceptional month. Although the straight-time work week of workers in manufacturing was reduced to an average of 37 hours, this was more than made up by the increase in overtime. Only 9 percent of full-time workers were employed less than 40 hours a week; about 50 percent worked 40 hours; and the balance—some 41 percent of the full-time work force—worked much longer.[16]

The workers in the General Motors Chevrolet Plant at Lordstown, Ohio, worked out their own way to beat the inhuman monotony and suffocating tension of repeating the same mechanical operation over and over again. They decided to "double-up," that is, to take over a mate's job as well as their own for half-hour stretches in return for a similar favor the next half-hour. In this way they worked twice as hard half the time in order to get a complete rest the other half. "The only reason we started doubling-up was to break the boredom of the damned line," explained Dennis Lawrence, the shop committeeman in the body shop.[17]

This is no real answer to the problem. Doubling up half the time also extracts its pound of flesh. On top of that, the company will now press all the harder for workers to double-up all the time. This was already happening even before the mass layoffs in auto in 1974. Joe Alfona, absentee replacement operator at the Lordstown plant, described the process: "First they tell you, 'put in ten screws,' and you do it. Then a couple of weeks later they say, 'Put in fifteen,' and next they say, 'Well, we don't need you no more.'"[18]

The only solution lies in workers' control over the speed of the line and in reduced hours of work. All the professed management concern with "humanizing the work process" and ending blue-collar alienation is just so much rhetoric if it dodges these solutions, and they are being dodged.

Corporations are concerned, of course, with reducing absenteeism and keeping a stable work force with uninterrupted efficient production— uninterrupted, that is, except when it is in their interests to interrupt it. The companies realize, as Gramsci pointed out in his study of Fordism in the twenties, that the workers of a given enterprise are a collective human machine "which cannot, without considerable loss, be taken to pieces too often and renewed with single new parts."[19] The answer, therefore, cannot simply be the firing of workers. Establishments must hold on to the basic core of skilled and experienced hands or the human machine may cease to operate efficiently.

The corporations tend to respond to this dilemma in the way that Henry Ford did when the auto assembly line was first introduced. He found that the ranks of the workers "almost literally fell apart," and the company could not keep its working force intact, let alone expand it. Ford admitted to a 380 percent labor turnover for the year 1913. To add 100 men to the work force required hiring 963, "so great was labor's distaste for the new machine system."[20] Ford's answer was to offer the workers a somewhat higher than average hourly wage in exchange for their acceptance of the grinding, inhuman speed-up and monotony.

Since World War II this has become the established policy of the huge monopoly corporations. There are three reasons for this: First, they now have to deal with organized workers and therefore must be prepared to "give" somewhere. Secondly, the corporations more than make up for the increase in wages through the increased intensity of labor. And lastly, with price-fixing practices and general inflation, they can partially cover wage increases through price increases. Hence, in the mass-production industries under monopoly or near monopoly control, wages are generally higher and fringe benefits larger than in the more competitive branches of industry.

## Where Wages are Higher

A study conducted in 1971 showed that higher than average wage rates tend to be associated with three factors—the size of the establishment, the degree of concentration in the industry, and the degree of unionization. In realtively small and unorganized firms the average wage was $2.58 an hour. Where the manufacturing firm had over a thousand employees, this added 50¢ an hour in pay. Where 40 percent or more of the given industry's output was accounted for by the four largest companies, another 42¢ an hour could be added. And where 50 percent or more of nonoffice employees was covered by union contracts, there was a further 72¢ an hour hike in pay.[21]

Thus a worker in a plant with the above three characteristics earned an average of $4.22 an hour, or some 60 percent more than in those plants where they were lacking. (Workers in the South earned 41¢ an hour below the national average.) Bearing in mind that the large monopoly corporations are also the best union organized, the above three factors are usually found together.

The difference in wage rates between the highest- and lowest-paying industries is even wider. In 1969 the average textile worker earned only half the wage of an auto worker. In 1947 she/he had earned three-fourths as much.[22] The trend, therefore, has been toward a widening of the gap. It should be remembered that many workers receive above the "average high" or below the "average low."

Clearly, the workers in the monopoly dominated industries are significantly better off wage-wise than those in the lighter and more competitive branches of industry. Of course, there are exceptions to this rule. Where skill is a key requirement, where the rhythm of teamwork requires an extremely stable, experienced and dependable work force; where specific jobs have to be completed according to an inflexible time schedule; and where unions hold a monopoly over the skilled labor force and are the suppliers of it, wage rates may even be higher than in monopoly industries. In branches of construction, printing, mining and shipping, hourly wages are above those in manufacturing, although in many of these areas, unemployment also tends to be greater. Conversely, industries and occupations in which women predominate universally pay less.

## Key Role of Workers in Basic Industries

But it would be wrong to conclude that the workers in the large monopoly industries hold back the militancy and class-consciousness of the rest of the class. It has already been shown that these workers are the most exploited in the sense of producing surplus value. Furthermore, the production workers in the basic industries are the best organized, with confidence which comes from experience in struggle and from testing their strength on numerous occasions. By the very concentration of their numbers they are obliged to think more in terms of collective action than workers in smaller enterprises. Finding themselves inside the bowels of the corporate beast, they can more easily grasp the nature of the monopoly system as a whole. The "boss" for them is no longer a single individual, but an impersonal far-flung industrial empire. A worker at GM, for example, does not rub shoulders with the company president—whoever he may be—nor have delusions of "rising to the top" or opening a competing auto plant. The house painter and carpenter, on the other hand, can still indulge in the dream of becoming a small contractor.

Workers in the mass production industries are also more aware of the immense profits being raked in by the corporations. Even the most conservative union newspaper or magazine will, from time to time, remind the workers of the huge profits made by the corporations in their industry. Furthermore, the intensity of labor is so great that these workers feel their exploitation in more than monetary terms. This bears out Marx's observation in *Capital*, that the increased wear and tear of labor-power can be compensated by higher wages only *up to a certain point*. "But beyond this point the wear and tear increases in geometrical progression and every condition suitable for the normal reproduction and function of labor-power is suppressed. The price of labor-power and the degree of its exploitation cease to be commensurable quantities."[23]

This is now happening on a larger scale than heretofore. It explains the new consciousness about the need to change working conditions and the quality of life. It also explains the new demands for workers' control of machine speed and for the right to challenge management prerogatives in the work place. Although the corporations are trying to stem this discontent with mini-concessions—and, only where compelled to, with more substantial ones—tension on the job is likely to increase. The employers are determined to intensify exploitation still more, and to use the growing numbers of unemployed as a club over the heads of those still working. They will oppose interference with what they consider their sacrosanct rights to run plants as they please.

### The Gap Between Skilled and Unskilled

Simultaneous with the above development is a narrowing of the wage differential between skilled and unskilled workers. A study of wages in the building trades indicates that the wage gap between skilled and unskilled has been "reduced substantially since the turn of the century." In 1907, the earliest year for which statistics are available, the average union wage rates for journeymen craftsmen was about twice that of laborers and helpers. In 1950, it was 48 percent higher, and in 1974, 32 percent higher.[24] The same trend is apparent in manufacturing. In 1907, skilled wage rates were double those for unskilled. By 1947 they were only 50 percent higher. This trend holds for each separate industry for which data are available. In construction, the cents-per-hour differential grew from 80¢ in 1950 to $2.02 in 1974 but the percentage difference declined. In manufacturing also, the cents-per-hour differential increased but the percentage difference also "narrowed substantially."[25]

It should be noted, however, that in comparison with the European countries the wage differential between skilled and unskilled workers is still great. Everett M. Kassalow, in his comparative study of national labor movements, 1969, estimates that the wage differential in Europe is between 15 and 20 percent. Significantly, Kassalow finds that one reason for this "more egalitarian approach" is the greater influence of socialist thinking and the existence of "a wider worker solidarity."[26]

The narrowing of the wage gap within industries occurs alongside of its being widened as between the large unionized establishments and the smaller unorganized ones. Also to be considered are the millions of workers employed on so-called marginal jobs, and on part-time or seasonal work. These are extremely low-paid and are largely minority workers, women and youth.

Furthermore, while the wage differential between the skilled and unskilled production worker is narrowing, the revolution in science and technology has raised the earnings of a technical, professional élite far above those of the average worker. Two tendencies are at work. Many engineers, technicians and research personnel find themselves more and more in the category of "hired hands"—or perhaps, "hired brains"—becoming part of the class which sells its laboring power in order to live. Lacking organization, many of these find themselves with less protection than the unionized production worker. Contributing to this is the fact that many former skills are now being broken down or eliminated through the introduction of ever newer technology.

On the other hand, the same process enhances the role of a more limited number of highly specialized technicians. There is evidence that management seeks to "buy off" this élite from the immensely greater fount of automation profits.[27] Already there are a few manufacturing firms where labor costs are down to approximately seven percent of total costs.[28] In such conditions the attempt to bribe the more highly trained technicians is a foregone conclusion. This is already to be seen in chemical, oil, electric power, seafaring and longshore.

EXPLOITATION in the United States is fact, not fiction. What workers gain in modern conveniences, they often lose in the quality of life, the relationship with nature, and the ability to find a reflection of their own personalities in the work they do.

# 5 : WORKERS ALL — BUT NOT THE SAME

THE very atmosphere of our society breeds competition and animosity even between working people. This characteristic of capitalist society was noted by Frederick Engels in his study of early English working-class conditions. The struggle for existence, he wrote, "is waged not only between different classes of society but also between individuals within these social groups. Everybody competes in some way against everyone else and consequently each individual tries to push aside everyone whose existence is a barrier to his own advancement."

"The competition between workers," he stressed, "is the sharpest weapon" of the employing class against labor. "This explains the rise of trade unions, which represent an attempt to eliminate such fratricidal conflict between the workers themselves."[1]

Trade unions have done much to eliminate the worst features of this conflict, but only a minority of the working class is organized. And competition between workers still exists alongside of, and within the framework of unionism itself; union jurisdictional disputes are one example of this.

The greatest lag in white-collar organization, ironically, is to be found in the very industrial plants where blue-collar labor is strongly entrenched. A major reason for this lies in the special measures taken by the corporations to give the office workers a feeling that they are "different,'' ''better,'' and that salaried workers are of a higher breed than the hourly wage earner. Even when office and technical workers see the advantages of unionism, they often balk at entering the plant-wide industrial union local. They fear that their own special interests may be overlooked, and they object to mingling with manual workers, since they look down on them. In turn, blue-collar workers often show disdain for those who push pencils and typewriter or calculator keys in air-conditioned offices. Likewise, male supremacist attitudes are an obstacle in white-collar organizing. The result is that manual and clerical workers are frequently divided when confronting the company.

Discord expresses itself even between different categories of workers in the same union. In auto, for example, the skilled craft workers have their own division. Although a minority in the union and industry, they have considerable influence on contracts submitted for ratification. This right was won by a threat to disaffiliate from the United Auto Workers. Lower paid workers seek wage increases that are the same across the board — penny for penny. Higher paid skilled workers want these increases granted on a percentage basis.

Hostility develops sometimes between workers on straight hourly pay and those on individual or group piecework. Night-shift workers understandably believe they are entitled to a higher hourly pay than day-shift workers. Young workers often have a different approach to seniority, fringe benefits and overtime work than older workers. They want a contract to give them more now, being less concerned with such matters as retirement pensions.[2] And workers on dangerous jobs, where life, limb or health are threatened, believe, and with good reason, that they deserve the highest compensation of all.

Friction frequently develops between men and women workers. Men often resent women doing what they narrow-mindedly consider ''a man's job.'' Many of them believe that women should be laid off first and that their natural place is ''in the home.'' Wages and salaries for women are consistently lower and few unions put women in positions of leadership or fight for their full equality on the job and in the union.

Sometimes the momentary interests of workers in private and public employ seem to collide. Bus drivers, for example, demand higher wages to meet higher living costs, but bus riders, mainly workers, fear this will mean another fare hike for them. And when transit workers go on strike it is the workers of the city who are the most inconvenienced.

One of the most serious areas of friction is that between the more steadily employed, mainly white workers, and those on welfare. Working-class homeowners often blame the poor people on welfare for their high property and payroll taxes. Poisoned by racial prejudice and consciously misled by the media, many of these workers believe that all welfare recipients are Black, even though a substantial majority are white.[3] They accept the myth that those on welfare do not want to work, and that they live a life of idle affluence.

Hostility is engendered between workers in union and nonunion enterprises. In runaway and nonunion shops in the South the workers are told that their only hope of keeping their jobs is by enabling the company to compete successfully with Northern industry. At the same time, workers in Northern unionized plants are told that their wages cannot go up because of the competition from Southern unorganized shops. And often it is the selfsame corporate interests who play both sides of this street.

## Disparities in Income

Different levels of income among workers often generate different approaches to questions. Workers' living standards vary considerably, depending upon the number of members of a family; whether both husband and wife work, whether older children go to college; the nature of the occupation or industry; whether it is union or nonunion; in the North or South; and whether employment is full-time, part-time, seasonal, temporary, or with overtime hours and rates of pay. In January 1975 average hourly earnings for industrial workers ranged from highs of $7.13 in contract construction, $5.63 in mining, and $5.74 in transport equipment, to a low of $3.15 in apparel and other textile products.[4] These are averages, obviously many workers earn above the "highs" and below the "lows."

When one takes into account that poor families tend to have more children and pay higher prices for equivalent, or, in many instances, inferior, purchases than workers in better income communities,[5] the difference in wage scales can mean the difference between living reasonably well, just squeezing by, or not getting by at all.

Sharp disparities in income relate to more than wages. Whether a worker's family is covered by hospitalization and medical care, and by supplementary benefits in case of injury, illness, layoffs, and retirement, has also a great deal to do with the standard of living. The stronger unions in the mass production industries, some civil service unions, and a few craft unions, have been able to meet these needs to a far greater extent than most. Such coverage is considerably less or totally absent in the more competitive branches of industry and in the retail and service sectors, or where unions are weaker and workers employed only part-time or intermittently.

The system of social security was inadequate from the start, but nothing compared with what postwar inflation has done to it. Social security payments are based on average earnings going back over a 15-year period, when dollar wages and the cost of living were only a fraction of what they have since become. It is estimated that a retired worker in 1971 received "less than 25 percent of his terminal or maximum salary or wage."[6] Congress has since increased social security payments, and in 1974 cost-of-living adjustments began to be added, but it is doubtful whether the percentage of terminal wage has greatly increased.[7]

## Fringe Benefits

When organized labor began to push for so-called fringe benefits the situation started to change — but only for workers whose unions were strong enough to win substantial supplementary benefits. By 1971 some 28 million workers were covered by private employer-employee pension plans. The amounts received vary, as do the number of years of employment required for eligibility. But it has created a new situation, in which the income of some workers after retirement is larger than that of many workers while fully employed. The UAW retirement plan, as of early 1973, "enables a worker with 30 years of service to retire at age 56 on $500 a month."[8]

The differential in unemployment compensation is also great. General Motors, for example, guarantees its laid-off workers with two years' seniority 52 weeks' coverage at approximately 95 percent of their straight-time earnings — inclusive of government unemployment compensation. The U.S. Steel Corporation added a maximum of $52.50 a week in supplementary unemployment benefits.[9]

There is one hitch in all this. Supplementary payments last only as long as the fund has a surplus. The period of extensive unemployment, which began 1973-4, has largely evaporated these funds.

Nonetheless, they represent important gains won through collective bargaining. But they have not been an unmixed blessing. To the extent that fringe benefits were won, the unions involved lost interest in the fight to bring about a radical updating of unemployment and social security laws and the establishment of a comprehensive federal system of free hospital and medical care for all. As only the unions with muscle could win the most substantial fringe benefits, their withdrawal from the battle for a more effective federal system of social security has hurt that fight badly.

The United States lags far behind other capitalist countries in such reforms. In Western Europe most retirees "get 50 to 70 percent of maximum pay received just before retirement."[10] In Canada, just across the border, all workers are covered by a national system of free hospital and medical care. As for the socialist countries, even small, as yet economically underdeveloped Cuba has a system of universal free hospital and medical care that puts this country to shame. And this is even more true in the Soviet Union and other Eastern European socialist countries.

Fringe benefits have also often been used to tie workers closer to management. Workers fear that a loss of job would mean a loss of fringe benefits and, most important of all, their retirement pensions. It should be recalled that company-sponsored pension plans predate unionism. In the 1910s and 1920s large corporations deliberately developed such plans to keep workers from organizing or striking.[11]

While present-day pension plans are jointly sponsored by the unions and the companies, it has been aptly noted that "They create a setting in which labor and management people live together and make common cause."[12] This has become a source of corruption in more than one union.

### Racism—Main Cause of Tension

The most acute tension in workers' ranks is racial. This is so notwithstanding the continued solidarity of white and Black workers when confronting the company.

We have previously indicated how technological change coupled with discriminatory practices has helped bring into being a primary labor force of higher-paid, better skilled and more steadily employed workers, and a secondary force of lower-paid, underskilled, temporary and part-time workers. A disproportionate number of Black and other minority workers find themselves in this peripheral labor force. It is this structural racial discrimination in the employment market that explains the intense poverty among racial minorities.

As more white youth gravitated toward white-collar and professional jobs, less desirable blue-collar jobs went by default to minority workers. Such industries as steel, auto, rubber, shipping, garment and public transit have large components of Black workers. Even in industries where they have fewer marginal and more steady jobs, and some accumulated seniority, Black workers are still relegated to the heavier, dirtier, more dangerous, less skilled and lower paid work. Foundry workers, for example, are nearly all Black. In the women's clothing industry the Puerto Rican, Black and Chicano women are operators on the very cheapest garments, where piece-work rates are lowest and speed-up greatest. And in agriculture, Chicano, Haitian, Dominican and Asian farm hands—men, women and children—are treated worse than beasts of burden.

Racial discrimination is a fact, therefore, in hiring, job assignment, wages and upgrading, and in the failure of unions to recognize the nature of the problem and to combat it in full seriousness. Most building-trades unions practice outright exclusionary policies. Other unions either collaborate with management in discrimination or, what amounts to the same thing, give but token lip-service to the fight against it. Only a minority of unions fight vigorously for and practice full equality in their own ranks, including the election of Black and other minority workers to top leadership posts.

Many white workers have been led to believe that Black people have really "made it" in recent years. Some of them actually argue that Black people are now the privileged, while they, the white workers, especially the white "ethnic workers," are the underprivileged. A study of a white neighborhood in Philadelphia indicated that a majority felt that Black people were "getting too much." When pressed for evidence, they pointed to news stories about antipoverty programs for Black communities while there were none in their own. Many of the same workers, largely of Italian, Polish and Ukrainian extraction, with the Italians making up the largest group, worked in two large electrical plants in the area. In these factories the workers stood black shoulder to white shoulder in recent protracted strikes. Yet, at about the same time, the white community gave George Wallace a large vote.[13]

White workers do not really believe that Black workers have it better than they. Irrationality on this score is explained by something else— racist prejudice combined with a growing feeling of insecurity. These workers see automation and depression eliminating more and more blue-collar jobs. They also see Black people fighting militantly for full equality, including job opportunities. They are fearful that between these two pressures they may lose their somewhat more privileged position as compared with that of Black people. Thus, "By exaggerating the results of Negro aggressiveness, the white worker is saying, 'Why doesn't someone speak for me?' "[14] As rising prices eat into family income and unemployment increases, discontent grows. But failing to identify the real source of their woes, racial prejudice leads them to make Black people the scapegoats.

This situation underlines once again how capitalism pits worker against worker and why this competition, in the words of Engels, is the"sharpest weapon" of the ruling class.

## Ethnic Differences

Another aspect of this problem is the continued presence of ethnic and religious differences and prejudices. Despite melting-pot theories and the reduction in large-scale immigration, workers of different European backgrounds, including the second and third generations born here, continue to think of themselves as hyphenated "ethnic-Americans." They frequently live in their own ethnic communities, belong to separate religious and cultural organizations, gravitate often to the same kind of occupations, and vote frequently as a bloc, especially for ethnic kin— whether for mayor, congressman, or local union president.

This pattern of conduct is explained by a number of interrelated factors. Feelings of national pride (and prejudice) and cultural and religious traditions carry over into generations long removed from the soil of their foreparents. This is particularly so where a sense of continued inequality and insecurity prevails. And this feeling subsists despite a certain degree of upward mobility and cultural assimilation. For one thing, the dominant Anglo-Saxon, Protestant culture does not permit those from other origins to forget their more "lowly" estates. And, for another, insecurity is endemic to capitalism—especially to its manual workers. Sticking together and practicing mutual assistance by "ethnics" are natural reactions, therefore, to feelings of group insecurity.

Conflicts also arise between ethnic groups for control over jobs, unions, or political office. Where this involves Jewish individuals or groups it often expresses itself in anti-Semitism. In unions where the majority of workers were once Irish, German, or Jewish, the change in the racial and ethnic mix of the work force frequently leads to a clash between an old leadership, no longer representative of the ranks, and the new workers. In all too many instances, the old leaderships hold on until death itself separates them from their power.

## The Changed Immigration

European immigrants who have come here since World War II are different from those of an earlier period. Among the many millions who came to these shores prior to World War I, there were large numbers of revolutionary, socialist-minded people. The first Marxists in this country were co-workers of Marx and Engels who fled Germany after the unsuccessful bourgeois revolution of 1848-49 and during the Bismarck period of anti-socialist laws in the 1880s.

German immigrants formed the first Communist Leagues, led the Socialist Labor Party, and built many trade unions. The Brewery union under their leadership was one of the very first industrial unions and was built on class-struggle principles.[15] In the early 1900s it was the Jewish and Italian immigrants who organized the needle trades, with Jewish workers making up 60 percent and the Italian workers 30 percent of union membership.[16] The two largest Italian-speaking locals of the Ladies Garment Union, Local 48 and Local 89, were named in honor of the revolutionary years of 1848 and 1789.*[17]

In 1910, East European Jews were one-fourth of New York City's population but nearly one-half of its labor force.[18] In the twenties, a majority of New York needle-trades workers were Jewish. Jews also constituted "over one-sixth of the printers, nearly one-fourth of the building-trades workmen, one-third of those employed in the jewelry, amusement, and ornament trades, and over half of the labor force in the leather trades, and virtually all the members of the retail salesmen's unions." Many of their leaders sought to build a labor movement in the socialist image.[19] Finnish socialist immigrants built the first unions in the Minnesota Mesaba iron range, and Southern and Eastern European workers built the first stable miners' union in the Pennsylvania coal fields.[20]

But the European immigrants who came to this country since World War II were largely of an opposite strain. A welcome mat was put out by the State Department only for tried-and-true anti-Communists, which has really meant antidemocrats of every vintage. Thus the postwar influx of European immigrants had a quite opposite effect from that of an earlier epoch.

---

*The year 1789 was that of the Great French Revolution and 1848 the year of the German bourgeois revolution.

Recently, some change has taken place. The modification of the immigration laws has increased large-scale immigration from a number of European countries such as Greece, Italy and Portugal. These immigrants have more varied ideological and political views, although the State Department still bars those who were associated in any way with Communist parties. There has also been an exceedingly large influx of Latin American and Asian workers. Those from Cuba, Indochina, South Korea and Taiwan are reactionary. Those from Puerto Rico—the largest immigration of all—and from Mexico and Caribbean countries are ordinary working people coming largely from the peasantry and without socialist traditions. They are, in large numbers, now acquiring a socialist consciousness, especially from the impact of the Cuban Revolution.

FROM the foregoing, it can be seen that the working class is by no means a homogeneous mass. Workers are not all alike. They make up a common economic and social class because they lack independent means of livelihood and are compelled to sell their work ability to the highest bidder.

Like most people, workers generally act from motives of self-interest. Because of differences of income, education, type of work, cultural and national backgrounds, personal problems, and varying levels of class and social awareness, their own interest is seen differently by different workers and sometimes it is in collision with other workers.

These differences tend often to obscure the most important common interests of workers and to stand in the way of the working class becoming a class "for itself." The American workers are highly practical and most often view self-interest in narrow, momentary, and strictly economic terms alone. But long-term basic interests are not always identical with short-term ones.

When workers go on strike they violate an important momentary interest—the need to draw weekly wages. Should they lose the strike, they could lose their jobs. Even when they win, it may take years of steady employment to make up for the wages lost during a protracted work stoppage. Capitalist ideologues have tried to convince workers over many generations that strikes "don't pay" in dollars-and-cents terms. But most workers know better. They do not lightly use the strike weapon. Experience has taught them, however, that temporary sacrifices at times are necessary if they are to make any lasting gains. Should they shrink from fear of sacrifices, they would be pushed down to the level of abject slaves.

Self-interest can be assessed accurately, therefore, with only a degree of knowledge and foresight. White workers in the South, for example, well know that they have certain advantages over Black workers. They have access to better jobs, higher wages, more opportunities, and greater freedom. But the average wage in the South is still about 20 percent below that in the North, for precisely the very reason Southern whites think they have advantages. Karl Marx was profoundly right when he said that workers in the white skin cannot be free so long as workers in the black skin remain branded.

SEEING the overriding common class interests has not been easy for workers in this country. The whole history of American capitalism has reinforced petty-bourgeois ideas in the working class. The greater class fluidity and the generally higher living standards have pulled against working-class and socialist consciousness. As long as the system seemed to be functioning normally there was less motive for coming to grips with its seamy sides. But in the thirties, when conditions of general decline and increasing elements of crisis became apparent which could not be ascribed to just individual or group failings, working people then found more common ground; secondary differences and prejudices were put aside, and unity and consciousness grew in struggle. For the great majority the times were bad and the responsibility was seen as definitely not their own.

Today we are at the beginning of a similar phenomenon. The entire capitalist world is in crisis and the movement against capitalism grows with leaps and bounds everywhere. In the United States, uncontrolled inflation, large-scale unemployment and attempts to control wages are eroding working-class incomes rapidly. The standard of living in this country is now sliding downward, both absolutely and relative to those in other countries. Despite continued competition between workers, they are compelled increasingly to act as a class in defense of their living standards and rights.

# part
# TWO

SINCE World War II the conditions of working-class struggle in the United States have altered considerably. The classic form of employer attack used to be the direct wage-cut. Many of the most militant workers' battles of the twenties and thirties were precipitated by wage-cuts or an increase in hours of work, or both. At one time these accounted for up to 50 percent of all strikes. But in two years only since World War II did they account for more than 1 percent of all strikes. Hence, according to one writer, "they have all but disappeared."[1]

Wage-cutting still took place, but in a less direct and more subtle fashion. A glance at the different price patterns of the post-World War I and post-World War II periods will indicate the problem. After World War I, prices climbed until 1920, slumped sharply with the depression of

73

1921, wobbled up and down in subsequent years, but never regained the 1920 price level until 1946—a full quarter-of-a-century and a new world war later.[2]

Since World War II, however, prices have risen every single year, with the exception of one. And the climb has been accelerating. Even the major depression which began in 1973-4 did not bring with it a fall in prices; they continued to rise.* Employers have not felt, therefore, the same need to cut wages *directly*. Under workers' pressure they have even agreed to raise them. Most new union contracts have contained some wage "gain." But in most cases this was soon eaten away by inflation.

The main reason for the chronic inflation is the ever increasing concentration of economic power in fewer and fewer hands. In 1969, the top 200 corporations owned over 60 percent of all manufacturing assets—a larger share than that held by the 1,000 foremost corporations in 1941. The U.S. Senate Subcommittee on Antitrust and Monopoly believes that even these figures "significantly understate the level of concentration in the economy."[3]

Hence, fewer and fewer firms dominate more and more of the national economy.** The process of concentration has come through massive mergers in which 21 percent of all manufacturing assets were gobbled up in the period from 1953 to 1968.[4] These mergers were also different from those of the past. Previously, mergers were "vertical," that is, corporations bought up competitors in their own and related product lines. The postwar mergers were more "horizontal" and also of a completely new type, merging firms in unrelated lines into gigantic octopus corporations. The tentacles of these conglomerates reach into even minor competitive branches of industry, formerly considered outside the direct sphere of monopoly conquest. But with computerized means of gathering, storing and analyzing data instantly, it is possible to monitor and direct hundreds of different kinds of enterprises scattered over vast areas. One conglomerate executive claims that a central staff of 90 experts could "run any company in the world, any company."[5]

By holding a monopoly position in one or more product lines, the large

* The government's consumer price index, using prices for the year 1967 as 100, rose from 42 in 1940, to 72.1 in 1950, to 88.7 in 1960, to 116.3 in 1970, and to 158.6 in April 1975. (*Handbook of Labor Statistics, 1974; Handbook of Basic Economic Statistics*, p. 102, May 1975, Bureau of Economic Research, Washington, D.C.)

** "Of the 500 largest industrial corporations there are 167 in the $1-billion club, 27 more than last year, and their sales represent 75 percent of the total. Seventeen companies are now in the more exclusive $5-billion club." *Fortune*, May 1974, p.230.

conglomerate can use its higher profit yields to finance forays into other fields. In addition, because of its buying and selling relationship with other giant firms, "large conglomerates exchange reciprocal favors with one another to the detriment of smaller firms."[6]

*Fortune* magazine observes that "trade relations between the giant conglomerates tend to close a business circle." The U.S. economy "might end up completely dominated by conglomerates happily trading with each other in a new kind of cartel system."[7]

This works not only to the "detriment of smaller firms," but to the public at large. The large monopoly corporations constitute an increasingly autocratic, antisocial corporate fiefdom over the country. The more immediate effects are disastrous, contributing greatly to the constant rise in living costs.

As we indicated, price competition tends to disappear at high levels of economic concentration. If the Ford Motor Company, for instance, were to lower its prices substantially, it would almost immediately gain a larger share of the auto market. But it would not be long before GM and Chrysler did likewise. The net result is that they would all be selling at a lesser profit. *"Therefore,"* said the Senate Subcommittee, *"firms in highly concentrated markets are more likely to price as monopolists rather than as competitors, that is, they will sell at prices that maximize their joint profits."*[8]

The result is more than a rise in price of monopoly-produced goods. *All* prices get pushed upward. Smaller producing and retail firms must pay higher prices for their machinery and durable goods. Then, as monopoly penetrates the retail field through huge chain stores and supermarkets, it sets price patterns. Furthermore, a rise in the price of monopoly products compels workers to demand a rise in wages. As the workers in the mass production industries are better organized, and as the monopoly firms are better able to absorb wage increases by passing them on to the consumer, wages rise.

In time this has an effect on wages generally. Workers in competitive branches of industry, in service trades and government employ find it harder to make ends meet, become restive, and also push for wage increases. The militant struggles of teachers, sanitation workers, hospital employees and farm workers, are examples of this. Hence, the main cause of inflation has not been the workers' push for higher wages, but the immense profiteering of the huge monopoly corporations. To think otherwise is to put the cart before the horse.

In addition to monopoly price-fixing, government deficit spending, particularly escalating expenditures on militarism and war, have upped prices year after year.* Thus, with each passing year, more workers realize that they are victims of a sleight-of-hand, now-you-see-it-now-you-don't game in which one hand gives and the other takes away. The hand that gives—rather, is forced to give—can be seen and grabbed, but that which takes away seems disembodied, an apparition, something surely there yet difficult to see and even more difficult to grapple with.

It is understandable that the class struggle, in the sense of direct worker-management pitched battles, seems somewhat blunted as compared with the past, but only because the struggle has become more complex and takes on more than one form. The hand that takes away belongs to no single employer but to the whole system of monopoly capitalism and its governmental power. To control prices and profits requires a political struggle, not only an economic one. Workers, therefore, need to broaden their view of the system they live under and learn to fight together as a class, not only as separated contingents.

## Conglomerates

The rise of conglomerates created new complex problems. Trade unions first made their appearance when the journeyman-apprentice relationship broke down into an employer-employee tie. The rise of modern industry necessitated a move from the narrower craft form of union to factory and plant-wide organizations. Still later, to make industrial unionism effective, industry-wide national unions had to be built. Now this framework, too is becoming restrictive. A strike which paralyzes only one of the many conglomerate tentacles is no longer capable of wounding the beast sufficiently to make it see reason.

For example, the ITT corporation had $1 billion in assets in 1961, mainly in telecommunications. Since then it has acquired over 100 corporations with combined assets approaching $4 billion, plus 50 foreign-based operations. Consequently, only 17 percent of ITT income in 1969 came from telecommunications.[9] ITT now bargains with 15 different major unions in this country, including electrical, auto,

---

*Government deficit spending feeds inflation by artificially increasing the amount of money in circulation. Military spending compounds this inflation by taking out of the national economy large quantities of human labor, natural resources and finished products, but putting back into it no equivalent values. It is as if, to make a comparison, some 20 percent of all wheat produced were to be dumped into the ocean. The price of bread would naturally rise.

teamsters, communications, steel, machinists, chemical, bakers and plumbers.

The research director of the United Steelworkers reported that eight major steel producers were involved in mergers in just two years' time. Six of them were swallowed by companies outside of steel. Jones and Laughlin was devoured by Ling-Temco-Vought, and Youngstown Sheet and Tube by the Lykes Corporation, a steamship company. The others were consumed by similar corporations. But, "At the same time, all of the steel companies themselves became conglomerates. . . . There is not today a major steel company that is itself not a conglomerate. In fact, most of them pride themselves on the fact . . . although they do not use the name because it has come in disrepute." The U.S. Steel Corporation calls itself a "diversified company." It now is engaged in producing plastics, chemicals, fertilizers, aluminum siding, cement, titanium and housing.[10]

As the large conglomerates have the muscle and the fat to absorb union pressure along single unit lines, there is great emphasis in union ranks on the need for "coordinated bargaining." But this is not easy to achieve even in single plants or multiple plants of a single industry corporation in which more than one union operates. A major breakthrough in this respect was the coordinated action of eleven separate international unions in striking GE plants in 1969. But this unity is a thousand times harder to realize between scores of diverse unions and occupations in completely unrelated industries.

The Ling-Temco-Vought conglomerate is said to have a myriad of interests "from rocking horses to jet fighters, from sausages to space vehicles, and from pills to catchers' mitts."[11] The Jones and Laughlin steel plant is one ingredient in this strange conglomerate goulash, so its workers have something in common with workers in these other industries, far removed from steel-making though they be. Yet the relationship of J and L workers to those in other steel plants—though these are ingredients in still other conglomerate pots—is necessarily close, and their coordination of efforts even decisive.

One conglomerate president predicts that there will be only 200 major manufacturing companies in the United States by 1980.[12] As conglomeration represents a sophisticated, determined effort to attain complete monopoly domination over the *entire* economy, it is clear that the problems posed for the labor movement are increasingly more complex. Some observers believe that this development may ultimately compel a massive reshaping of the trade union movement. The industrial union form of organization is here to stay, but it is no longer sufficient by itself. The conglomerates demand some form of union coordination across craft and industrial lines, some form of corporation-wide contacts and coordination of many different unions in diverse industries and occupations.

## Coordinated Bargaining

Coordinated bargaining has long existed between multiple employer associations and single unions. Trucking, shipping, longshore, garment, and building trades are only a few that employ this method. Both the employers and the unions favor it. The employers believe this strengthens them, since it makes divisions in their ranks more difficult, and it guarantees uniform labor costs for all of them.

But multiple union bargaining with a single corporate employer is not to the liking of the conglomerates, for it enables all the workers in all the branches of industry owned by the conglomerate to act in unison. Even where employers are compelled to accept this form of bargaining, it is extremely difficult to coordinate the interests and demands of many thousands and sometimes tens and hundreds of thousands of workers, employed in hundreds of different plants and scores of diverse industries.

Even when all the unions of a conglomerate have gathered their representatives into one room for bargaining discussions, they may find that the corporation has acquired or merged with still another company only a few hours before, or even in the course of the deliberations themselves. That has actually happened more than once.[13]

The Industrial Union Department of the AFL-CIO has undertaken the difficult task of keeping unions informed of the rapid changes in corporate ownerships. It has developed a computerized information center to provide up-to-the-minute information. Some unions are also taking steps to have their contracts culminate at approximately the same time, to facilitate coordinated bargaining.

But all this requires a different kind of labor movement to be really effective. Paul Jennings, president of the International Union of Electrical Workers (IUE), has correctly stated that it will take new methods to deal with what he calls, ''new look business,'' and that ''Coordination, if it is to reach its full potential, must be a year-around effort.''[14] This demands the closest cooperation between unions, and the building of workers' unity on a scale and to a degree not seen heretofore.

WHEN a conglomerate takes over a firm or when radical new technology is introduced, major questions also arise relating to the size and site of the given production unit. These are posed by the very nature of the new technology which enables greater centralization of control with greater decentralization of production. Because many of the new, more automated plants require a smaller work force, some of the older huge plants of highly concentrated production become more expensive to maintain. "Thus, when advanced technology is introduced it probably will be in a new plant located in an area that meets a broad range of economic requirements."[15]

The newer plants are more specialized, closer to the source of raw materials and regional consumer market, and located in outlying small towns where both labor and land are cheaper. The migration, therefore, is not just from the central city to the suburb, but also from the metropolis to rural and semirural communities.

This is most strikingly illustrated by the process of industrialization in the South, where the fastest industrial growth is in the rural countryside. One study shows that "manufacturing jobs increased by 43.7 percent in the South's metropolitan areas during the nineteen-sixties, but by 61 percent in the rural counties 50 miles or more from the nearest metropolitan area."[16]

Thus, in the meatpacking industry, the traditional gigantic stockyard complexes, formerly in Chicago and Kansas City, have now given way to a multiplicity of smaller, more specialized plants. They are no longer bunched together, but spread over many small towns, each tied to its own livestock and consumer market. "Similar developments have taken place in the auto, paper and textile industries."[17]

This, too, confronts workers and unions with many new problems. Even where the corporation agrees to recognize the union in the new location, it does not solve the problems of the laid-off workers in the old plants. Many of them cannot pull up roots and move to new communities even where the union contract gives them the option of similar jobs at the new locations. For middle-aged and old workers the results may well be tragic. They are tossed out like the junk of the dismantled plant. Many of the nation's distressed areas are due to this geographic redistribution of employment opportunities.[18]

Problems also exist in the new plants. Where workers find themselves unionized through a top labor-management agreement, certain basic union conditions are assured. But a union local created without the active

intervention of the workers themselves is at best a deformed organization. And where the new plant is a runaway from unionism, as are many
of those in the South, the national union is further weakened and labor
conditions in the industry are undermined.

## The Multinational Corporations

The rise of the multinational corporation has created even a greater
host of new problems for workers than the emergence of the conglomerate. The very same technology that enables conglomerates to centralize
control over enterprises across the country, enables them to supervise
industrial plants scattered across the globe.

Huge corporations such as GM, ITT, GE, IBM, Exxon and others are
"national" only in the sense that American nationals own majority
stock in them; otherwise they are transnational. Exxon, Mobil, Woolworth, National Cash Register, among others, derive more than half their
earnings from foreign sales. Eastman Kodak, Caterpillar Tractor, International Harvester, to name a few, sell from 30 to 50 percent of their
products in other lands.[19]

Before World War II, U.S. foreign investments went mainly to exploit
sources of raw materials abroad and to build the necessary transportation
and communication infrastructures. Since then, however, an increasingly larger percentage of U.S. foreign investments goes into manufacturing. In 1950, one-third of U.S. direct investments abroad* went into
production plants; in 1970, this had risen to 43 percent.[20] Direct investments in manufacturing abroad jumped from $4 billion in 1950 to $32
billion in 1970.[21] By 1970, Ford was producing 40 percent of its cars
abroad; Chrysler, 30 percent; GM, 25 percent.[22] "From a business point
of view this makes good sense, but it also means there is less trade in
exports from the United States."[23]

While the United States is not as dependent on world trade as are
countries such as England and Japan, exports are still very important. In
1969, 20 percent of bituminous coal, 41 percent of tobacco, 37 percent of
medicines, 19 percent of chemicals, 10 percent of autos, 29 percent of
construction machinery, and 16 percent of office machines went into
exports.[24] In recent years, however, the United States' share of world

---

*Direct investments, according to the Department of Commerce, are long-term investments
that go *only* to private foreign enterprises controlled or managed by American interests.
They do not include investments in foreign firms not so controlled or managed.

manufacturing exports has been declining—from 25.3 percent in 1960 to 18.2 in 1973.[25]

Multinational corporations undercut exports and the domestic market. One may buy a GE portable radio in the belief it was manufactured here, only to find that it was made in Hong Kong. It could have been produced in nearly any of the 98 different countries in which GE plants operate. Nor does the multinational corporation have to bear an American name tag. Olivetti, for example, is thought of as Italian. But there is an Olivetti General Electric, an Olivetti Underwood, a British, French and German Olivetti, and Olivetti subsidiaries in 23 countries.[26]

The *New York Times* of May 7, 1970, quotes the American director of the Motorola electronic assembly plant outside of Seoul as saying that production costs were one-tenth what they were for similar production at Motorola's plant in Phoenix, Arizona.

## "Cheap Labor" Competition

An article in the April 1970 *Fortune* reported that multinational corporations were "secretive" about a new pattern for investments in underdeveloped countries. These, it is said, have an important resource scarce in industrial countries—cheap labor.

What is meant by "cheap labor" is made clear by a glance at hourly wage rates in Southeast Asia. In 1969 these ranged from 41 ¢ to 35 ¢ for skilled construction workers in Hong Kong, South Vietnam and Singapore, and from 17¢ to 13¢ for ordinary labor in Taiwan, Thailand and South Korea.[27] A Department of Commerce report on trade notes:

> The increase of imports of manufacturers has resulted in part from the establishment of plants of U.S. firms in low-wage countries to produce for the U.S. market as in the case of TV picture tubes. . . . The more rapid increase of imports than exports implies a larger problem in the future. Some of these imports will come from foreign subsidiaries or affiliates of U.S. firms.*[28]

This is happening. Estimates indicate that in 1971 imports accounted for about 18 percent of steel sales in the United States; approximately 24 percent of autos; something like 35 percent of TV sets; more than 60 percent of phonographs; about 86 percent of radios; almost all tape recorders; nearly 60 percent of sewing machines; 80 percent of electronic microscopes, and 33 percent of shoes. "Baseball is an American game,

---

* It is in the direct interest of U.S. workers, therefore, to have foreign nations nationalize the holdings of American corporations. This enables the standard of living to rise in these countries and puts an end to "cheap labor" competition.

but about 95 percent of baseball mitts sold in the U.S. in 1971 were imported."[29]

The gravity of the problem looming ahead can be appreciated when we note that in the 25 years between 1945 and 1970, U.S. firms established 8000 subsidiaries abroad, mostly in manufacturing.[30] This does not include hundreds of manufacturing plants established in Puerto Rico, which are not considered as being in a foreign country because the island is a colony of the United States. But it is also a source of "cheap labor."

IN 1970 the Industrial Union Department of the AFL-CIO convened a special national conference on "The Developing Crisis in International Trade." Attended by 625 participants, of whom 525 came from unions at the national, state and local levels, the subject on everyone's mind was the multinational corporations.

Many examples of their effects were given. A Zenith Corporation electronics plant in New Jersey had been shut down after a similar plant opened in Taiwan employing 6,500 workers. U.S. corporate subsidiaries were springing up along the Mexican border and in the Far East "to produce components for products made in the U.S." An aluminum plant in Ghana, similar to one operated by the same company in the United States, paid only "a small fraction of U.S. wages."

Labor delegates were highly critical of the present effect of international trade on the workers they represent. But "there was no formulation of a feasible, concrete program."[31]

Not a single voice was recorded as taking issue with a pro-imperialist foreign plicy that serves the interests of the multinational corporations, yet it is impossible to oppose cheap labor competition in Korea, Taiwan and Indochina, while supporting the oppressive role of U.S. imperialism everywhere in those areas.

However, voices were raised at the conference in behalf of a "Buy American" campaign. Some unions, such as the ILGWU, hard hit by foreign imports, have made this their main answer to the problem. But it is a false answer. A jingoist, racist campaign directed against the products of other lands, will only engender similar responses abroad. It is more than self-defeating; it is inflammatory and dangerous. It pits workers of one country against workers of another. Employers use this to divert workers' ire from the employers themselves. Despite the fact that 20 percent of General Motors' assets are abroad, and its German-made Opel is the third largest car import, GM blames foreign capitalists and workers for the loss of jobs at home. It does this to prod U.S. workers to greater productivity.[32]

The multinational corporations are not "foreign." They are as "American" as Nelson Rockefeller. The enemy to be fought, therefore, is here, not abroad. But just as capital is international, so must labor be. Labor must be international to maximize the common fight against exploitation and to unite the workers of all lands for peace and friendship.

## The Need for World Labor Coordination

In recent years even conservative-led unions have had to face up to the need for some form of world labor coordination in confronting the multinational corporations. The UAW was one of the first to recognize this need. Through the International Metalworkers Federation, meetings of representatives of auto workers of different countries have taken place. They agreed to cooperate to narrow wage differentials between different countries and to assist one another in case of strike by preventing the transfer of work from one country to another.

At the end of 1972 the International Metalworkers Federation (IMF) convened a meeting in San Francisco of union leaders from 23 different countries. Plans were mapped to seek worldwide contracts with nine giant conglomerates, six of them U.S.-based, including Ford, Chrysler, GM and GE. The large UAW delegation favored an international minimum wage. The meeting agreed that if a union in one country is unable to strike in support of workers of another country, it should be asked to contribute to the strike fund and to join in a boycott of the product being struck. One metalworkers federation official optimistically concluded that the meeting had "laid the basis for multinational bargaining with nine international enterprises."[33]

A three-day IMF conference was held in New York City in the spring of 1973 in connection with the approaching contract negotiations of U.S. unions with GE. Sponsored by the Coordinated Bargaining Committee (CBC) of U.S. GE-Westinghouse workers, the meeting discussed ways and means of more effective international cooperation. A CBC pamphlet entitled, "Where in the World Are Your Companies?", ended with the hopeful note, "Perhaps, in some future time, the CBC will also be worldwide, and multinational corporations like GE and Westinghouse will do their bargaining with a coordinated committee drawn from around the globe."[34]

Hence, the first steps toward worldwide coordinated efforts have been taken. But we are still some distance from the day when international bargaining will actually take place. The main obstacle is the AFL-CIO top leadership, which has opposed international trade union unity with a determination and consistency worthy of better things. When the cold war broke out, the AFL leadership instigated and engineered the split in the united World Federation of Trade Unions (WFTU). Both the AFL and CIO helped initiate a counterfederation, the International Confederation of Free Trade Unions (ICFTU). But the AFL-CIO has now broken relations with this second federation, too, because the ICFTU has been compelled to move toward unity with the WFTU and its affiliated unions.

There can be no completely coordinated fight against the multinational corporations and for world peace without an end to the split in the world labor movement. This requires an end to AFL-CIO collaboration with the CIA in breaking up unions in other countries—those that are not to the liking of the U.S. State Department and its multinational bosses. In Europe, the split is gradually being healed. A first meeting between representatives of the WFTU and the ICFTU was held in January 1974 in Geneva. But the reactionary position of George Meany still determines the official U.S. trade union policy.

Without the fullest international cooperation aimed at raising the wage and living standards of workers everywhere, it is impossible to effectively fight against the multinationals. In the name of fighting competition from foreign "cheap labor," the steel union has surrendered the right to strike, and collaborated with the steel corporations' drive for increased productivity. This can only lead to even more speed-up, work accidents, new labor-saving machinery, rising unemployment, and the steady erosion of workers' living standards. Nor are the unions that call for import quota limitations fighting realistically and effectively. Such efforts will only sharpen the international trade war.

The independent United Electrical Workers Union has formulated a more struggle-oriented approach to meet what it calls "the foreign runaway menace." It favors a flat prohibition of runaway plants to other countries and calls for an excess profits tax levied on American corporations whose foreign-owned plants have wages and working conditions inferior to those in this country. The UE also demands the closing of tariff loopholes which give U.S. companies special exemptions on import duties on goods produced abroad. It also calls for a drastic reduction in military spending as an important step in the fight against inflation.[35]

The growing consciousness that multinational corporations are exporting jobs is to be seen in a provision of the Trade Act of 1974. This makes possible the group-filing of claims for "Trade Readjustment Allowance" to workers who lose their jobs because of increased imports. The first group of workers to be approved for such cash benefit adjustment assistance were 300 employees of the Allen Quimby Veneer Company of Bingham, Massachusetts.[36] A much larger claim was filed by the UAW for 39,000 unemployed Chrysler workers in 10 plants, who lost their jobs because of an increase in the import of Chrysler cars. If successful, this claim would yield more than $100 million in additional lay-off benefits for these workers.[37] An official of the International Association of Machinists has predicted that within 12 months of June 1975, 600 more plants, employing 100,000 American workers, will close down because of foreign imports.[38] More unions will thus be claiming adjustment assistance for their laid-off members.*

The fight is twofold: to take the superprofits out of the export of capital abroad, and to unite the workers of all countries so that they are as one in fighting their common enemies.

"Workers of all countries unite!" urged Marx and Engels in the *Communist Manifesto*. This slogan is as timely now as when it was first pronounced. The menace of multinational capitalism has made it a practical necessity.

---

*Where granted, such assistance enables a discharged worker to receive up to 70 percent of former earnings but no more than the average weekly wage paid manufacturing workers. As only $350 million was allocated for this purpose, it is at best only a stopgap measure.

IT IS hard to believe that the word "automation" was still unknown when World War II ended, that the first computer control system was yet to be installed, and that the term "cybernetics" had not yet been coined. So breathtaking has subsequent technological advance been that it is commonly referred to as "a revolution in science and technology."

When the implications of the new technology were first perceived, many people assumed that in a decade or two tens of millions would be left permanently idle.[1] Norbert Wiener, the "father" of cybernetics, in *The Human Use of Human Beings*, estimated in 1950 that it would "take the new tools 10 to 20 years to come into their own." If war came, he surmised, the automatic age would be upon us "within less than five years." He feared that unemployment would increase so rapidly that "the depression of the thirties will seem a pleasant joke."[2]

In January 1962, in face of a rise in joblessness, the President's Advisory Committee on Labor-Management Policy made its report on problems incident to automation and other technological change. Composed of leading representatives of management, organized labor, government and academe, the committee concluded that automation did indeed threaten employment. Two years later a group of prestigious individuals issued a statement on the "Triple Revolution," which alarmingly predicted that automation would cut down a majority of jobs in a short period of time.[3]

As the fearsome auguries failed to materialize, an opposite view, minimizing the effects of the new technology, gained official ascendancy. The invention of the steam and gasoline engines, it was asserted, had greater total impact on society than the new automatic work processes were likely to have.

At the time of the Presidential advisory committee's report, two members made public their disagreement with its over-all finding. Henry Ford II challenged the committee's assumption that "technological advances are in and by themselves causes of unemployment." Automation displaces some individuals from their jobs, he conceded, but "its overall effect is to increase income and expand job opportunities"[4] Arthur F. Burns, the economics expert, likewise disagreed. He deplored "anything that adds to the greatly exaggerated fears that many people have of what is loosely called automation."[5]

As the apprehension of working people continued to mount, a top-level campaign was begun to dispel such fears. Within a few days, in early 1965, "*Look, Fortune* and the *New York Times Magazine* issued glowing stories on the blessings of the new technology."[6] Professor Peter Drucker's article in the *Times' Magazine* entitled, "Automation Is Not the Villain,"[7] set the tone. Many corporations also decided as policy to shun the very use of the word automation. It was regarded as "inflammatory, misleading and inaccurate."[8]

On the surface, Ford, Burns, Drucker, and the others who agreed with them, seemed to be right. The new technological upheaval did not bring mass unemployment on the scale originally predicted. But it is somewhat too soon to rejoice. When the economy is in upswing it is possible to balance a loss of jobs due to technological change with a total rise in employment. This was the case, for instance, in the printing industry for at least two decades. But with the country facing an extended period of chronic slump and/or stagnation, the cumulative effects of the new technology are bound to strike with devastating force.

There are additional reasons why the earlier dim forecasts did not materialize. Production under capitalism, it should be remembered, is for profit, not philanthropy. Where automation costs prove cheaper than the purchase of labor power, corporations will invest large sums of cold cash today for greater total profits through the reduction in the work force tomorrow. But greater automation becomes impractical where human labor remains cheaper than the new technology, or where a firm is too small to utilize it economically.

Automation should also be seen as an ongoing process, not limited to computerized feedback systems. In fact, all technological innovation that transfers some part of human labor to machine (automatic) performance is part of the automation process. As the new technology tends to be very expensive at first, only the very largest units avail themselves of it. But as relatively cheaper second and third generation models appear, and as competition intensifies, the smaller firms find the means to automate rather than face elimination.

Despite claims to the contrary, automation has already taken its toll. Government unemployment statistics are notoriously unreliable. They conceal the existence of a vast army of hidden unemployed. A 1962 survey found that 31.5 percent of those listed as employed were working only part-time or intermittently.[9] Another survey taken in 1966 found that more than five million persons who "wanted a job" were not included in either labor force or unemployment figures because they were not "actively" seeking work. About 1.5 million of these were women.[10] Hence, in working-class homes, ghetto streets, rural back roads, and in high school and college classrooms millions who would be working if remunerative work was available are to be found. These are now listed as housewives, students, unemployables, or not listed at all, as with jobless ghetto youth. Nor do the unemployment figures include the over four million persons in the armed forces and working for the military.[11]

## Rising Labor Productivity

Deception is also widely practiced in the juggling of labor productivity figures. To "prove" that technological change is nothing to fear and technological unemployment only a phantom, it is even asserted— despite Labor Department figures—that labor productivity has been declining instead of rising.

Man/woman hour productivity in manufacturing industries for the years 1947-57 increased at an annual rate of 2.5 percent. But from 1960 to 1973 the annual rise was 3.4 percent.[12] As a 1 percent increase in annual productivity doubles productivity in approximately 72 years, a 2 percent rise in 36 years, and a 3 percent rise in 23 years, the additional increase is quite significant.[13]

But even this does not tell the whole story. Government productivity indices lump production workers with executives, officials, advertising personnel and other nonproductive strata.[14] The scene is muddied further because the Department of Labor includes "self-employed and family workers as well as wage and salary workers" in its calculations.[15] Thus labor costs are artificially inflated and productivity deflated.

Average labor productivity is determined by lumping together and flattening out figures for widely diverse industry increases and decreases. In 1973, for example, official figures showed a 3 percent rise in private sector labor productivity. But this average concealed the fact that ten separate industries showed a decline for the year while others showed a sharp increase. Steel productivity increased, for example, by 10.8 percent and aluminum rolling by 12.3 percent.[16]

Just as great a variance exists between production units in the same industry. The most advanced technology is spearheaded by the firms with the greatest financial reserves. Labor productivity will vary immensely, therefore, depending on the level of technology. The textile industry, for example, has seen rapid technological changes. From 1949 to 1957 annual woman/man-hour productivity rose by 2.9 percent. But it leaped to 7.3 percent a year between 1960 and 1965. This development was not uniform. The difference in productivity performance between the "more efficient" and the "average" textile mill ranged from 40 to 140 percent. The difference between the "more efficient" and "less efficient" mill was far greater—from double to 4.5 times as great. Hence, some mills lagged far behind others. Yet technological change reduced total employment in textile by 28 percent, or about 340,000 workers.[17]

THUS automation reduces the work force as it increases production. Faster looms, self-correcting winding machines, continuous dyeing—all computer guided and controlled—are making the changes in textile. In coal, a mechanical giant called the "Push-Button Miner" stands three stories high and weighs more than 1.5 million pounds. "It cuts and loads as much as 266 tons of coal an hour in one continuous operation, without drilling or blasting. . . . The entire operation requires a crew of only three men and is performed by remote control from a panel outside the mine shaft."[18] The number of miners has thus been reduced from some 600,000 at the end of World War II to about 130,000 today.

In maritime, highly automated ships now sail the seas with but a handful of men as complement, while containerization has radically cut down the size of the longshore force, greatly simplifying the unloading and loading of cargo and its transport on both land and sea. In printing, photo-offset machines use punched tape and new forms of computerized electrostatic printing. The laser beam and the cathode tube eliminate direct-contact technology completely.

In auto, the huge Chargomatic machine swallows sheet-metal blanks in one mouth and spits out doors or body frames from another. In steel, the basic oxygen furnace produces steel six to eight times faster than the open-hearth. And continuous casting "eliminates pouring, molding, transporting, and reheating." It is faster, saves space and fuel, produces a stronger steel, cuts scrap loss, and "reduces labor requirements per unit of output."[19] The same phenomenon can be found in one industry after another.

Computer control of industrial processes was first introduced in 1958. By 1968, about 1,700 process computers had been installed or ordered. Some 6,000 are now in use. The years needed to install a computer system in 1970 ran from two years for a simple system to 21 years for a highly complex one. The cost of installation ranged from $200,000 to $1,500,000. Two trends are evident, one toward a multiplicity of small, relatively low-cost computers capable of controlling a single process, and large-scale computers able to simultaneously guide numerous complex processes. It is expected that as process computers spread into more labor-intensive industries, their job displacement effect will become more pronounced.[20]

STRUCTURAL unemployment due to technological change can be partially counteracted by conditions of large-scale industrial expansion and growth. But in a period of general economic slowdown and stagnation, technological displacement merges with, and greatly swells, the ranks of general unemployment. In the present period the process is only in its early stages. The combined conditions of inflation, slowdown, and increased world competition, press upon corporate management to seek additional measures to increase labor productivity. Because price wars between the industrial giants are usually ruled out as a matter of policy, competition is centered on technological innovation that can squeeze more out of workers.

That big business spokesmen see increased productivity as their "answer," can be seen by their own recent statements. William F. May, chairman of the American Can Company, responding to the question, "What can business do?" replied: "About the only thing I can see that we can do is to push as strongly as we can for increased productivity. . . ." Lynn A. Townsend, chairman of the Chrysler Corporation, asked that government do something to "give business a chance to improve its efficiency and increase its productivity." Robert W. Sarnoff, then chairman of the RCA Corporation, likewise stressed "the need for major capital spending efforts to expand capacity, reduce costs and increase productivity." And Leif Olsen, chief economist for the First National City Bank of New York, saw the drive for productivity "as a long-term remedy against inflation."[21]

## The Government's Push for Increased Productivity

As early as 1972, faced with a growing foreign trade imbalance, the Nixon Administration began pushing the productivity theme. A special National Commission on productivity was established with Task Forces for each separate industry group. These were given the responsibility of finding the bottlenecks holding back increased productivity, and advancing proposals for their elimination. Each separate Task Force prepared its own special report for the Commission. These varied from industry to industry but overlapped on two questions—the financing of the new technology, and the problem of labor "inflexibilities" that stood in the way of changes in work rules.

A proposal on financing suggested that the cost of new plants and new technology be paid for by tax deductions; in other words, by making the public foot the bill. It was conceded that this would reduce tax revenue, but, it was argued, this would only be temporary, for "less labor would be utilized in more efficient facilities."

Labor "inflexibilities" discussed were the reluctance of workers "to accept new work standards," "seniority without regard for skill," "difficulty in terminating undesirable employees," and "restrictions on testing of new employees." Proposed solutions included the guaranteed annual wage and greater union-management cooperation through the establishment of a network of plant productivity boards composed of management, labor and public representatives. The goal was that "no labor contract or practice would be permitted which restricts or reduces productivity." It claimed that this would foster and enlarge "new technology" and make the United States "more competitive in world markets," for "labor would be replaced by higher technology."[22]

## Lack of Labor Counterstrategy

Obviously, the drive to replace labor with higher technology is well organized and coordinated. The labor movement cannot say the same for a counterstrategy. Yet the threat to both workers and unions is bound to grow. More jobs will be eliminated, more work standards undermined, and more unions greatly weakened, unless a militant and effective counterstrategy is devised and implemented.

Labor's most effective weapon—the ability to shut down production—is now being newly threatened in the more automated industries. Often a mere handful of employees, usually supervisory, can maintain production at near normal levels for long periods, despite strikes involving the great majority of workers. This is now true in such industries as telephone, gas, electric utility, chemical and oil refining. A strike in the Shell Oil refinery in Houston, Texas, lasted a full year, yet the plant "continued to operate at high levels of capacity." During a 28-day strike at the Brooklyn Gas Company, "there was not a single cold pot of chicken soup in Brooklyn."[23] Automatic dial service kept phone lines open during a nationwide long-distance telephone operators' strike. The Hammond, Indiana *Times*, moved new automated equipment into its plant in the dead of night, kept it hidden in a basement storeroom, and, when ready, locked out 113 composing room workers. The paper continued to appear without interruption.[24]

Some conclude that the strike weapon is now antiquated and passé. George Meany (who never participated in a strike) has long held that the strike is on its way out. And I. W. Abel, president of the powerful steel union, rushed to surrender the strike weapon even though steel is not in the category of automated industries cited above. Not that there is need to abandon strikes even in the most automated industries, although the conditions for successful strikes have been altered somewhat. Strikes are likely to be of longer duration, to be fought with no holds barred, and to require a broadened base of worker participation and support.

Wherever technological change has shifted the balance in favor of management, the labor movement must find the strategy and tactics to shift it in its own favor. Wherever craft unions, as in printing, are hard-pressed to win battles on their own, or where attrition from automation has reduced the numerical strength and financial reserves of an industrial union, it is imperative to combine the forces of a number of unions and to confront the employers with united joint action.

As early as 1963, the late Elmer Brown, then president of the typographical union, urged unification of the printing unions to meet the challenge of company mergers and technological change. With considerable foresight he warned, "As newer tools, equipment and processes are employed, the jurisdictional lines of demarcation will tend to disappear.

. . . Such evolution must bring with it additional frictions over jurisdictions, competition for members and lack of effective cooperation among the crafts."[25] Since then two mergers have taken place in the industry. The pressmen and stereotypers joined to form the new International Printing and Graphic Communications Union; and the lithographers, photoengravers and bookbinders united in the Graphic Arts International Union. But even this is not enough to halt strikebreaking in the industry, as the typographical union, the most militant and most hard pressed in the printing crafts, recognizes. At its 1974 convention it called for merger, amalgamation or federation with other printing or communication unions.

Rapid technological change in the meatpacking industry was also a major factor in prompting the entrance of the militant United Packinghouse Workers into the Amalgamated Meat Cutters and Butcher Workmen's Union. In the same year, 1968, four operating railroad brotherhoods merged to form the United Transportation Union. The independent Left-led Mine, Mill and Smelter Workers Union, undermined by repeated raiding, was finally compelled to enter the steel union.

More mergers would have taken place were it not for objective and subjective difficulties. The merging of disparate unions "is not a simple task," notes Prof. Seligman. "A craft outlook must be fused with industrial unionism, official posts must be redistributed, voting rights must be adjusted, and the various funds must be comingled." Yet he believes such changes are essential, "if unions are to face up to the impact of an ever changing technology."[26]

Often employers fear such mergers and their possible effects in organizing the unorganized. This is shown by the reaction of employers in the printing industry. In early 1974, the organization of open-shop (anti-union) printing trades employers, addressed a letter to printing firms. It stressed that the printing industry "is seriously threatened by moves . . . to establish one giant international union covering the entire industry." It pointed to the mergers that had already taken place which "greatly increased [union] power to organize your employees and to enforce their demands at the bargaining table. And the merger of two of the big three, the ITU and Pressman-Stereotypers, currently is under discussion." Finally, it urged "that aggressive action be taken to combat efforts of printing industry unions to completely unionize and dominate the industry."[27]

Notwithstanding this exaggeration of the immediacy of the threat to open-shop printing—still the dominant form in the industry—it does indicate the justified fears that employers have of a unified and enlarged labor movement.

## Labor Mergers

Mergers, therefore, are on the order of the day, and in more industries than printing. A word of warning is needed, however. Labor history tells us that while mergers may be essential at times, what is decisive is the democratic and fighting character of a union. A multiplication of the size of subservient, corrupt, class-partnership unions is not an accretion of labor strength, but of weakness. The steelworkers, for example, are united in one union, but this does not prevent its leadership from working with management against the best interests of the steelworkers. The issue is not unity for the sake of unity, but unity for the sake of improving the workers' capacity to fight for their interests and rights.

A division of opinion arose in the ranks of the International Longshoremen's and Warehousemen's Union (ILWU) on this very question. Harry Bridges, the union's often courageous and militant president, came to the conclusion that automation's attrition had so weakened the union's bargaining power that merger was the best way out. He toyed with the idea of merging with either the International Longshoremen's Association of the East and Gulf Coasts, or the Teamsters. Both proposals had a certain logic in their favor. A merger with the ILA would bring about the complete unification of longshoremen on a national scale. A merger with the Teamsters would unite dock, warehouse and trucking workers, whose jobs overlap due to containerization, into one union. But the efforts of Bridges to explore these possibilities were not supported by the ILWU membership, and for valid reasons.

If the ILWU were swallowed up by either the ILA of Thomas Gleason, or the Teamsters under Frank Fitzsimmons, the fight against the shipowners would not be strengthened but weakened. Both of these unions are reactionary-led and notoriously corrupt. Merger with reactionary leadership and policies is sometimes unavoidable, and at times advisable, if there is basic inner-union democracy and thus the possibility of change. But where there is gangster-type union control and the bureaucratic head-chopping of those who disagree, organizational unity is counterproductive to real unity.

The problem of unity is not one for leadership alone. It requires the action of the rank and file; the conscious reaching out and the forging of unbreakable links to the workers in other unions. The starting point is simple solidarity; the mutual aid of workers to workers. To prepare the way for future mergers—or in lieu of them when they are impractical—it is possible to achieve agreement *between* unions. These could eliminate jurisdictional strife, coordinate bargaining, synchronize contract termination dates, establish joint strike strategy, develop a common approach to political action and legislative demands and, in some cases, pool resources for a massive organizing drive. When unity of this kind develops around specific, concrete objectives, merger arises as a natural consequence where it is feasible and necessary.

The coordinated action of the workers and unions, including the cooperation of two intensely competitive unions, the U.E. and I.U.E., in confronting the GE Corporation, is an example of such unity, though still limited. The Canadian sections of the ILWU and ILA have also shown how unity can begin to be forged among longshoremen. Under the aegis of the Canadian Labor Federation and the Canadian Labor Congress, both unions, with the support of their Internationals, formed a permanent National Committee on Common Problems. Technological change, which is used to undermine job security and working conditions, motivated this move.

Meeting in July 1974, the ILWU executive board unanimously decided to attempt a similar development in the United States. Vice-President William Chester explained, "I'm not talking about merger. I am talking about an alliance." Steps have also been taken to discuss jurisdictional issues affecting both the ILWU and the Teamsters. Both unions and their members have much to gain by an understanding. An issue of jurisdictional dispute has arisen over the workers in the newly created container freight stations, where the huge container boxes get packed and unpacked and readied for shipment by truck, train, ship or plane. These stations are being established in western regions where unionism is weakest. An agreement between the ILWU and the Western Conference of Teamsters to divide jurisdiction and to jointly organize these ports would represent an important step forward.[28]

Like the new problems arising from conglomeration and the multinational corporation, the problems flowing from automation call for trade union unity on a scale and to a degree never experienced before. This need goes beyond uniting workers in a single industry or in associated industries. The Hammond *Times'* lockout of its printers, for example, was a challenge and threat to other workers as well. Hammond is a working-class and union town. If Hammond's other unions had decided to break the lockout, it was in their power to do so. They could have massed thousands of workers on the picket line to prevent scabs from entering the plant. They could have stopped the distribution and sale of the paper. They could have organized a boycott against merchants who continued to advertise in the *Times*. But, as one typographical worker ruefully commented: "It's one thing to say you're in sympathy with those locked-out people. It's another to show that sympathy right here on the picket line."[29]

## A Class Approach to Technological Change

A major policy question facing nearly all unions is what attitude to take to technological change as such. This question has no easy answer. Opposition to all further advances in technology is impossible. It is futile and retrogressive. Technical change, in and by itself, is not the enemy. Automation could be a blessing if it freed workers from drudgery and exploitation. It is often a curse because under capitalism it is used to intensify exploitation and to throw additional millions on the jobless scrap-heap, all in the interests of greater profit.

The approach of workers to automation requires, therefore, a vigilant and consistent class approach. Workers cannot favor the introduction of new technology if in any way it threatens their own class interests. Yet to prevent such a threat is extremely difficult, because corporations invest in new technology to reduce unit labor costs. And this is also the reason that workers historically have been hostile to the introduction of new machinery.

Where unions have the muscle to influence the situation, they usually first respond to mechanization by saying "no," thereby indicating a determination to halt or slow the process. When the pressure mounts and fear grows of being outflanked, the "no" gets changed to "maybe." Unions indicate a readiness to consider automation if there is something in it for them. They agree to one form or another of what has been called a "buy-out."

In coal mining, the union under John L. Lewis did more than this. For it, mechanization was also a form of "buy-in." Unbeknownst to the miners, the UMW leadership had established a controlling interest in one of the largest coal-mining operations. It sat, therefore, on both ends of the bargaining table. And from this ambidextrous position it gave the coal operators the green light to mechanize. In return the miners got a boost in pay, some additional fringe benefits, and a per-ton royalty paid into the union's hospital and welfare fund. Within a few years some 70 percent of the miners were jobless and the word "Appalachia" entered the language as synonymous with mass poverty and hopelessness. But not for the mining conglomerates, which were practicing the alchemy of turning huge quantities of coal into large hoards of gold.

## The Longshore Mechanization Agreement

In longshore, the story is somewhat different. By 1957 it became obvious to union leaders that mechanization was gaining ground despite all attempts to prevent it. Harry Bridges then confronted the union with the alternative—either fight against mechanization a few more years until the inevitable showdown, or give the employers a free hand to mechanize in exchange for specific benefits for the workers.

After a prolonged period of discussion and negotiation, an agreement known as the Mechanization and Modernization Agreement (M & M) was signed in October 1960. This was to last five years and give the shipowners the right, within certain limits, to reduce the size of the workforce as mechanization advanced. The fully registered dockers— men with the highest seniority in division "A"—were guaranteed 35 hours of pay per week "even if there wasn't any work for them to do." Nor could they be laid off. "To give older men an incentive to leave the industry, the agreement provided for early retirement and a lump sum of $7,920, over and above their pensions upon retirement at 65." If they retired at 62, they could begin drawing on this sum at the rate of $200 a month. All this was to be paid from a yearly $5.5 million M & M trust fund provided by the shipowners. There were no provisions to protect jobs of men with lesser seniority in the "B" division, nor for casual workers. Nor were the shipowners obliged to replace men who left the industry through retirement, illness or death.[30]

Mechanization paid off handsomely for the shipowners. A ship that once took as long as two weeks to unload, could now be docked, unloaded and returned to sea in seven hours. "Of course, the steamship companies were quite delighted, as the new arrangements permitted quick turn-around and saved them days of port charges and seamen's wages. But the burden of displacement was placed on the shoulders of B men and the casuals. . . ."[31] And on workers who would otherwise be entering the industry.

Twelve years later, after a strike that lasted 134 days—the first West

Coast longshore strike in 23 years—the union summed up the results of
the 1960-1970 decade: "Cargo doubled, from over 19 million tons to
nearly 40 million tons. Manhours worked . . . dropped 17 percent. The
amount of cargo per manhour rose 138! Labor cost per ton dropped 30
percent, . . ."[32] And the size of the total longshore force declined by
nearly 50 percent.

The ILA on the East and Gulf Coasts followed a like pattern. It settled
for a guaranteed minimum annual wage for registered men, a promise
against lay-offs, and a cash incentive for earlier retirement. Reduction in
the size of the work force would come by attrition.

More recently, in 1974, the typographical union in New York settled
its automation dispute with newspaper publishers along somewhat similar lines. The agreement consisted primarily of "a lifetime job guarantee
and a six-month paid sabbatical leave for all full-time and substitute
printers, the unlimited right of publishers to automate, wage increases
and cost-of-living protections, and a long-term [eleven years!] contract
with two reopening dates."[33] This was a considerable improvement over
settlements elsewhere, and provided protection for substitute workers
also. But this "buy-out," too, was at the expense of workers who
otherwise would be entering the trade in years to come. When Harry
Bridges was once asked if there was an alternative to mechanization, his
reply, in effect, was: What do you expect? This is capitalism. For another
alternative you first have to change the system.[34]

It is true; there is no full answer to automation short of socialism. Yet
this does not obviate the need for a consistent class approach to the
struggle under capitalism. The shipping corporations certainly did not
consider the M & M agreement as in any way jeopardizing their interests.
This is seen in their attitude toward Bridges. For many years treated as an
ogre in human disguise, he was now a "responsible labor statesman."
The vice-president of a shipping company said, "I used to think he had
horns and a tail and long fangs, but now I must say his word is
good. . ."[35]

## A Partial Solution

Recognizing the immense complexities of the problem of automation,
and the difficulties of finding even a partial solution to it under
capitalism, the advisability of unions giving management a free hand to
automate is questionable. By surrendering their ability to check and
control the process, they inevitably create conditions in which their

bargaining position becomes steadily worse. This is one reason the typographical local in New York accepted an eleven-year contract previously considered unthinkable. It feared that if a basic conflict arose before that time, it could place in jeopardy the job guarantees it had won. By the time the contract expires, however, a large percentage of present printers will have retired, for the average age in this craft is unusually high. Then, either the union recoups some of its lost strength through unity and merger with other unions, or its bargaining position will atrophy.

This process is already at work in longshore. In the 1966 ILWU agreement the employers were able to insert a new section known as "9.43." This gives them the right to hire "steady, skilled mechanical or powered equipment operators without limit as to numbers or length of time in steady employment." These "steadymen" can be shifted from job to job without having to return to the hiring hall. The democratic hiring hall is thus by-passed as the means by which equal job opportunities are made available to all longshoremen.[36] "Steadymen" become something of a new labor aristocracy with close ties and allegiance to management. As the size of the work force declines through attrition, these technicians given certain circumstances, can be used against the rest of the workers and the union.

A MUCH overlooked partial answer to automation lies in a more determined fight against a reduction in the size of the total work force. This requires going beyond job security for those currently employed and cash inducements for earlier retirement. It is obvious that employers are going to profit immensely from automation. But some benefits of a lasting kind could accrue to the workers if they think in class terms and adopt a more radical approach to the question of the length of the work week.

If the level of technology in the mid-thirties enabled the general adoption of a 40-hour work week, what should this mean 40 years later when technology has moved forward with jet-like speed? It is anachronistic that miners should be compelled to work approximately the same hours as formerly, when mechanization has made possible much greater output with only one-third or one-fourth of the previous work force. When the hazards of life, limb and health—and the unconscionable profits of the coal and fuel magnates—are considered, it is barbaric to view the present workday or work week as sacrosanct and inviolable. New technology also makes it possible for ships to unload and load in a fraction of the former time. In printing, the most advanced hot metal typesetting machine could set only seven to ten characters a second, but the new computerized phototypesetters operate at speeds up to 1,000 characters a second.[37] Why then should miners, longshoremen and printers, and all working on hazardous and nerve-wracking jobs, not think in terms of a 20- or 25-hour week without a reduction in weekly pay? This is possible, of course, only in industries that are fully organized.

Nor is it to be expected that newer industries will absorb the technologically displaced. Present-day automation is different from the gradual technological advances made since the first industrial revolution. And secondly, the new industries, such as plastics and chemical, tend to be more automated from the start. Prof. Ben Seligman was justified in asking: "Where are the vast new industries we have been promised to take up the slack?"[38]

## The Shorter Work Week – a Partial Solution

A major reduction in the work week cannot be won all at once. Corporations will resist such reform because once gained it cannot be easily taken away. It enters into the historic standard of living. The steel workers and New York printers won extended sabbatical leaves for workers with long years of seniority. Employers preferred this to a reduction, even nominal, in the workday or work week. They realize that such a reduction would become contagious. Won by one group of workers, it would soon spread to others.

Both the ILWU and the Typographical Big Six Local in New York raised the demand for a shorter work week during their negotiations. But this was never meant to be treated seriously. It was raised for the record, to be dropped at the first sign of oppostion from the employers. Had it been a serious proposal, the unions would have been campaigning over a longer period and preparing their ranks and the public for a lengthy battle in its behalf.

From time to time, other unions, especially in convention resolutions, raise the question of a shorter work week. In the UAW's 1961 negotiations, they listed a number of possible approaches to this question, but did not pursue them. Because employers prefer to pay time-and-a-half as against hiring another worker, the UAW proposed that this be countered by double time for overtime, with triple pay for work over ten hours or on Sunday. Again these proposals were never followed up.

With automation spreading, unemployment growing, working conditions and health standards deteriorating, the issue of a shorter work week without reduction in weekly earnings emerges once again—as in previous periods of crisis—a major struggle to be waged on both the economic and political front.

## Socialism – the Answer

A shorter work week is not the only answer to the automation problem. Material goods and services are still needed in vast quantities, because tens of millions in this country lack decent living standards. Furthermore, as Prof. Seymour Melman has stressed, the United States is fast becoming a depleted society in essential social services—it lacks decent housing, rapid public transportation, adequate health and educational facilities, and even air and water fit for human consumption. There are also the immense needs of world humanity, for the overwhelming majority of the people on earth live in abject poverty. Many socioscientific problems need solving, from the prevention of cancer and heart disease to the desalination of sea water and the tapping of solar energy.

Hence, there is still great need for human labor. But what stands in the way of its proper use is the capitalist system of production for private corporate profit. In a socialist society, with production for private profit eliminated, the problems arising from automation can be met with relative ease. There are enough socialist countries without unemployment to provide irrefutable evidence of this.

The changing of social priorities by placing human needs before profits cannot await a future socialist society—it should be fought for now. The auto industry, for example, is in a deep and chronic crisis. It is questionable whether many thousands of laid-off workers will ever again find work in the auto industry as presently constituted. The flood tide in auto demand is receding. The increased cost of gasoline, the shift to smaller, more economical cars, and continuous introduction of labor-saving technology, spell ever fewer workers employed. Yet auto plants and workers could be used to build the rolling stock for a much needed national system of mass, cheap, public rapid transit. They could also be converted to the building of prefabricated housing units or panels. When World War II started, the auto industry was converted to the manufacture of planes, tanks, missiles and guns. It could be converted again, this time for peaceful purposes. But to attain this the labor movement would have to challenge the investment policies of the giant auto magnates and the spending priorities of the government.

Many jobs could also be made available for workers in shipping and manufacture if there was a foreign policy aimed at extending long-term credits to underdeveloped lands—and with no strings attached—and if there was a great expansion of trade with the socialist countries. But these, too, require the active intervention of the labor movement on questions of foreign policy, and in a completely different direction from that followed by Mr. Meany and his cohorts.

AUTOMATION can provide the mechanical means with which to free humankind from backbreaking, boring and degrading toil, or from being a mere appendage to a machine. Men and women could be freed from the need to spend a major portion of their waking hours and the better part of their lives just "making a living." The revolution in science and technology is creating the material possibilities for the "human use of human beings." But this can never happen so long as the powerful productive forces of society are harnessed for private, corporate enrichment.

Automation can be a blessing instead of a curse.

## 8 : THE THIRD PERSON AT THE BARGAINING TABLE

THE STATE has never been a neutral observer of the class struggle in the United States. Despite the facade of government neutrality, our history is replete with examples of strikes broken by court injunctions, police clubs and troopers' bayonets. It is only in more recent decades that government has openly assumed the role of regulator of capital-labor relations and trade union procedure and function. The state is, indeed, the third person at the bargaining table.

This is part of a general reversal of the old Jeffersonian axiom that the less governed, the better governed. The government now intervenes in economic and political life on a scale not previously believed possible. This process began with the Great Depression, intensified during World War II, became steadily more pronounced in subsequent years, and promises to accelerate even further in the period ahead. The root of this phenomenon lies in the chronic crisis of the system, for capitalism is no longer capable of functioning in the old way. Its economic furnace has to be stoked and banked by ever greater direct government intervention.

The vested interests always expected, and got, special favors and handouts from the government—vast natural domains, protective tariffs, subsidies, fair-trade laws, and tax exemptions. Still they looked with suspicion upon "government meddling" in general economic affairs. In fact, it took some time for ruling class ideology to reflect the new reality.

Now only Neanderthal remnants adhere to the old laissez faire prescriptions, and even these do so for demagogic reasons and as a means of pressure for or against specific government policies. As long as the government acts in their behalf, they graciously concede it the legitimacy to do so.

There is now so close an interlocking between big business with big government that some call it the "new partnership," the "corporate state," and the "new industrial state." More than a half-century ago, V. I. Lenin foresaw the trend and aptly termed it "state-monopoly capitalism."

Richard Barber, in his study of *The American Corporation – Its Power, Its Money, Its Politics,* observes that the monopolies and the government "accentuate each other, producing a unique brand of corporate state in which the government and private sectors threaten to coalesce in a way that would be antithetical to democracy."[1] It is more than a threat; it is a historical reality. It is exemplified most vividly by the person of Vice-President Nelson Rockefeller, who is the living link between Exxon, the Chase Manhattan Bank and the White House.

The crisis of the system requires that the government concentrate a large portion of national income into its own hands in order to intervene effectively in the national economy and foreign affairs. This is seen by the growth in government spending. In 1950, government spending on all levels—federal, state and local—represented 21 percent of national income. In 1973, it was 32 percent—jumping from $61 billion in 1950 to $407 billion in 1974.[2] The government is now the largest single conduit of funds into the economy.

This has led to a situation in which the third person at the bargaining table is also the uninvited guest at the dinner table. The huge sums spent by the government come mainly from taxation derived from working and middle-class people. The income tax, originally adopted as a form of progressive taxation based on ability to pay, has now become regressive. Before World War II most working-class families paid no income tax whatever. In 1928, for example, a year before the Great Depression broke, only four million tax returns were filed. The population of the country then was 120 million. In 1972, with a population of 208 million, 77 million tax returns were filed, covering over 120 million taxpayers.[3] Many states now have income taxes as well, and in 25 cities with populations of 150,000 or over, including New York City, there are also city income taxes.

The super-rich are adept at finagling their tax returns, using every conceivable loophole to avoid payment. Nelson Rockefeller, member of the richest family in the land, paid no federal income tax at all for three whole years. Workers, however, get their income taxes deducted from their pay envelopes—a little-noted form of class discrimination.

When a corporation loses money on an undertaking, it declares a comparable tax deduction. But when a worker is laid off, works only part-time, or is ill, this is not considered a deductible loss, only reduced income. In addition, there are scores of sales taxes and dozens of hidden excise taxes that eat away at the workers' dollar and add to the general inflation.

The government redistributes a portion of income, therefore, but not in favor of working people. The working class is made to pay for far more than the social benefits it receives.[5] Hundreds of billions of dollars go into channels that are retrogressive, parasitic and extremely harmful to society, even though highly beneficial to the monopolistic interests.

Military expenditures multiplied over six times since 1950. The government also picks up the tab for more than 50 percent of the $34 billion spent annually on research and development. "As a consequence," notes one scholar, "domestic research has in a very real sense been 'nationalized.' " But it is a strange kind of nationalization, "a massive transfer of funds from the Treasury to universities, nonprofit organizations and especially industry."[6]

When a huge corporation runs into financial straits, the federal government is on hand to bail it out to the extent of hundreds of millions of dollars. The Lockheed Corporation and the Penn Central Railroad were the beneficiaries of this kind of "socialism for the rich." There is parsimonious, penny-pinching assistance to the poor, the needy, the social services, but lavish largesse to the powerful and opulent.

Government purchases take place largely in a closed-circuit market in which the government is the only buyer. Yet instead of nationalizing industries such as armaments, aerospace, and highway construction, and thereby saving the public billions of dollars paid in exorbitant corporation profits, the government pursues a policy that is exactly opposite. Atomic energy, first developed as a publicly financed government undertaking, was later turned over to private industry. The research in this field, however, is still paid for by the government. Likewise, hundreds of the most modern industrial plants built with government funds during World War II were later "sold" to private corporations for less than a song.

Generally, these plants were turned over to the largest corporations, thereby furthering the process of economic concentration.

The more than trillion dollars spent on militarism since World War II went for the production of goods that added nothing to national wealth. It drained this wealth. It was like dumping a thousand billion dollars of goods and services into the ocean. Again, the vast bulk of military contracts went to the largest corporations. Had these huge sums been spent on housing, some 40 million single family homes could have been built. Millions of additional jobs would have been created, because housing construction is labor-intensive while atomic, missile and plane production is capital-intensive. This was not done because armament production is far more profitable for the monopoly corporations and because a huge military machine is needed by U.S. capitalism to pursue its aggressive designs abroad.

Thus the uninvited guest at the workers' dinner table has the most ravenous appetite of all, but also robs the family till.

## The Government's Industrial Relations Business

When the Wagner Labor Act became law in 1935, it represented an important victory for the workers. After generations of bitter conflict, they had won the legal right to form and join and to be represented by unions of their own choosing in bargaining with their employers. The law also provided for the establishment of a National Labor Relations Board to implement this right and to codify and regulate employer-labor relations. This opened the door all the way for the government's full participation in the industrial relations business.

At first it was to the advantage of the newly formed industrial unions that such a board existed. Its members were appointed by the President, and as the Roosevelt administration depended on labor support for reelection, its rulings were frequently helpful to the fledgling unions.

However, over the years, this brought with it some negative consequences. The unions became far more dependent than previously on the favors of the politicians of the party in power. With the new regulatory machinery growing into an intricate system of often conflicting rules and procedures, it became increasingly important to have influence at the White House. This meant going all-out to get your so-called politician friends—usually the Democrats—into power while at the same time doing nothing that would turn your non-friends into open enemies.

The industrial unions of the CIO were caught in this mesh even more than the craft unions of the AFL. The latter, because they were craft unions, were less dependent on NLRB decisions and federal legislation. Their dealings were usually not with the large industrial corporations, but with smaller and more local enterprises. Representing skilled craft workers, they had fewer problems in gaining employer recognition for they held more control over local labor markets. The building trades unions, for example, were completely immersed in city, county and state politics (for many construction jobs came from these sources), but generally shied away from national politics.

The passage of the Taft-Hartley Law in 1947, and the Landrum-Griffin Law in 1959, entangled the labor movement even more extensively in federal legalisms. According to Benjamin Aaron, professor of labor law and a former director of a government labor board, the United States "has a more comprehensive and bewildering array of restrictive laws regulating the relations between employers and unions than does any other industrialized country."[7] In the industrial countries of Europe there is far less statutory labor law, far less use of arbitration, and less use of the courts in labor disputes.[8] The number of cases filed annually for NLRB processing will give some indication of the magnitude of the problem. In the first year of the NLRB—fiscal year 1936—1068 cases were filed. These grew to nearly 7,000 in 1939, 12,000 in 1946, 21,000 in 1959 and over 42,000 in 1974.[9] In 1963, 54 percent of all Board decisions went on to the court of appeals; in 1967, it was 60 percent. Hence, the process tends to become more legalistic over the years.[10]

By establishing the "rules of the game," the NLRB and the courts determine how and when unions are to be recognized as bargaining agents, what constitutes an acceptable labor election unit, where and how they should be formed, and the conditions under which a union's jurisdiction can or cannot be challenged. Hundreds, even thousands, of often contradictory rules and regulations have been spawned. Thus, highly skilled lawyers, trained and versed in the intricacies of labor law, NLRB rulings and Labor Department practices, became necessary. These attorneys increasingly make their weight felt in union decision-making, tying the unions ever tighter into the legalistic straightjacket.

In time new issues arose such as those under the heading of "fringe benefits." Each of these required still more rules and regulations. The adoption of the Taft-Hartley and then the Landrum-Griffin Laws further added to the labyrinth of legal wheels within wheels. Labor was told when it could and could not strike and the exact procedure for doing so.

Secondary boycotts and sympathy strikes were outlawed. The NLRB was reorganized, removing its limited independent powers and leaving it an abject tool of the given Administration in office. The Secretary of Labor was designated as the sole authority to judge if remedial action was called for where union elections were tainted with fraudulence.

In this way, step by step, the unions gave up a great deal of their independence, and their leaders became increasingly dependent on the good will, graces and favors of politicians, especially the occupant in the White House. Labor leaders would hesitate to ruffle the Administration when they knew that the Secretary of Labor had the power to lower the boom on the way they ran their unions.

The government encroached further on collective bargaining by imposing arbitrary "guide lines" respecting wage settlements. In other words, no longer were workers entitled to get what their organized power could win, but the Administration in Washington decided how much employers were permitted to give. Yet no such control was enforced over prices and none whatever over profits.

## Conflicting Labor Board Decisions

Labor Board rulings have often had a pernicious effect on the labor movement. Some rulings that appeared to be positive and necessary in earlier years, turned out to be the opposite in later years when conditions had changed. For example, one of the first major policy questions thrust upon the newly formed Board was what to do about jurisdictional disputes between unions. These were handled in two ways. First, the "majority rule" doctrine stipulated that the union which won a majority vote of a designated bargaining unit was the sole representative of *all* the workers of that unit. This was desired by the newly formed industrial unions, anxious to consolidate their strength, avoid continuous internecine warfare, thwart company inspired dual unions and AFL "raids," and guarantee a common front of workers in negotiations. Those employers who had decided to come to terms with the new unions also preferred the exclusive representation formula as assurance of greater stability in labor relations.

In 1942, a second formula, the "contract bar" doctrine, aimed to give a union protection for a reasonable period after winning an election. Both union and employer representatives unanimously decided that petitions for a decertification election could be filed only in a designated 30-day period prior to the expiration of a contract or two years after it was signed, whichever came first.Later, the two-year rule was amended to three years, "no matter what degree of dissatisfaction may exist."[11] This change, too, had the support of both union and employer representatives.

In past decades dual unionism has frequently been a trap into which militant and radical-minded workers fell, permitting themselves to become separated from the rest of the workers. Yet there can be no doubt that the "contract bar" doctrine has been used by unscrupulous union leaderships to treat their rank and file as helpless peons with nowhere else to go. It is extremely difficult for workers to change jurisdiction even when the three-year period is up. They must first file a petition bearing the signatures of at least 30 percent of the workers in the bargaining unit. Many workers hesitate to put their names on such petitions for fear of reprisals.

Nor did the NLRB and the courts hesitate to reverse themselves when it was politically expedient. One such occasion was in 1950, during the CIO's raiding drive on Left and progressive-led unions, particularly on the UE. As the "contract bar" formula was an obstacle to permitting new elections before the expiration of a contract, the Board just shoved it aside. It conveniently discovered that implicit in every company contract with a Left-led union was its continued affiliation with the CIO. This no longer being the case, it argued, there was reasonable doubt as to who represented the workers.[12]

It became unnecessary for raiding unions to prove their strength by collecting signatures from 30 percent of the workers, because the Taft-Hartley Law had given employers too, the right to petition for a new election. In 1952, a top GE lawyer, testifying before a Senate Committee, admitted that the company had taken the raiding IUE "off the hook by filing our own petition for an NLRB election. "This, under NLRB rules," he pointed out, "made it unnecessary for the IUE-CIO to show any membership at all."[13]

The courts also decided the question of the rights of locals to secede from an International under the same "implied contract" doctrine. Up to 1949 a local could not secede from its International and take its assets with it. These, the courts held, belonged to the International. But when the attempt was being made to prod and intimidate locals to leave Left-led Internationals, the rules of the game were changed. Locals could now hold on to their assets.[14]

The responsibility for determining the size, scope and character of a bargaining unit rests with the Labor Board. The unit may take varied forms, based on employer, craft, plant, or subdivision thereof. It may also be composed of workers in plants of multiple employers, or in multiple plants of the same corporation. The Board, therefore, has considerable leeway in exercising its discretion to authorize the type of bargaining unit. And this, in turn, sometimes determines whether a union wins or loses an election. It also has a bearing on whether a unit is an integral whole or a clumsily and undemocratically constructed one.

As mixed bargaining units containing both professional and non-professionals are prohibited by the Taft-Hartley Law unless the professionals vote separately to be included in them, further ground is provided for Labor Board gerrymandering. The Board has been charged with being "unnecessarily severe" in its interpretation of these restrictions, making it all the harder to organize professional and white-collar workers. During union shop elections in the aerospace industry, for instance, it was "startling to learn" that the bargaining unit had been so chopped up that 40 percent of the workers were not in it.[15] Thus Labor Board rulings have considerable influence on the shape and course of the labor movement.

## The Landrum-Griffin Law

The Landrum-Griffin Law has further ensnared the labor movement in governmental red tape. Ostensibly adopted to curb labor leadership corruption and lack of union democracy, it has given "national union headquarters a strong justification for supervising local affairs more closely than ever before."[16] By compelling unions to file their financial records with the government, it has enabled employers to ascertain the ability of unions to withstand lengthy strikes.[17] However, the law does not compel corporations to open their books to similar public perusal.

Most harmful of all of Landrum-Griffin's provisions is its Title IV. This gives the Secretary of Labor the exclusive authority to determine, *after* a union election has been held, whether such extreme and flagrant violations of democratic procedures have occurred as to place in question the outcome of the election. If he should find this to be the case, he can "bring suit to set the results of the election aside and order it to be rerun."[18]

This section was in conflict with Title I, which gave union members the right to ask the courts for direct intervention. But in December 1964, the Supreme Court ruled that union members could not protect their rights relating to elections in any other way than by appealing to the Secretary of Labor.

The Supreme Court's decision was to the liking of both the government and the AFL-CIO top command. The AFL-CIO had filed a "friend of the court" brief in which it argued that if there were to be any outside intervention into organized labor's internal affairs, it had best be the Secretary of Labor, whose "expert's appraisal" could be counted on "to avoid improper interference." The Solicitor General submitted an amicus brief for the Department of Justice, which likewise argued in favor of the Secretary of Labor.[19]

The choice of the Secretary of Labor as guarantor of inner-union democracy is logical from the point of view of both the government and the labor brass. First, he is a political appointee of the Administration and beholden to it. At the same time, he is chosen because he is acceptable to the labor leaders closest to the Administration, and is credited with the ability to win the support of others.

Labor leaders have an interest in desisting from fighting the Administration, and the Secretary of Labor has an interest in avoiding conflict with them. It is an ideal arrangement. It explains the love affair between Frank Fitzsimmons of the Teamsters and Richard Nixon. It also explains why the Secretary of Labor ignored rank-and-file miners' appeals to do something about Tony Boyle's dictatorship in the miners' union until Jock Yablonski and his wife and daughter were murdered.*

The best-laid plans of employers, politicians and labor officials often get upset. Even the worst labor bureaucrat must keep at least one eye on his membership and its mood. Politicians may want to work closely with labor officials, but they also have other commitments and constituencies that cannot be ignored. Employers may want their union "colleagues" to play ball with them, but there is not always full agreement on the rules of the game and how much each team is to get. Employers do not care how unions are run, so long as it does not interfere with production and profit-making. Sometimes it does, and even employers who encourage corruption in labor officials do not want it to get out of hand for fear of blackmail.

Sometimes it is possible for the rank and file to take advantage of these contradictions. This has been the case with sections of the Landrum-Griffin Act which, in their very wording, reflect the pull of somewhat contradictory forces. As a consequence, rank-and-file caucuses, which were formerly forbidden by union constitution and/or union leadership,

*Jock Yablonski was the rank-and-file supported candidate opposing Tony Boyle in the union's election.

now have a legal right to exist. Union elections must also take place regularly, and now and then the Secretary of Labor must move to order a new election when the election is so blatantly fixed that it may stir up a storm.

## Tied to the Two-Party System

This increased role of government in the economy, in labor-management relations, and in internal union affairs, is a major factor in keeping the labor movement tied to old politics and, particularly, the Democratic Party. As a deterrent to labor's independent political action, it is second in importance only to the lack of developed class consciousness in the ranks of the workers.

The need to have an "in" in Washington, a state capitol or in city hall, is often seen by labor leaders as having precedence over all other political considerations. It is considered "practical," and what is practical is supposed to be good and virtuous, no matter how unprincipled and pernicious it may be. This view is not a monopoly of the right-wing of the labor movement. Some of the political endorsements of Left-led and progressive unions reflect the same position. Local 1199, the militant New York drug and hospital local with a generally excellent record, found it expedient to support Nelson Rockefeller when he ran for governor of the State of New York. It was part of a trade for legislation that aided in the organization of hospital workers. And Harry Bridges has switched party registration a number of times—endorsing the 1960 Presidential candidacy of Richard Nixon, and having had his own deal with Democratic Mayor Joseph Alioto of San Francisco.

Since the thirties the bulk of the labor movement—particularly the industrial unions—have been wedded to the Democratic Party. Having won the right to organize during the days of the Democratic New Deal, the unions have relied on an alliance with the northern Democrats as their main form of being on the "in." In turn, the Democrats have seen the support of organized labor as essential to their victory at the polls.

This is considerably different from the political development in most countries of Western Europe. There, the popular franchise, free public education and the right of workers to organize were won by the direct political struggle of the workers through the agency of their own Social-Democratic or Labor parties. In a number of European countries, working-class political parties appeared on the national scene prior to the establishment of nationwide confederations of labor. In fact, many early trade unions were directly affiliated to, sponsored and aided by the Social-Democratic Parties, only much later forming their own distinct centers, yet continuing to maintain close fraternal ties with the parties.

Developments in the United States were considerably different. For a number of historic reasons we touched on previously, class consciousness here did not reach the same level. While the workers conducted their own extremely militant fight for the right to organize, and for unemployment benefits and social security, it was not done through the medium of their own mass political party. The winning of these reforms therefore became identified in the public mind with the somewhat more liberal of the two major capitalist parties, the Democrats.

Peculiarities of the United States electoral system also make independent class politics more difficult. It is a "winner-take-all" system; no provision is made for proportional representation. This was illustrated graphically in 1912, a year in which two minor parties got sizeable chunks of the popular vote. The "Bull Moose" Progressive Party of Theodore Roosevelt received 27 percent of the national vote, and the Socialist Party of Eugene Debs received six percent of the vote. But with 33 percent of the national popular vote between them, they won only 4 percent of the seats in the House of Representatives.

Unlike most European countries, the national administration in this country is chosen by direct popular vote, not by the legislature. As it remains in office for four years and holds the decisive reins of political power in its hands, all economic and social interests try to get a bite of this juiciest of all political plums.

The "winner-take-all" and presidential-election systems tend to reinforce each other in making each major party into a catchall coalition of the most varied and peculiar assortment of social, class and regional group interests, essentially united for winning elections. This has placed a premium on the unprincipled kind of politics in which party platforms and election promises are meaningless.

The advantages of this system for the ruling class are innumerable. It encourages a political flexibility in which compromise is the name of the horse-trading game. And because compromise is essential to get ahead politically, it serves as a guarantee against "extremism" and any substantive challenge to the economic and social system of monopoly capital.

This is seen in the ability of the electoral system to make adjustments which enable it to pass through stormy periods. One such adjustment, the winning of the primary ballot, has made the selection of candidates somewhat more democratic, enabling more representative individuals to win now and then. This does two things: It bolsters illusions that the present electoral system can be made to serve the people by reforming either of the two major parties, and at the same time it compels even some of the more progressive of elected officials to compromise with the powers that be.

All this can work as long as the capitalist system appears capable of meeting the basic needs of the great majority of the people. But as capitalism's crisis deepens and the standard of living is driven down and mass unemployment becomes a "normal" state of affairs—and not just for racial minorities—the method of compromise and political horse-trading also reaches a crisis.

This can be seen by what was beginning to happen in 1939. The New Deal had come to an impasse. Reform measures that seemed radical compared with Herbert Hoover's antediluvian conservatism, now appeared halfhearted, feeble, and contradictory. This became especially apparent when the economy hit bottom again in 1938 without passing through the prosperity phase of a normal economic cycle. The new depression just piggybacked on to the previous one.

FDR's administration was being buffeted by two increasingly powerful winds, blowing from opposite polar extremes. Big business demanded an end to reforms it considered "creeping socialism." It called for a tougher stand toward labor, lower taxes for the corporate rich, and a halt in government spending. Labor, too, demanded change. Purchasing power had not increased sufficiently to make up for either the considerable rise in labor productivity or for the continued lag in world markets. Only by greatly increasing mass purchasing power could the economy be stimulated sufficiently. Hence, labor called for more, not fewer, reforms and for more radical ones. It demanded that the Administration provide more jobs for the unemployed and give full support to labor's critical battle with the giant corporations.

The CIO had become increasingly impatient with Roosevelt's halfway measures. At a meeting of the CIO executive council, Lewis expressed his thorough disenchantment. "The country is still in crisis," he said. "Economically we now stand little ahead of where we stood four years ago." He insisted that democracy must put men back to work if it is to continue to exist. He intimated "that he indeed might be interested in forming a third political party."[20]

C. K. McFarland, a historian of the period, believes that Lewis set out to build such a political coalition. He points to Lewis' control over Labor's Non-Partisan League, his influence in the American Labor Party of New York, and his active wooing of progressive agrarian and Black leaders.

No one can say whether a new political coalition would have materialized and from it a new labor-based political party. There is reason to doubt that Lewis ever intended to go that far. More likely he was seeking alliances as a means of exerting greater pressure on the Roosevelt administration. One thing, however, seems evident: things could not go on much longer as they had. The times demanded more radical solutions and a more basic regrouping of social and class forces to bring these about.

Some years later the historian Richard Hofstadter asked a rhetorical question: "What would have happened to the political fortunes of Franklin D. Roosevelt if the war had not created a new theater for his leadership?"[21]

## Independent Political Action

Events since then have tied the labor movement even more closely to the two-party system. It has made it even more dependent on the good will and favors of politicians in office. As a consequence, the workers are the least represented segment of our society, though they are the majority. Having so-called friends in government does not take the place of having direct representatives there. Black people understand this. There is a Black Caucus in Congress that meets regularly to weigh all questions. But there is no labor caucus because there are no labor people in Congress. Even the multimillionaires, always over-represented in government by their corporation lawyers, are now putting their own scions into public office. Nelson Rockefeller now dirties his hands in sordid politics, whereas this used to be a chore assigned to hirelings. But organized labor has not even reached the point of putting labor lawyers, let alone working men and women, in political office. Yet one militant worker coming directly out of a work place and speaking for working people would do more to break up the lawyers' club that is Congress than all the so-called friends bought with labor—that is, workers'—votes and money.

Many people still believe that the Democratic Party can be transformed into a peoples' party and fear that by leaving it for a third-party movement the progressive-liberal vote would split to the benefit of extreme reaction.

This fear cannot be dismisssed lightly. Yet, at a time when a majority of people are fed up with politics as they know it, and do not even take the trouble to vote, passivity and cynicism may produce the very results most feared.

In this respect something may be learned from the tactices pursued by extreme reaction. The Conservative Party in New York, for example, is organized both outside and inside of the Republican Party. It has its own line on the voting machine, its own spokespeople, its own financing and propaganda, yet also operates within the Republican Party by participating in primaries and using its power of veto to pressure the Republicans into choosing candidates more to its liking.

This is even more true of the George Wallace movement. He maintains his own separate organization, conducts his own financial campaign, runs in the presidential primaries of the Democratic Party, and threatens to—and has—either run on a third party line or sat out an election if the Democratic ticket is not to his liking.

Were the labor movement and its allies to do the same, it would immediately begin to change the political climate and add greatly to labor's political weight. But this is not likely to happen as long as the labor leadership is allied with some of the most conservative forces, and those who oppose its policies fear taking open issue and bringing these disagreements to the trade union membership for debate and resolution.

The labor movement has the potential power to become a major, leading political force in the country once it decides to. It has natural allies that would gladly coalesce with it if they felt that the organized labor movement was taking a new, more militant and progressive course. Such allies are the racial minorities, mainly workers; the young people, fed up with things as they are and looking for new directions; the working farmers being pushed to the wall by agribusiness; and large sections of the intellectuals, professionals and middle classes.

The labor movement also has a political weapon that no other segment possesses. It has great numbers and solid organization, and is so strategically located that its legitimate demands on behalf of the people cannot be ignored when it makes up its mind to press for them. It can also use its most potent weapon—the strike—for political objectives. In Europe this is commonplace. In Italy, for example, national strikes have compelled governmental action on housing for working people, on reformed and updated social security legislation, and on other social-class issues. In the United States, only the coal miners use this weapon, and with telling effect. It was the shutdown of mining in West Virginia that finally "convinced" the State legislature to pass the "black-lung" legislation favored by the miners. The miners also used the strike weapon to force an end to the artificial gas shortage that afflicted them in the winter of 1974.

There are a number of reasons for the failure to use economic power to compel political action on inflation, jobs, taxation, housing, or the updating of unemployment and social security legislation. First, there is a reluctance to think in new and more militant terms commensurate with the needs of a new period. Second, there is a lack of the genuine unity and solidarity among unions that could make joint politcal action effective. Third, the labor officialdom is frightened of the very legalisms it permits to be written into contracts, especially the no-strike pledge. And lastly, there is little done to educate the workers to act on their own when necessary, since the bureaucrats fear this most of all. But when the miners shut down the mines they didn't ask for permission to do so, and both the courts and the employers were helpless to do anything about it.

There is today an intermixture of economics and politics, of big business and big government. Federal agencies so intervene in the labor movement itself that for unions to fail to take on the employers in the political arena as well in the economic, is like fighting a powerful antagonist with one hand tied behind you. Clearly whatever issues confront the workers, they are above all political.

# 9 : THE CRISIS OF ORGANIZED LABOR

THE CRISIS in the labor movement has been recognized for a long time. Symptoms of this crisis began to appear during World War II, grew immediately afterward, became dominant with the expulsion of the Left-led unions from the CIO in 1949, and were formalized and fossilized with the AFL-CIO merger in 1955.

When the merger occurred, most people naturally assumed that a re-united federation would pave the way for another great labor advance. They looked for a massive organizing effort in the South and for a rise in organized labor's prestige and political weight in the nation. But instead of growth there has been further unrelieved stagnation.

The CIO, during its heyday of militancy, was more than a federation of autonomous union principalities fighting for their own particular share of the jurisdictional domain. It was a crusading social movement—a class movement—dedicated to the welfare of *all* workers. The Mine Workers, Amalgamated Clothing Workers, Typographical, and other unions, pledged themselves to help organize the mass-production industries. Toward this end they pooled resources, united efforts, and came to the assistance of unions and workers engaged in bitter conflict. In time, they even affected the crisis-ridden, conservative, hidebound AFL, infusing it with new life, ending its stagnation, and compelling it to come to terms with industrial unionism.

The CIO was a trade union movement dealing with economic matters but also something more than that. It reacted to national and international issues. It opposed fascism. It fought for progressive social legislation. It was in the forefront of the civil rights movement of the period. It built its own independent political machinery—first, in 1936, Labor's Non-Partisan League; later, in the forties, the network of Political Action Committees (PAC). Although largely concerned with electing pro-labor and New Deal candidates, the PAC was meant to play an independent role in relation to both major parties. Sidney Hillman of the Amalgamated Clothing Workers, the man largely responsible for leading the CIO PAC movement, told the executive board of his union that no one in the Roosevelt administration knew that Labor's Non-Partisan League was to be formed until it was announced publicly. "The Administration was not notified," he said, "because some of us believed that pressure would be used to stop it."[1] CIO unions actively participated in independent political formations such as the American Labor Party in New York, the Farmer-Labor Party of Minnesota, and the Washington Commonwealth Federation.

The CIO saw itself and was seen by others as the fulcrum of a wider peoples' movement. It consciously sought alliances with farm, Black, professional and youth organizations and movements. Many people viewed the CIO as the hope and conscience of the nation. Others feared it as a potential radical and revolutionary force. Few were indifferent to it.

Today, the organized labor movement neither inspires its friends nor frightens its foes.

## Class Partnerships

The crisis in the labor movement has been the subject of many books and articles. As early as 1959, Sidney Lens, a Chicago local labor leader, wrote *The Crisis of American Labor*.[2] He traced the crisis to the loss of idealism and the subsequent victory of "business unionism" as against "social unionism." Other writers, such as Paul Jacobs, showed the relationship of the crisis to the cold-war anti-Communist witch hunt and the expulsion of the Left-led, progressive unions from the CIO. Daniel Bell pointed to the loss of "élan," and C. Wright Mills to the loss of "insurgent impulse." These characterizations, although apt, do not put their fingers on the class significance of what occurred.

The decade of the thirties was different from the preceding one, as from those following World War II, in one major way: it was a decade of bitter, unrelenting class struggle. The entire labor movement was affected by this struggle, which set the tone and style for the period.

Even some individual leaders who rejected the class struggle in theory were swept into its powerful current. When John L. Lewis told Akron rubber workers that "labor and capital may be partners in theory but they are enemies in fact," he was touching the heart of the matter.

The roots of today's labor crisis are concealed in the word "partnership." As in the twenties, labor leaders no longer see capital as the enemy and, as in the twenties, internal crisis is the inevitable consequence. The policies of leadership collide with the essential class nature and purpose of the movement. In Selig Perlman's words written in 1928, in *The Theory of the Labor Movement*, "the labor movement must be an organized campaign against the rights of private property, even where it stops short of embracing a radical program seeking the elimination, gradual or abrupt, 'constitutional' or violent, of the private entrepreneurs.,,[3] When labor does not fill this role, it is in trouble.

This may not be apparent all at once. But in time, especially when economic conditions worsen, a collision develops between the ranks and leadership. "The union member is extremely suspicious of an inordinately cozy relationship between his officers and management."[4]

The loss of idealism, élan, insurgent impulse, can all be traced to the succumbing, in theory and fact, to the blandishments of class partnership. So insidious and pervasive has this tendency become that even many labor leaders who think they are free of it, in fact are influenced by and bow to it.

While some labor leaders may have a twinge of conscience, the top hierarchy faces no such moral problem. Believing in class partnership, for them this is still the best of all possible worlds. Salaries and elastic expense accounts place many of them in the income brackets of corporation executives. Some actually think of themselves as such and the unions they head as their private enterprises. They wholesale labor peace to the employers and retail bargaining services to the workers.

Dave Beck, former president of the Teamsters Union, responding to criticism of undemocratic union practices, said, "Unions are big business . . . Why," he asked, "should truck drivers and bottle washers be allowed to make big decisions affecting union policy? Would any corporation allow it?"[5]

Jimmy Hoffa, his successor, saw nothing wrong in his ownership of a fleet of trucks employing his own union members. His argument before a government committee was simple: "If he had the money to invest," he asked, "why shouldn't he put it into the industry he knew best?"[6]

Most members of the hierarchy are not that frank, at least not in public. A majority of them do not engage in such extreme crudities. Many are even shocked at them. Those labor leaders who consider themselves "social unionists," disagree that unionism is a form of business. For them it is a "calling." They think of themselves as professionals who graciously and unselfishly give of their great talents to uplift the worker. Because they know what is best for the workers, they believe they should have the right to run the unions without interference from them. After all, think of all they have done and still will do *for* the workers! Those who once held radical or even socialist views deny abandoning their youthful idealism. Only, they assert, those goals are now being realized in different and even more effective ways!

## The Ladies Garment Union

Some inkling of this "social-unionist" approach can be found in a book that appeared in 1967. Written by Gus Tyler of the ILGWU, *The Labor Revolution* expressed shock and disbelief that anyone could consider the labor movement in crisis. No, says Tyler, it is participating in a great revolution. Labor's "massive impress is changing the face of the nation."

But in this jolly tune there is also a mournful note. The "timing of the revolution is ironic," states Tyler, "It comes at a time when labor's repute is at a nadir among progressive intellectuals and militant youth. Labor's " 'friends' in academia" pour out works "decrying the state of the unions and depicting the crisis of unionism."[7]

The "timing of the revolution," was not ironic, for none occurred, of course. The irony is that this Tyler-made product appeared when no one would buy it. Its author is an official of a union whose record in behalf of its workers is dismal, to put it mildly. If Tyler wants to know why some militant youth are turned off by labor leadership, he need but glance at his own union.

A large portion of the ladies' garment industry is unorganized. Yet the union's score in new organizing is less than zero. According to its own official convention figures, the union had 445,000 members in 1956 and 18,000 fewer than that in 1975.

Certainly many garment shops have run away to the South to avoid unionism. But what about organizing the South? And if the union cannot accomplish this by itself, what is it doing to bring about the fighting unity between unions that can do it? The fact is that the officialdom prefer things as they are. It enables them to cover up their failure to get decent wages and conditions from organized shops, with the argument about competition from unorganized ones.

The ILGWU leadership has been one of the most vociferous supporters of the cold war, of anticommunism and anti-Sovietism, and of every U.S. military aggression abroad. It supported armed intervention in Korea, Taiwan, the Dominican Republic, Vietnam, Cambodia and Laos. Yet it complains about garments flooding the U.S. market from areas where American capital super-exploits workers. And it says nothing against the colonial status of Puerto Rico from which U.S. capital obtains cheap labor.

A majority of the ILGWU, like the industry, is composed of women workers. But men run the union from top to bottom with only one woman on the International Executive Board. An increasingly large percentage of the union is made up of Puerto Rican, Black and Chicano workers, yet these workers are excluded from any positions of power in the union and have only token representation on the Executive Board.

## Walter Reuther and the Auto Workers

At approximately the same time that Tyler's book appeared, another "social unionist" took issue with its euphoric claims about a "labor revolution." Walter Reuther, president of the powerful auto union, admitted the existence of a labor crisis. Breaking ranks with his former colleagues on the AFL-CIO Executive Council, he charged it with "complacency," "indifference," and "lack of social vision." He accused its members of becoming "increasingly the comfortable custodians of the status quo."[8]

Reuther spoke from intimate knowledge. He had been a member of the exclusive executive club since the two federations merged. He was in an excellent position to pinpoint his accusations. But instead he couched his criticisms in generalities.

To say the Executive Council was complacent was true, generally speaking. But it was far from complacent or indifferent to the interests of American capitalism as it saw them. It was also Johnny-on-the-spot in its support of the cold war, the huge arms budget, and the hot wars in Korea and Vietnam. Pentagon brass had no more zealous friends than labor brass. Nor was the Council totally lacking in vision—the myopic vision of the ruling class.

What Reuther said about the labor hierarchy could also, with some modification, be said about him. Reuther was one of the first to jump on the cold-war bandwagon. He led the fight to expel the Communists and the Left from the CIO. The UAW rushed to take advantage of the Taft-Hartley Law by pouncing upon and dismembering unions that refused to knuckle down. And Reuther went out of his way to prove his loyalty to the system of so-called free enterprise. At a time when it was assumed that war was imminent between the United States and the Soviet Union, Reuther wrote an article for *Collier's* magazine about how the American trade union movement would follow American troops into the Soviet Union to help establish "free" unions there.[9]

It is true that Reuther drove his own cheaper model auto instead of riding in a chauffered limousine. No one could accuse him of living like a corporation executive or rifling his union's treasury. This was to his credit. But when it came to basic policy matters and to relations with the corporations, Reuther was no different from the rest. At the time of Reuther's tragic death in 1970, Virgil Boyd, vice-president of the Chrysler Corporation, praised Reuther's ability "to keep the situation under control" and expressed the hope that "whoever his successor may be can exercise equal internal discipline."[10]

In 1966, when his brother Victor charged the AFL-CIO under Meany with being a CIA conduit, funneling money to Latin America to counter Communist influence in unions, columnist Thomas W. Braden disclosed that he had turned over $50,000 to Walter Reuther in behalf of the CIA. Walter Reuther acknowledged receiving the money, but characteristically copped a plea. It was an "emergency situation," he said, because the "weak European labor unions" were especially "vulnerable to Communist subversion."[11]

The difference between Meany and Reuther boiled down to this: Reuther was ready to do the bidding of the CIA in "emergency" situations, while Meany believed the "emergency" was permanent. Neither saw anything wrong in subverting labor unions in other countries in the interests of American capital.

William Serrin, in his book on the UAW, *The Company and the Union*, makes a devastating indictment of the UAW under Reuther's stewardship. The UAW, he says, became a right-of-center union with a left-of-center reputation. "It was for others to lead the campaigns; the union was not in front, nor, at times, even in the parade." Workers' sons were being claimed by the war in Vietnam, "but the UAW did not attack the war until attacking the war became acceptable, even popular."[12]

Reuther marched in civil rights demonstrations, admits Serrin, but the UAW "refused to discuss with its members the nature of racism, refused to explain to them that many of America's problems are class, not racial, problems; refused to demonstrate to them how working-class whites and Blacks are confronted by the same enemies."[13] Although some 30 percent of the UAW's membership is Black, and Black workers make up "60 to 70 percent of the workers on many urban assembly lines," only two Blacks are on the UAW's Executive Board and "both are hand-picked."[14] Serrin notes that many Black workers accuse the UAW of doing little for them. He quotes one as saying, "That's what the plant is—short for a plantation!"[15]

With about 14 percent of the auto workers women, few are active in union leadership and only one is on the Executive Board.[16]

In July 1968, Reuther led the UAW out of the AFL-CIO and into a coalition with the Teamsters Union. Together they formed the Alliance for Labor Action (ALA), which was to be a new labor center but not a new federation. The ALA called for a massive organizing drive, for modernizing bargaining to meet the new conditions of corporate con-glomerates, for support to the agricultural workers, for exploring the possibilities of a huge mutual defense fund for unions engaged in bitter battle, and for the establishment of "community unions" in poverty and ghetto areas. It declared itself against the Vietnam War and called for a shift in priorities from militarism and war to peacetime social needs.

These planks represented an important advance in labor's thinking. It seemed that at last Meanyism was going to be challenged from within the labor movement itself. Certainly a huge organizing effort would soon get under way.

These hopes never materialized. The ALA was a ship that never left dry dock. Reuther tried to repeat what Lewis did when he broke with the AFL in 1935, but he failed. This was evident even prior to his death in 1970.

Why did Reuther fail? The issues raised by the ALA were valid and timely. Two of the largest and strongest unions in the country formed the new alliance. A few smaller ones joined and others would have followed if something had really happened.

The ALA failed because it was a bureaucratic attempt to induce change without involving or taking into account the thinking of the rank and file. The convention that formed the ALA was composed of a few hundred hand-picked delegates. UAW and Teamster locals were not even invited to elect their own delegates. The ALA was to be Reuther's great gift to the workers, something *for* them but not *of* them.

This was not how the CIO movement was launched. Lewis, the traditional Republican, the typical business unionist, the man who ran his own union like a private fiefdom, was shrewd enough to realize that without enlisting the enthusiastic support of the workers he would fail; he knew he would neither succeed in organizing the mass-production industries nor give the labor movement a new and more favorable image. He therefore went out of his way to appeal to the instinctive class feelings of the workers and to their hatred of the corporations. Every step he took was carefully planned with this in mind—to reach the workers, to arouse them, to win their confidence.

Saul Alinsky, Lewis' biographer, tells the story of the fisticuffs that broke out on the floor of the 1935 AFL Convention. At one point in the heated acrimonious debate, Lewis rose and punched the 300-pound William Hutcheson of the Carpenters' Union squarely on the nose. It was a headline in newspapers across the country.

Years later, Lewis told Alinsky, "I never walked across the aisle so slowly and grimly as I did in the 1935 Convention. An act of some kind, an act dramatic to the degree that it would inspire and enthuse the workers of the country was necessary. Did I say necessary? It was essential. With this in mind I laid my plans. . . . Bill Hutcheson, unknowingly, was to be one of the main actors in the cast."[17]

Lewis could have been even more candid. A dramatic act was needed also to rehabilitate himself in the eyes of workers—to prove to them that he was no longer part of the old gang. When his fist collided with Hutcheson's nose, a message was telegraphed to the workers that the fight was in earnest, the break in leadership's ranks, real.

But, unlike Lewis before him, Reuther did not even confront Meany face to face. He made no fight at Executive Council meetings or on the floor of the AFL-CIO Convention. He preferred to level his attacks from the safer ground of Solidarity House, the UAW headquarters, in Detroit.

Whether Reuther could have won more support in the Executive Council by an open fight at its sessions is beside the point. He may not have succeeded, although a number of Council members sympathized with his views on foreign policy, the crisis in the labor movement, and Meany's one-man rule of the federation. Meany's power was great. He controlled the federation's purse strings. He was the federation's go-between with the White House and Congress. Meany was the man to see if a union needed support in a strike, with finances or a boycott; if it wanted help to bring about coordinated bargaining; if it desired intervention in its behalf with the Secretary of Labor or to get Congress to raise bars on some imports. Meany could get things done. This has been the secret of his success. Even his severest critics have given him credit for knowing how to function within the strict rules of the trade union game. He is the bureaucrat's bureaucrat.

But even had Reuther gained no further support in the Executive Council, he could have used it and the AFL-CIO convention as sounding boards with which to reach the workers with the issues involved. He preferred not to do that. It is no wonder that workers felt this was just another squabble "up on top" with no great meaning to them.

IT IS true that Reuther was more sensitive to rank-and-file moods and respected the latent power of workers once aroused to action. His socialist background, his rise to leadership in the turbulent revolt of the thirties, and the greater democratic traditions of the auto union left their influence on him. Yet he was not one to encourage rebellion, especially when it could infect his own ranks.

Had he lashed out at "sweetheart" contracts, sell-out deals, and the general cozy relationship between union and corporation leaders, workers would have listened. Had he exposed what blind anticommunism had done to the labor movement and how the unions were sacrificing their independence to increasing government intervention, he also would have struck a responsive chord. Had he spoken to the situation of the racial minorities, women and young workers and urged them to join in a great crusade to make the labor movement more responsive to their needs, it would have registered. And had he exposed the lack of democracy within unions and called upon the workers to begin to take things into their own hands, workers would have known he meant business.

But how could he do these things when his alliance with Fitzsimmons of the Teamsters Union was an unprincipled betrothal that could never lead to a meaningful marriage? The Teamsters Union had done relatively well in improving the lot of teamsters. It had also grown into the largest union in the country. But its reputation was tainted with many charges of corruption. The union's organizing methods were questionable. Often it used its power to halt truck deliveries, not as a means of supporting workers' struggles, but in order to extract "sweetheart" contracts from employers. This led to a far from honest and democratic unionism. Thus the alliance with the Teamsters did not inspire workers with the image of a new, more democratic and militant unionism..

## Rank and File Upsurge Lacking

There is even a more important reason for the failure of the ALA. The formation of the CIO was a response to a powerful working-class upsurge. The economic crisis had shaken workers out of their lethargy. They realized that they would have to organize and fight if they wished to improve their conditions. Years of battling for jobs and unemployment compensation had created a militancy that swept over the plants once employment began to pick up. A left-wing, largely organized and led by Communists, participated in numerous strikes and helped organize the first nuclei of the new industrial unions. The historic San Francisco General Strike, to cite one example, took place in the summer of 1934, a full year-and-a-half before Hutcheson's nose became the target of Lewis' ire and showmanship.

But when the ALA was formed in 1968, there was no comparable rank-and-file upsurge, not to mention a Left-led rank-and-file movement. There were increasing signs of labor discontent. Black workers were forming their own labor caucuses. Young workers were using absenteeism as a means of protesting unbearable working conditions. Where workers had the right to vote on a new contract, a record number were being turned down. Among Southwest farm workers there were the inspiring organizing efforts led by Cesar Chavez. Among coal miners an internal union revolt was brewing. These were the signs of a new stirring, but not yet the crystallization of a conscious mass movement for class-struggle policies.

The ALA could have been a catalyst to help bring such consciousness and such a movement into being, but it would have required a different kind of leadership and a different perception of what was wrong and how to correct it. The ALA was doomed to failure. It was another symptom of organized labor's growing crisis; not an answer to it.

# 10 : THE LABOR ESTABLISHMENT (1)

ARNOLD Miller's election as president of the United Mine Workers (UMWA) in 1972 represented the most important rank-and-file victory over an entrenched, corrupt union machine in decades. The incumbent Tony Boyle gang had usurped power. It had used the union for its own mercenary ends and in the service of the largest mining conglomerates. The election of Miller and his rank-and-file slate was a triumph, therefore, for union integrity and democracy.

## Tony Boyle and the Miners

The miners had more than ample cause for revolt. The victims of "black-lung" disease had doubled in two decades. Approximately 125,000 miners were suffering from it. Mining disasters had also taken a ghastly toll. In the year 1967 alone, 220 miners perished in explosions and more than 6,000 men were left disabled. When 78 miners were buried alive in the Consolidation #9 disaster in Farmington, West Virginia, in 1968, the nation suddenly learned that 82 percent of underground mines lacked proper safety precautions.

But this meant little to the UMWA officialdom. Three weeks prior to the Farmington entombment, a federal court in Kentucky found the UMWA guilty of conspiring with the Consolidation and other large coal companies to create a monopoly in the industry. Even after the tragic event, Boyle had nothing but praise for the company. It was "one of the best companies to work for as far as cooperation and safety are concerned," he said. "The company here has done all in its power to make this a safe mine. . . . We don't understand why these things happen, but they do happen."[1] In the very midst of the grieving wives, mothers and children, Boyle's heart bled for the company.

The union reeked with corruption. Boyle's salary was $50,000 a year plus an unlimited expense account. A neat sum of $850,000 had also been stashed away in a special fund to provide retirement at full salary for all International officials with ten or more years of union service. In contrast, retired miners, after a lifetime in the mines, were at the time entitled to only $115 a month pensions. Men incapacitated by "black-lung" were entitled to no compensation.

Nepotism was rampant. Boyle's brother was appointed district president in Montana, a post formerly held by Tony Boyle. It paid $27,000 a year not including expenses. Boyle's daughter, a lawyer, drew $23,000 a year, though "there was some question as to what she was supposed to do." John Owens, the union's secretary-treasurer, received $40,000 as salary, an unlimited expense account and a suite of rooms in the Sheraton-Carleton Hotel in Washington. Owen's two sons were also on the union payroll. An assistant general council for the union had three members of his family on payroll, and John Kmetz, an executive board member, had two sons on union staff. There was also a special contingency fund to handle incidental items over and above regular salaries and expenses. Owens' son, Willard, for instance, received a "grant" of $10,000 in 1967 for an unstated purpose.[2]

Nepotism, corruption and dictatorial rule were not new to the miners. Time and again they had fought for district autonomy and a greater control over their union. But now the issue of union democracy had become a life-and-death matter. To clean union house was an urgent imperative.

As discontent was rife in the union and all locals were entitled to elect delegates, the convention seemed to be the logical place for a showdown. The leadership, however, had other thoughts on the matter.

The 1964 convention was called for Miami, Florida, a site far removed from the northern coal fields. This immediately had the effect of limiting the number of delegates from the larger locals, frequently the most militant. The union constitution provided for transportation expenses for only one delegate per local, so additional ones had to be financed by the local unions themselves. Many locals could not afford to do this, because it also entailed meeting the lost wages and living expenses of their delegates.

Another, even greater, barrier to a fully representative convention existed. About 600 locals were composed exclusively of retired or inactive miners. Although the union constitution provided for the closing down of such moribund locals, this was not done. Hence, there were as many "bogie" or "blue-sky" locals as active ones. It was easy to get these locals to send delegates because the International paid the travel costs and there was seldom any lost-time pay to make up. The delegate was "usually a man who could be counted on to be friendly to the hierarchy." Where a delegate could not afford to come, the International helped in other ways. It could provide a job on one of the seven convention committees or as one of the 168 convention messengers, ushers and sergeants-at-arms. These jobs paid a flat $60 a day. There were 500 such jobs that Boyle could assign "to whomever he pleased." If a delegate still could not come, his credential was passed on to some worthy staff member.[3]

These practices were all in violation of the union's constitution, but a convention composed largely of fraudulent delegates was not likely to declare itself unconstitutional.

The officialdom took no chances. All voting was done by voice vote. A delegate representing a defunct local had as much voice as a delegate coming from a live local representing hundreds of active miners. Convention guests, the wives of officers and delegates, "and even a few coal operators," were also seated among the delegates.

One delegate from a large local in Ronco, Pa., asked for the floor to complain. "Delegates and spectators are all together," he pointed out. "When it comes time to vote, the spectators' voices could outnumber the delegates' voices."

Boyle's response was caustic. "Let me assure you that I don't think we have to worry too much, from the demonstration you saw here this morning, as to the closeness of the votes that might occur." Thus, no matter what the question before the house, the votes had already been counted! When delegates tried to reach floor mikes to protest, they were physically assaulted. One delegate from New Eagle, Pa., recognized a foreman from the U.S. Steel mine at which he himself worked, sitting just behind him. He tried to reach a mike. He was led bleeding from the hall.[4]

It is not surprising that the 1964 convention only further tightened the oppressive grip of the machine over the union. The term of office for International officers was lengthened from four to five years. The number of local union endorsements needed to nominate a candidate for International office was increased from five to fifty.

Four years later the convention was more of the same. Boyle was given power to fill vacancies in International officer posts and the executive board was given the right to postpone conventions.

In 1972, the Boyle machine was finally ousted. What it took to accomplish this will be dealt with subsequently.

## Joe Curran and the Maritime Union

The situation in the UMWA under the Boyle regime was not typical of that in most unions. Yet it was not so atypical as to be treated as a sole horrible example. Joe Curran's methods of rule in the National Maritime Union (NMU) were no less dictatorial than those of Boyle. He, too, knew how to live high off the membership. His salary topped $100,000 a year in addition to expenses. He moved about in a telephone equipped limousine chauffeured by a $15,000-a-year NMU "field patrolman." He was an absentee landlord over his union plantation, living most of the time in his sumptuous winter residence in Boca Raton, Florida, or his summer residence in Dutchess County, New York. An assistant ran the mundane affairs of the union for Curran at an additional salary of $30,000.[5] And when Curran retired from the union presidency in the spring of 1973, it was discovered that he had feathered his retirement nest with a million dollars of union pension funds.[6]

It would seem that this last outrageous rip-off should have called forth condemnation from Curran's cronies on the AFL-CIO Executive Council. But George Meany, the hefty warrior against corruption, did not bestir himself from his easy chair to thunder damnation on errant Brother Joe. Actually, there was more than a little empathy with Curran. After all, what kind of democracy is this that denies union presidents the same right God gave corporation heads to make their pile. It's the American way.

Tony Boyle and Joe Curran held no monopoly on union-leadership corruption. One need but mention the International Longshoremen's Association's Tommy Gleason, the Teamsters' Jimmy Hoffa and, worse, Frank Fitzsimmons; or the Carpenters', where the scepter of union rule was handed from Willian Hutcheson to his son Maurice as if it were a family heirloom.

But the degeneration of Joe Curran has a moral all its own. The Miners, ILA, Teamsters and Carpenters have long histories of corruption and dictatorial rule. The NMU, however, was a CIO union built in the thirties from the bottom up. It was one of the most militant and democratic unions, under Left-wing leadership. The debasement of Curran and the deterioration of the union are closely linked with, and the products of, the cold war anti-Communist witch-hunt.

Shipping being considered a "defense" industry, a drive was launched to exclude all radicals and militants in the name of "national security." It did not take Joe Curran long to take on the new coloration. He cooperated with the FBI, CIA and Naval Intelligence to rid the ships and the union of all so-called undesirables. An NMU member, writing in the fifties, described the procedure: "When a seaman applies for a job, his name and seaman's number is sent over a teletype machine to the Marine Index Bureau." Here the files were collected for the shipowners with NMU cooperation. The NMU also kept its own dossiers.[7]

It was not long before Curran succeeded in emasculating the constitutional safeguards for democratic control. In 1959, he began to use the strike fund to finance buildings named after himself. In 1960, he pushed through a constitutional amendment giving himself the power to appoint convention committees. In 1963, the constitution was amended further to give him the power to appoint patrolmen. Prior to this time, these waterfront "business agents" were elected by port memberships. The constitution was again amended to deprive the rank and file of its right to vote in secret referendum on major policy issues and on proposed constitutional amendments. Members who had not served at least one full term as salaried officials were also barred from running for national office. With each consolidation of personal power, Curran surrounded himself with paid lackeys who, like himself, used the union for personal enrichment.

The issue of undemocratic election procedure was taken to the courts by a rank-and-file group in 1966. Two years later, Federal Judge Constance Baker Motley handed down a 57-page decision upholding the petitioners. She found that the union constitution had been so mangled that "it now takes a *minimum* of 10 years to become eligible for national office." [Emphasis in original.] Striking down the most undemocratic provisions, she ordered a new election, which took place in 1969.

Once again a true test of rank-and-file sentiment was impossible. The sea-time requirement for voting, which had been 200 days up to 1966, was boosted to 800 days in 1968. About 40 percent of the members were thus deprived of their right to vote. Even then, the opposition candidate, James Morrissey, received 43 percent of the national vote and 54 percent of the vote in the port of New York.[9]

THE great majority of unions are not Curranized. Yet more than a few are infected by its bacillus. When Judge Motley wrote her unvarnished opinion of NMU practices, she also pointed a finger at the ILGWU. "No other union studied," she stated, "except possibly the International Ladies Garment Workers Union required so much time for its members to qualify for national office."[10]

This was a significant inclusion. The ILGWU prides itself on its "social unionism" and on being democratic and respectable. Yet Judge Motley linked it with the NMU as a union which had established institutional guarantees for the self-perpetuation of the leadership clique.

To be eligible as candidate for president or general secretary-treasurer of the ILGWU, a member must be a delegate to the convention, a member of the union for at least 10 years, and a paid officer of the union for at least five years. To be eligible for the general executive board, a member must be a delegate to the convention, a member of the union in good standing for five years, and a paid officer for at least three years.[11]

Hence, only paid bureaucrats can run for top union posts or for membership on the GEB. One must be on payroll for three to five years to climb still higher on the rungs of the bureaucratic ladder. So, no one can rise except by the grace, and through the medium, of the hierarchy. An Arnold Miller would have no chance in this "democratic" union, no matter what his support in the membership. He could not even get his name on the ballot.

To prevent dissensions within the ILGWU paid officialdom, another safeguard is imposed. Officials are required to sign undated resignations, presumably to keep them honest so "that no breath of scandal should disrupt the International."[12] Actually, it keeps all lower echelon officials toeing the line—or else.

These measures serve to perpetuate a top leadership that has long lost touch with the membership and whose racial, ethnic and sex composition no longer has any relationship to that of the industry or union.

## The Use of Anticommunism

Many others, like Joe Curran, embraced the anti-Communist witch-hunt to undermine union democracy, although not all to the same degree. The National Industrial Conference Board found that the most important restriction in International constitutions are those dealing with Communists. It claimed that 156 unions out of 200 national unions had such constitutional bars.[13] A 1954 Bureau of Labor Statistics survey indicated that out of 100 union constitutions studied, 55 of them, with over 60 percent of national total union membership, barred Communists from office, and 40 unions barred them from membership.[14]

The restrictive clauses vary in wording. Most have muzzles so wide that pellets can strike just about any militant rank-and-file worker whom the leadership dislikes. The UAW Constitution does not bar Communists per se from membership. Instead, it denies membership to those "whose principles and philosophy are contrary to those of this International Union as outlined in the Preamble to the Constitution."[15]

One need but glance at the UAW preamble to see what this could mean. Part of its philosophy is that "organized labor and organized management possess the ability and owe the duty to society of maintaining through cooperative effort, a mutually satisfactory and beneficial employer-employee relationship." It further holds that, "The worker does not seek to usurp management's functions or ask for a place on the Board of Directors of concerns where organized."

But what if an auto worker disagrees with some of this? What if he or she believes that the interests of capital and labor cannot be harmonized, or that labor should challenge corporate prerogatives, or that socialist public ownership is preferable to capitalist private ownership? According to a strict interpretation of the provision, such a worker could be excluded from union membership.

Like many others, the UAW Constitution specifically excludes members of "Communist, Fascist or Nazi organizations" from holding appointive or elective office.[16] Provisions such as this have been used in many unions to deprive Communists—or those charged with being such—of their rights, but not in a single instance have similar measures been applied against those in racist- or fascist-type organizations.

The result has been a stifling of dissent, the creation of an atmosphere conducive to stultified thinking and bureaucratic control. With provisos such as the above it becomes more difficult, and in some cases impossible, to discuss working-class and trade-union problems from a longer-range vantage point and in a deeper way. The discussion of socialism has become proscribed, for socialism itself has become a "subversive" idea. Discussing the problem of apathy in unions, one writer made a telling point. "If you destroy the right of a dissident minority," he noted, "the majority can easily be manipulated. What appears as 'apathy' in many unions is not the *cause* but often the *result* of a disintegration of democracy, the end-product of the suppression of the dissenting spirit that is an essential ingredient of democracy."[17]

It has been said that the exclusion of Communists from the right to hold union office was necessary in order to defend unions from "subversion." But the very unions charged with having been "Communist controlled" were among the most democratic in the country. They barred no one from membership or the right to hold office because of political or philosophical beliefs. Most of them held conventions annually or biennially; constitutional amendments were submitted for membership ratification; and conventions were places where policies were debated, not festive gatherings where delegates were drowned in oratory during the day and in liquor at night.

### The UE and the ILWU

Discussing the "miracle" of the survival of the United Electrical Workers (UE) as an independent national union of importance, despite all the attempts to destroy it , Professor F. S. O'Brien, writing in *Labor History* (Spring 1968), asks how it is that the UE has even made "something of a comeback." He cites a Bureau of Labor Statistics report indicating that the UE grew from 115 locals in 1955-6 to 140 locals in 1961-2. Without attempting a definitive answer to his own question, O'Brien offers a few thoughts: "The UE is a democratic union, as unions go, and its leaders seem dedicated and hard-working. It employs only a relatively small number of organizers, relying primarily on the rank and file to spread organization in their immediate vicinity. It appeals to new members entirely in terms of local economic issues rather than ideologies."

Len De Caux, the editor of the *CIO News* during the CIO's crusading years, cites other examples of UE democracy: "Annual election of officers; election of all negotiation committees, with full rank-and-file participation; contracts voted upon by the workers they cover; strikes called and ended only by membership vote; a shop-steward system aiming for one steward for every foreman; salaries for officers and representatives in line with a skilled workers' wages," and so on.[18]

The International Longshoremen's and Warehousemen's Union, the other important national union that successfully withstood the anti-Communist witch-hunt, is also one of the most democratic in the country. A recall petition signed by 15 percent of the membership can immediately suspend any officer from office pending a recall election—from President Harry Bridges down. Union officers at all levels are elected every two years. Local unions meet regularly every two weeks. Every major policy is submitted to a membership referendum. When controversial questions requiring rapid determination arise, special meetings are convened by the union until consensus is reached. When 50 percent of the members are on strike, the salaries of International officers stop for the duration of the strike.

At the 1971 convention of the ILWU, Bridges sought to convince the union of the advisability of a merger with the East Coast International Longshoremen's Association. Later, Bridges went to Washington to talk merger with the Teamsters. He had to back away from that proposal as well. He knew he could not carry a union referendum.[19]

Thus, while Bridges is the respected and unchallenged leader of the union, with great personal authority, there are democratic checks against an arbitrary dictation of policy from above. This is far from the situation in most other unions. These examples of greater union democracy in the progressive-led unions should not suggest that they are perfect. But they are still among the most democratic unions in the country.

## 11 : THE LABOR ESTABLISHMENT (2)

THE MAIN tendency in trade-union administration has been an ever increasing concentration of power in the hands of top officialdom. This is a general phenomenon, although not uniform. A great deal depends on the nature of the industry, the history and tradition of the union, the politico-ideological characteristics of its leaders and, most frequently on a combination of these factors.

### The Trend Toward Centralization

The earlier, laissez-faire period of capitalism gave birth to a corresponding form of unionism. Bargaining and decision-making were decentralized and vested in each separate local. Modern, highly centralized monopoly capitalism, has produced a counterpart in a highly centralized type of unionism. The local union is no longer the sole or main center of decision-making where bargaining is conducted on a multiplant, nationwide scale, as in the basic mass-production industries, or where it takes place with regional or national employer associations. This has shifted to interlocal structures under the direct aegis of national leadership.

Local unions may be represented on national bargaining committees, and may even have the right to a referendum on proposed contracts, yet they are no longer independent entities making their own decisions. They are now part of a larger organization in which each local is but a fraction of the whole and subordinate to it. Were each local to bargain separately and come to its own terms with the corporate monolith, the advantages would all be on the side of management. It could divide one local from another and thereby drive them all down to a least common denominator. The oneness of corporate power dictates the oneness of labor response. Decentralization cannot be applied mechanically, therefore, or as an abstract principle.

The situation in unions operating exclusively in local market conditions is quite different. Craft locals in the building trades, for example, although usually more conservative than industrial locals, have far greater autonomy in matters of bargaining. This reflects itself, in turn, in more frequent local union meetings, better attendance, and greater freedom to initiate job actions, including work stoppages. Since construction jobs are temporary, and projects have to be completed in specified periods of time, a union threat to upset the time schedule is frequently sufficient to make employers see reason. This is particularly so where the local union has a monopoly of the work force and all hiring is done through it. A similar situation exists in unionized print shops, especially in newspaper plants. If a given job has to be completed by a certain hour of the day, it is the chairman of the shop union chapel who is "boss," and the company foreman has no right to interfere while work is in progress.

The need for centralized bargaining arises also in highly competitive industries where the labor force is fragmented and the setting of uniform wage scales extremely difficult to attain or enforce. Such was the situation in the trucking industry. Low capital requirements made possible thousands of large and small cartage firms. Over 17,000 interstate for-hire carriers operated under Interstate Communication Commission permits in 1960. In addition, there were thousands of smaller, intercity hauling firms that operated under state licenses. With stiff competition and labor representing a high percentage of operating costs, cartage firms resisted unilateral, or even one-city-at-a-time, wage increases for fear of being priced out of the market. The union, under Hoffa, undertook to bring "order" into the industry. He pressured the local unions to give their bargaining rights to regional district councils of the union under his control. He convinced the employers that by acting in unison and cooperating with him they could hike prices and more than make up for higher labor costs.

The corrupting side effects of these efforts are well known. Hoffa's organizing of the carriers led to sordid business deals. And the pressuring of local unions to fall in line was accompanied by a further deterioration of membership and local union rights. Yet Hoffa could not be faulted for seeking to centralize area-wide bargaining to replace the chaotic conditions that existed before. Centralization of many aspects of bargaining was essential if teamsters were to raise their living standards.[1]

The character of an industry has a great deal to do with the pressure for or against centralization. Given the constant acceleration of economic concentration, the number of separate bargaining units tends to decrease while their size tends to increase. There is a danger, therefore, that the process of collective bargaining may become ever more removed from the local union and the rank and file.

This danger is heightened as the enlargement of bargaining units also increases the scope of the issues dealt with. In addition to bare wages and hours, these now include complex items such as cost-of-living escalators, overtime rates, premium pay for Saturday and Sunday, guaranteed hours of work, shift differentials, vacation rules, paid holidays and sick leave, wash-up time, technological changes, seniority rules, layoff and severance pay, grievance and arbitration procedures, and pensions, health and hospital insurance. Bargaining is also hemmed-in by multiple bureaucratic often conflicting National Labor Relations Board rulings, written in typical legal gobbledygook.

This leads to an increasing dependence on professional experts of one kind and another—lawyers, economists, statisticians or insurance specialists. The process of bargaining becomes ever more obfuscated and remote from the perception of the average worker. This adds to the feeling that the union is a professional service agency for which the workers pay a monthly fee, and not a class movement of the workers themselves. Even the payroll dues "check-off" replaces a personal, voluntary act with a computerized compulsory deduction akin to payroll taxes.

## Centralization Manipulated

These factors have fed the tendency toward increasing centralization of power in union affairs. But there is still another factor—the role of leadership itself. Labor leaders have manipulated certain objective needs for greater centralization into a pattern aimed at further undermining union democracy, at destroying all forms of decentralization, and at enhancing their own personal power.

In an increasing number of unions the chief executive officer concentrates enormous arbitrary powers in his own hands. In the International Longshoremen's Association, for example, the president does all the hiring and firing of representatives, organizers, and administrative and technical employees. These "hold their positions at the will of the International President," says the union constitution. He also fixes the salaries of all persons employed by him; appoints committees not otherwise provided for in the constitution; designates duties and directs performance of district officers, organizers and vice-presidents. He has the power to examine, inspect or audit all books, records, papers, etc., and he has such undefined additional powers "as are usual to his office." He also has the power to interpret the constitution, and his decisions are binding unless overruled by a two-thirds vote of the Executive Committee. The same vote can amend the constitution itself.[2]

The president of the steelworkers union "shall have authority to appoint, direct, suspend or remove, such organizers, representatives, agents or employees as he may deem necessary. He shall fix their compensation subject to the approval of the International Executive Board." He appoints all convention committees. These meet in advance and consider all resolutions, appeals, reports and constitutional amendments.[3]

Appointing convention committees in advance is a general practice. It is effective in conducting a smoothly run convention, yet it can easily be used to manipulate the convention into becoming a rubber stamp of leadership. A study made of the convention proceedings of 100 unions over a period of 20 years found that through the appointment of convention committees, union leaderships were able to control the conventions. Of 93 unions "in which the procedure used to select committee members could be identified," 85 gave this authority to the union president or the executive board.

In only 28 of nearly 2,000 appeals examined did convention delegates overrule the committee decision in favor of the appellants. Only twice was an administration beaten in "politically crucial appeals." And this occurred because of a factional split in the top leadership itself. Otherwise, appeals from individuals expelled from membership because of political dissent were "uniformly denied," as were "appeals from disciplinary action for engaging in or supporting communist activities, striking illegally, or committing other acts 'disloyal' to the union and its leadership."[4]

Concluding this point, the author notes: "Defective appeals review at the convention means that there are no internal safeguards against use of disciplinary procedure to purge opposition factions from the union. . . In doing this, the leaders can prevent the minority from ever becoming the majority and thus frustrate the democratic process inside their organizations."

Conventions get stacked by other means as well. In the Teamsters, the rules for naming delegates to conventions were changed in 1961 "to give automatic delegate status to all elected local officers and business agents." This change was in line with Hoffa's view that the union's business was the prerogative of professionals.[5]

So pervasive is the tendency to concentrate power in the hands of the chief executive officer, that even a newly formed progressive-led union, the National Union of Hospital and Health Care Employees, took similar direction. Its constitution states that the president "shall coordinate and administer all the affairs and activities of the National Union"; appoint directors, representatives and organizers; fix salaries, have the power to appoint additional vice-presidents; and appoint all necessary convention committees. However, there is one safeguard not present in the ILA, the Steelworkers and some other unions—all these powers are subject to the approval of the executive board. But the executive board is required by the constitution to meet a minimum of twice a year, while the president performs his duties every day. Moreover, the constitution lists the first responsibility of each national officer as being to "aid and assist the President" in the administration of the union.

There are reasons for this stress on one-man executive authority. Emergencies arise. Pressures are great. Decisions have to be made rapidly at times. The union must speak to management with a single voice. Yet over-centralization tends to deform the collective role of leadership and the democratic processes in the organization.

Unions in the United States are traditionally top-heavy, with a larger proportion of full-time officials than in any other country. Salaries of union officials are also much higher. Most large unions have no working members on their executive board. Yet, in England where unionism also suffers from bureaucratic practices and class partnership policies, the two largest unions have working members on their boards.

The British National Union of General and Municipal Workers has two leading bodies—a general council and a smaller national executive chosen from members of the general council. The council is composed of two representatives from each district of the union. One is the district secretary, who is full time; the other is a "lay member"—a worker in shop or office. The four largest districts each have an additional "lay" representative.The national executive has one representative per district, but one-half of these must be "lay members."

The Transport and General Workers Union in Britain goes even further. It "does not allow any full-time officials to sit as voting members of the Executive, which is made up of one 'lay' representative for each region and one from each of the national trade groups in which membership is divided functionally."[6]

Few unions in this country make it possible for workers from the bench, assembly line, pit, machine or office desk to function as integral parts of national policy-making leadership. Such direct worker participation is not, of course, a guarantee of either correct policies or democratic unionism. Corruption seeps down. Workers, too can be bribed and corrupted. They are also influenced by ideas of class partnership. Especially is this so of more privileged sections of the workers, who think that by going along with the system and with the leadership they can gain more for themselves. Some workers also get seduced by the temptation to become union "big shots."Still, their participation on top committees is an important check against certain kinds of excesses. Full-time officials are made aware of thinking in the ranks, and the ranks can apply even greater pressure on their "lay" representatives in top councils.

## The Quality of Leadership

To this must be added a subjective element—the character and quality of leadership. People who remain in full-time union posts for a number of years no longer live the lives of ordinary workers. Even when their incomes are no greater than that of a wageworker, there is still an important difference. James Matles spoke of this to the delegates of a United Electrical Workers' convention:

> When you walk through a plant gate every morning, most of you hate to do it. If you did not have to earn a week's pay, few of you would ever go near that gate. . . . Instead of going to work every morning for a boss, and hating it, I've been getting up every morning and going to work at a job I like to do. That's where we officers have it all over you.[7]

Because this is undoubtedly true, the desire to hold on to a full-time position can become exceedingly strong. One may sincerely believe that he or she can serve fellow-workers best in a full-time capacity, but one cannot be sure that this is the only or primary concern. After all, most top and middle layer union officials never return to the workbench when defeated for union office. They now have professional skills. Some of them seek appointment on union staffs. Others seek more lucrative employment in other fields. A significantly increasing number accept employment as "lay consultants" to firms they face on the other side of the bargaining table.

While officers' salaries in the United Electrical Workers, the United Shoe Workers, the International Longshoremen's and Warehousemen's Union, and some others, are kept down to the level of skilled workers in the industry, this is far from the situation in most unions. The constant socializing with corporation and government executives also leaves its mark. Slowly at first, and then more rapidly, an informal first-name relationship develops, more akin to friendship and harmony than to worker-employer confrontation. Conferences and consultations are arranged at hotels and restaurants with the finest of cuisines, and appetites get whetted by the heady wine of flattery.

Many top labor leaders pride themselves on their incorruptibility, but few remain unaffected by their way of life. There are honest, conscientious union officials who work long hours, are always on the run from one trouble spot to another, and who strive to serve their members in the best way they know how. To remain dedicated, however, requires recognizing that there is a difference between their way of life and that of the average worker. Above all, it requires class consciousness — a committment to the working class in its struggle against the capitalist class.

## Wearing Two Hats

The practice of appointing International representatives and organizers from the top, instead of having them elected from the ranks, makes possible the formation of inner-union political machines. Where the hiring and firing is the sole responsibility of the chief executive officer, a personal machine of hundreds of full-time organizers can be built. This is often turned into a means of personal rule.

Also corruptive of the objectives and principles of democratic unionism are the new kinds of roles thrust upon union leaders. Unions today are the depositories of immense treasuries, often running into the hundreds of millions of dollars. In addition, billions of dollars of pension trust assets are managed by joint company-union boards, on which each side has equal representation. Often, the union president, as in the case of the International Ladies Garment Workers Union, is the chairman of the board of trustees. The billions of dollars in trust are invested in government bonds and, more frequently, in "blue-chip bonds and stocks and a sprinkling of high-quality and (generally) insured mortgages."[8] Some unions invest for so-called social purposes, such as cooperative housing. But even in this latter form of investment, the safety of the monies involved depends upon the prosperity of the economy and the given industry.

Willy-nilly, union leaders often begin to wear two hats. To the workers they appear as labor leaders; to banks, insurance and realty companies and Wall Street brokers, they are large-scale investors. The Teamsters' and Mine Workers' experiences indicate how corrupting this can become. Hoffa, as chairman of the pension board of trustees, soon began to have his own ideas as to how, where, and to whom money should be loaned or invested. It was not too difficult to get company trustees to go along with him. They knew that favors are usually returned. In the Miners' union the fund was administered by trustees who employed dozens of friends and relatives of union officers. On top of this, 78 million dollars in cash was deposited in the union-controlled bank in Washington in noninterest-bearing notes. In this way the union brass had a sizeable chunk of cash to use any way they chose.[9]

Even more sinister than the element of personal corruption, is the effect all this has on the union and its ability to defend the interests of its members. One top executive of a firm of consultants and actuaries on employee benefit plans put this succinctly. He noted that when company and union representatives sit together regularly to jointly invest huge sums of money, this creates an atmosphere that "helpfully" spills over into collective bargaining itself.[10]

BASIC change in the labor movement will not be easy to achieve. Even replacements in top union personalities are not enough. What is needed is a change in outlook; a change which sees unions as class organizations fighting for class ends. Without this, even well-intentioned individuals tend to drown in the inertia of bureaucratic, institutionalized opportunism. Minor squalls can help shake things up, but only a tempest can sweep clean the Augean stables.

## 12 : THE BASE OF THE PYRAMID

THE LABOR movement at its summit has a different look than at its base. What appears as frozen dormancy from one view, sometimes looks like perpetual motion from the other. At the top, officials are changed infrequently; at the bottom of many unions, they are changed repeatedly.

The average yearly turnover of local union officials is an estimated 20 to 25 percent.[1] As most locals hold elections every other year, this means a turnover at each election of from 40 to 50 percent. This estimate seems rather high, but the turnover is undoubtedly considerable.

The rate varies in different industries and unions. It is highest in single-plant industrial locals, and lower in craft locals and in industrial locals covering multiple workplaces (amalgamated locals). In many of the latter, the top leadership hardly ever changes.

Even where there is a regular turnover of local union leaders, it is usually little more than a changing of the guard. Discontent is always present to one degree or another, and a great deal of local union power has been usurped by the internationals, so voting the "ins" out, and "outs" in, is a ritual whose positive function is keeping local leaders on their toes. This is particularly so where a more basic program for union change is absent.

Of the estimated 71,000 union locals in the country, no two are exactly alike. They differ according to industry, occupation, union location, size, and their own peculiarities. More than 20,000 locals have less than 100 members each, but a few hundred have more than 5,000 members each. Some large locals have more members than some small internationals. About 55 percent of all locals are in the large internationals with a thousand or more local unions each, many of these are in unions with more than 2,000 locals each.

But the tendency toward ever greater concentration of union power is by no means absolute or uniform. It is greatest in industrial unions; less so in craft unions. Local unions possess considerable assets—more than half of all union funds. They are scattered among the hundreds and thousands of locals in a given international, while the funds controlled by the international are centralized and concentrated. Moreover in case of a dispute, the international has the legal right to take possession of a local's assets. And in most industrial unions the corporations send the checked-off dues payments directly to the international union which, in turn, sends the local unions their share.

Material wealth is not, however, the main asset of the local union. Its real strength lies in its being the basic organization to which all members belong and from which all power ostensibly stems. It is the constitutional, structural foundation upon which the entire union rests.

## The Local Union

A great majority of local unions are run without any full-time paid functionaries, except for hired clerical help. The leaders of the local are workers on the job. This is so in most single-plant industrial locals, although in the larger plants the chief union officer is usually full-time.

Most craft and amalgamated locals have at least one paid official. They wield considerable influence and power, especially in the building trades and wherever the local has control over the labor supply. Yet, even in these cases, most local officers and executive board members work on the job. The local union is a natural juncture for spare-time and full-time officials to commingle and function together.

In amalgamated locals, and in teachers', government employees', printers', transit, hospital, garment, retail clerks', and many other unions, intermediary structures function between the local and the membership. Sublocal shop organizations or committees exist, called chapters, chapels, departments, divisions, branches, sections or units.

Some locals of skilled, better-paid workers control sublocals of lower-paid, less skilled workers. For example, the business agent of dress pressers' Local 60 of the ILGWU was for many years also the business agent of the shipping clerks' Local 60-A. Local 3 of the International Brotherhood of Electrical Workers (IBEW), also in New York, comprises two divisions—a construction and marine division, and a maintenance, manufacturing and supply division. Twenty-three different classifications of workers are to be found in these divisions, each with its own subdivision committees and separate meetings. Skilled IBEW craft workers are "A" members, while production workers are in category "B."[2]

Some locals cover vast geographic areas. District 1199—formerly Local 1199— of the newly established national hospital union, covers New York, New Jersey and Connecticut. It has separate divisions for pharmacy, skilled and unskilled hospital workers, and separate chapters at each hospital. The chapters have little autonomy. Local 459 of the International Union of Electrical Workers (IUE), also based in New York, represents workers as far distant as New Orleans in the South, and Chicago and Milwaukee in the Midwest. Ethnic locals still exist in some cities, carryovers of the immigrant language problem. In a few unions there are still racially segregated locals—exclusively white and exclusively Black—the continuing pernicious influence of racism among white workers.

In some ways the single-plant local is the most democratic, despite the relatively smaller attendance at local union meetings. The local is more closely identified with the work site, functioning inside the plant, and union matters get aired in both formal and informal department and work-gang discussions. This takes place at work sites of amalgamated locals as well, but the relationship between the workers and their local union officials is closer and more intimate in a single-plant local. Many of these officers work in the plant, and all of them come out of the plant, so they are more subject to the direct, continuous scrutiny of the workers.

This is a different situation from that of most locals which cover multiple work sites, where the local union leaders are more removed from the body of the members. The local is something of a superstructure which ties together the various forms of union organization at the work sites, often by a network of delegate assemblies or councils. Such an amalgamated local takes on the appearance of an international to its members, for it stands as something *above* them, not *of* them.

Still another important difference exists between a single-plant local and a craft or amalgamated local. In the latter, the emphasis and spotlight are more centered on the individual leader—local president, business agent, or secretary-treasurer. But in the single-factory local, especially where the local leaders are unpaid officers working on the job, more power is vested in the collective—the executive committee, shop committee, or a combination of both. The nature of the collective that governs such a local depends more on the type of coalition that brought it into office, and less on the dynamism and charismatic qualities of a single personality, although in periods of crisis single leaders with great authority may arise. But the leaders of the single-plant local have less personal power in dealing with the company, and are less susceptible to the cruder forms of personal corruption prevalent in many craft unions.

Workers in a single-plant local are less dependent on the maneuvering skill of their top officer and more on collective strength and action, because of the difference in the power of the contending forces. In craft locals of skilled workers—and wherever the local union has control of the available skilled labor supply—the business agent wields considerable influence and is able to pressure employers and make his own deals with them. In this sense, the craft or amalgamated local which does its own bargaining and is not covered by national, regional or chain-wide contracts has more autonomous rights and greater freedom of action in dealing with the companies. In the larger industrial plants where production is capital-intensive, and where the constant pressure of the company is to turn the workers into mere adjuncts to machines, the power of capital represents a monstrous force that can be countered only by the workers' united strength and action.

## Local Changes

The structure and character of local unions have undergone considerable change. Many craft unions had their beginnings in workers' sick- and death-benefit clubs. Some began as secret societies at a time when all forms of workers' organizations were treated as illegal conspiracies against the sacred rights of private property. To this day some locals bear the ritualistic evidence of such origins; and locals in the machinists and railroad unions are still called lodges.

As craft unions became accepted, union halls began to serve as social, cultural and educational centers. This is rarely the case today. The auto has transformed the relationship between work place and residence. Workers in a factory or a mine no longer live in its shadow. Most large plants are situated in nonresidential areas and workers often travel long distances to work. The more skilled, better paid, mainly male workers may be spread over scores of suburban towns. The less skilled, more poorly paid workers, with less steady employment and incomes, particularly Black and Latin American, live crowded in deteriorating slums and ghettos of the inner city. Thus the sense of community that once existed when workers of an enterprise were also neighbors is now missing.

The auto and television have also radically altered cultural and recreation patterns, and have affected the relationship of workers to their local unions. Attendance at local membership meetings often entails traveling long distances after a day's hard labor or on a Sunday afternoon. Women workers, saddled with household chores, find it especially difficult. Thus normal pressures pull against large attendance. Only when something special occurs, or where, as in the case of the building trades locals, work sites and jobs are temporary and the local meeting is the place to learn of new job openings, is there a compelling reason to attend.

An even more important factor holds back larger attendance. Union meetings tend to be dull, uninspired affairs. The order of business is formal and stylized with procedure based on parliamentary rules, often some variation of Roberts Rules of Order. The aim is the expeditious dispatch of business with the least possible hassle in the shortest possible time. This is understandable, but does not provide the atmosphere for the average worker to take the floor and air his or her views. Instead, they feel inhibited. The factional in-fighting which often takes place at local meetings does not attract them, for the issues are frequently obscure or contrived. The situation is better in smaller locals, where workers know each other more intimately and where greater informality exists. But the tendency in many unions is toward a merger of smaller, multiple locals into one enlarged local.* Attendance is greater where fines are imposed for failure to attend, but it does not always result in greater active participation.

The fact that the union is now an established institution, no longer fighting for its life, removes that element of urgency that turned workers out in earlier decades—although then, too, attendance at local meetings was the exception, not the rule.

* The Hotel and Restaurant Employees and Bartenders International union is carrying through such mergers in city after city. In the Minneapolis-St. Paul region, for example, five locals were merged into one: "Why have five mimeograph machines when one will do; why pay rent on five office suites, when a small increase over cost of one will provide enough space for all?"[3]

TRADE union leaders often bewail this situation and employ harsh language to characterize the "indifference" of their members. Yet many of them prefer things this way. As politicians they would like more exposure before the members so as to be remembered when the next election comes around. But as administrators they find it more convenient to be the custodians of the union rather than its servants. The tendency is to give up the fight for fuller attendance and to opt for less frequent membership meetings. Local unions used to meet as frequently as twice a month, but now many no longer meet even once a month. Some meet once every three months, some only twice a year, and some only once a year.

The UAW Constitution stipulates that locals shall hold a regular general membership meeting at least once a month, except where the local decides otherwise. In such cases it is permitted to meet every three months, and meetings may be postponed during the summer. Where meetings take place only quarterly, the local is required to establish a representative plant or shop council or, where the local is an amalgamated one, shop councils. Such councils "shall meet and serve as the membership body in each of the intervening two months." The UAW Constitution also permits large locals to meet once a year, if the international executive board approves. Such locals are required to establish a representative council to serve in lieu of the membership body. The local union membership meets only once, every twelfth month.

Locals with thousands of members, sometimes tens of thousands, face special problems. If the attendance is relatively microscopic, it cannot be considered as representative of the whole. Such meetings can be manipulated by the leadership. But if the attendance is relatively large, the meeting loses its business character. It becomes a mass rally harangued by a few orators.

Gradually, the place and authority of the local membership meeting in the democratic structure of unionism has been weakened. When local union meetings were held regularly and frequently, they were important legislative bodies. They reacted to events more promptly, adopted resolutions on policy, initiated actions, submitted proposals to their international leadership, and sometimes brought these to the attention of sister locals for support. Many important popular working-class movements, such as the great struggle for unemployment compensation and social security in the thirties, were based at the local union level and then swept across the entire labor movement, in direct opposition to the stand of the moribund top AFL bureaucracy.

With local unions meeting infrequently it becomes more difficult to launch movements and actions in the same way. This will not be a major barrier to their development, however, where the issues are deeply felt, the proposed course of action simple and clear, and sufficient time taken for their gestation. But the starting point may be in the workshop itself rather than in the local meeting.

## The Union in the Work Place

The struggle for trade union democracy and class-struggle policies naturally begins at the work place. It is here that the workers are exploited, and it is here where the union must perform its class function. Here, too, the overcentralized power of the bureaucracy stands in sharpest opposition to the basic needs of the membership.

A union engaged in contract negotiations is often in the public spotlight. The membership is aware that important decisions affecting it are about to be made. But when the new contract is signed and hopefully tucked away for a number of years by the leadership, tension declines and the public assumes that peace reigns in the industry.

But contract or no contract, for the workers involved the struggle continues as a never-ceasing war. In fact, it is only some time after the contract is signed that workers learn its full meaning. They often discover that what was sold them as a monumental victory was in reality a great deal less. Inserted in fine print, or written between the lines, are sections surrendering to management the power to intensify labor exploitation.*

Even when it is not openly or tacitly agreed to in negotiations, management will try to interpret and enforce the agreement this way. I. W. Abel knew this well when he was campaigning to oust the steel union president, David McDonald. He admitted to the workers that what "appears to be won in national negotiations is often lost in local applications." But he did not admit his own complicity in this.

With both management and government pressing for increased

---

* Such treachery is written directly into Teamster union contracts in what is cynically referred to as their "plantation locals." The "sweetheart" contract signed with E. and J. Gallo Winery gave Gallo the following: "The right to hire, to determine the number of workers assigned to a task or particular operation; the means and accomplishment of any work, including subcontracting; to direct, to assign work, to supervise all of the workers; to promote and demote, to lay off for lack of work, to suspend, discharge or otherwise discipline for just cause; to decide the nature of equipment, machinery methods or processes used, to introduce new equipment, machinery, methods or processes and to change or discontinue existing equipment, machinery, methods or processes."

worker-hour productivity, job-related issues assume great importance. Centralized bargaining further aggravates this problem. Negotiations tend to revolve around general chain-wide issues to the neglect of specific local ones. In fact, most local issues cannot be resolved nationally, for in no two plants are the grievances identical. But the obeisance paid by labor officials to management prerogatives, plus the emasculation of the shop-steward system and the bureaucratic nature of the grievance procedure, make it extremely difficult for workers to resolve on-the-job issues in their own favor without some kind of direct action.

During the sixties a gradual "shift" took place in workers' concern over issues—from wages and fringe benefits to on-the-job-related ones. The grievances and complaints that arose were rarely considered to be contract violations and thus did not stand much chance of favorable consideration when admitted to arbitration. They became so-called "knee-pad grievances"—that is, the kind workers have to beg or pray for to get resolved in their favor.[4]

As runaway inflation ate away more and more of the workers' income during the early seventies, the wage issue became dominant once again in contract negotiations. But the continuing drive for increased productivity made local grievances the main issues of on-the-job daily disputes. Thus, the demand for a split-level system of bargaining, with local bargaining placed on an equal footing with national, gained considerable support, as did the demand for the right to strike over local issues during the term of an agreement.

REGULAR work-place meetings are not substitutes for local union meetings. But they are the most democratic expression of the union at the point of production, where the workers need the union the most.

Most amalgamated locals provide for periodic meetings of members on a work-place level. The chapel meeting of the Typographical Union is an institution. It can be convened at any time the chapel chairman thinks necessary, irrespective of the day's work schedule. In the State, County and Municipal Employees, and the teachers, chapter meetings are also customary. Such meetings, in shops, departments, offices, divisions, sections, yards, ships, garages, work crews, or units, are usually well attended. The participation of the workers is fuller, livelier, more informal. As others have noted, "The inhibitions that operate on the individual member at the local meeting do not operate at the unit meeting where he talks freely and holds his unit officers closely to account."[5]

While sublocal meetings of this kind are more frequent in amalgamated-type locals, they are less frequent in single-plant industrial locals. But even in the multiple workshop locals, such meetings tend to take place when emergencies arise, when stewards or committee members are chosen, or when the local leadership wants to raise some question. They are not *regular* meetings, not an integral part of union structure with the right to discuss and adopt positions on all questions of concern to the union and membership.

In many industries the companies are opposed to the use of "their" premises for union meetings. In some cases union officials also prefer that work-unit meetings be held in the union hall. In other countries the right to union work-place meetings is well established. In socialist countries it is a natural right, for the plants are not the private property of anyone. Even in some capitalist countries this right has been won. In France, it is guaranteed by law, won in the 1968 general strike. Workers in France are also entitled by law to one hour off with pay each month for such meetings.

In the earlier formative years of the CIO, shop stewards were urged to convene department meetings regularly. A pamphlet guide for stewards and committeemen prepared by the CIO Department of Research and Education in the early forties, emphasized that "the best steward in the world can't carry the union alone." "Your job will be easier," it read, "if you hold these [department] meetings regularly." It also urged informal lunch-hour classes for "heart-to-heart talks with the workers" and for listening "to their angles."

The "Manual for Shop Stewards," published by the AFL-CIO in 1972, no longer mentions departmental meetings. It urges the steward to keep the membership informed, but doesn't indicate how this is to be done.

## The Grievance Machinery

Regular department or work-unit meetings are directly related to the democratic functioning of grievance machinery. The aim of management and most union leaderships is to keep a grievance bottled up so that action by the workers affected is paralyzed.

A grievance procedure usually consists of four or five graduated steps. The worker and steward first confront the foreman. If they do not get satisfaction at this first step and decide to press the grievance further, it goes to the department superintendent. If still unresolved, it moves to the plant personnel director and/or a top-management committee. If it is turned down on this level, it goes to arbitration. The arbitrator, ostensibly impartial, has the responsibility of rendering a final decision.

It may take from a month to a year or longer, depending upon company stalling and the backlog of grievances, to proceed from step one through step four or five. And even at the last step, grievances can be denied or tossed out on grounds of not being covered by the existing contract.

During this protracted waiting period the workers are expected to cool their heels. They are warned against trying to break the bottleneck by collective departmental action. In cases where department meetings are regular occurrences, the workers are in a better position to press for speedy and favorable action.

Regular work-site meetings also affect the choice of stewards and their performance. In many unions the right of workers to elect their own steward griever, committee person, representative, or delegate has been whittled away. In a number of unions the election of stewards is carried out haphazardly and irregularly, and sometimes not at all. "It is not rare," states one report, "for the steward to be coopted by the local union officers."[6] And in such instances a certain amount of collusion between union officers and employers is also not rare.

The steward in the larger industrial plants is no longer a regular worker on a job. He is full-time, paid by the company to process the grievances of hundreds of workers, many of whom are employed on jobs far removed from his own personal acquaintance and former work experience.

The 1973 UAW-GM agreement specifies one chief steward for each 250 employees, but with a declining ratio in the larger plants. In plants of 5,000 to 7,000 workers, the union is entitled to seven chief stewards, and in plants with over 10,000 workers, to eleven chief stewards. Significantly, the agreement makes no mention of lower-rung section stewards, although the UAW Constitution provides for them. Thus, the ratio of full-time stewards to workers in the large GM plants is approximately one to 1,000.

The ratio in Ford plants is better; it is one steward for each 225 workers. But here, too, the stewards are no longer regular workers. They now "have the right to devote their full time to their duties."

Whether full-time stewards representing hundreds of workers are preferable to a considerably larger number of part-time stewards representing their own work unit, gang, or section, is a matter of dispute among trade unionists. Of course, one form does not necessarily exclude the other. It depends on the nature of the work and the detailed division of labor.

Those who favor the full-time steward to the exclusion of the part-time steward argue that the modern contract is a highly complex document and requires thorough knowledge of its provisions. They aver that filing a grievance requires considerable paper work, and the ability to find the exact clause that favors the grievance. They believe that the inducement of being on full-time makes for a better steward, for only then will he or she stand a chance of being reelected or reappointed.

There is merit to each of these arguments. But as a whole, they do not stand up to closer scrutiny. The replacement of multiple rank-and-file, part-time stewards with a handful of full-time, professional ones, reeks of the same bureaucratic thinking that has crippled the labor movement by making it a service agency *for* workers instead of a movement *of* them. It once again places a premium on elitist expertise as against rank-and-file participation and control. The end result of this trend would be to make contracts so unwieldy and complicated that no worker could understand them, and a union would have to engage an army of specialized Philadelphia lawyers to become shop stewards. As for inducements, if being full-time makes one a better servant of the workers, then all union posts should be full-time. If full-time officials were the answer, the labor movement of this country would be the best in the world, since it already has the highest proportion of full-time officials.

In most cases there is a qualitative difference between a steward who services a limited number of workers and remains a worker at the machine, bench or desk, and the steward who covers a number of departments and floors. In the first instance the steward's links with the workers are personal and intimate; in the second, they are formal and distant.

The policy of the UE on the matter of stewards seems to have the most merit. The aim is to establish one steward for each foreman, and for a simple reason. If an operation, department, or floor is too large for one foreman to supervise, it is also too large for a union steward to service. UE stewards work on their regular jobs and receive extra compensation at normal hourly earnings for the actual time lost in processing grievances. And the UE record of grievance handling is among the best of the industrial unions.

HOW workers in other countries view the matter of a democratic shop steward system can be seen by taking another glance at France. One of the first laws adopted after the liberation of France from Nazi occupation dealt with the rights of shop stewards. Article 4 of this law, adopted in April 1946, established an exact ratio of stewards to workers in places of employment. Every group of 11 to 25 workers is entitled to elect one steward and one alternate. A group of 25 to 50 workers elects two stewards and two alternates. As the size of the work force increases, the ratio of stewards tends to decline.

In both France and Italy, stewards are subject to recall if the workers are dissatisfied with their performance. Because the unions in these countries do not have exclusive bargaining rights, shop stewards are elected by *all* the workers of a given unit, irrespective of union or non-union membership. In addition to these stewards, the union members elect their own special delegates to watch over things and to help raise the level of workers' union and political consciousness.

The French workers have still another form of steward—the safety officer, or safety steward. This workers' representative is elected in industries where working conditions are hazardous to health. The safety steward represents all the workers of the enterprise and is responsible for protecting them from industrial accident or illness. He or she has the power to shut down production if workers' health or safety are endangered, and to ensure that injured or sick workers get the full compensation to which they are entitled. In the mining industry the rights of the safety stewards are guaranteed by law. He sends a daily report on safety conditions to the mine superintendent and the chief engineer. If his recommendations are ignored, he can get the mine committee to shut the mine down.

Thus, the shop steward (delegate) system in many European countries is highly developed and has facets unknown here. Of special importance is the shop delegates' council. It often represents something of an independent power base, depending upon whether class-struggle or class-collaboration views predominate. It may challenge the employer on production policy and even concern itself with who runs the plant lunchroom and how it is run.

In periods of acute social tension and crisis, the shop delegates' council can play an especially important role. Being closer to the rank and file and operating as the first rung of leadership, it often reflects more accurately the needs, mood and will of the workers.

# 13 : THE TWO SIDES OF UNIONISM

RECENTLY a number of liberal and radical intellectuals have concluded that the labor movement is now so much a part of the establishment that it is hopeless to try to change it. John Galbraith, for example, points to the role of unions as essential in assuring uninterrupted production and the elimination of wage costs as a competitive factor. Hence, he believes that the union belongs to an earlier stage of industrial development, and when it passes, "so does the union in anything like its original positions of power."[1]

Other observers see unions as now "aiding in the reconciliation of conflicting interests."[2] Still others stress the growing gap between workers and leaders. Some unions, it is claimed, even hire public relations firms to find out what their own members think. And one worker is quoted as saying, "What I need now is a union to represent me to my own union."[3]

## Union Viability

A New Left ideologue, Stanley Aronowitz, has taken this point of view further. He writes, "We are in the midst of a massive reevaluation by organized industrial workers of the viability of the union." This, he

157

believes, is "an action critique, rather than an ideological criticism of the union's role."[4]

If a massive reevaluation of the viability of unions is taking place *in action*, this should find some reflection in a weakening of workers' ideological commitment to unions. But there is no such evidence. Aronowitz states that "for the mass of working poor," unionism "seems to be a kind of deliverance from bondage," but "when grinding poverty has been overcome," the bureaucratic nature of unions is more discernible.[5]

It is true that many workers are highly critical of their unions. They have a right to be. They know about union bureaucracy, "sweetheart" deals, and the tendency of union officials to climb into bed with management. But there is no evidence that they are turning against unions, for they recognize that without them they would be at the complete mercy of the employers.

Every study of workers' attitudes toward their unions bears this out. Responding to a question about whether they would be better off without a union, rank-and-file workers of widely different unions all replied in a similar vein. One said, "Without the union we would have no contract, the company would run things the way they wished." Another, "Without the union we wouldn't have a leg to stand on." And a third, "If it weren't for unions we'd be working for peanuts."[6] Even when workers fear, hate or despise the union leaders who speak for them, they do not wish to "go no union."[7]

Two examples should suffice to prove this. When the postal workers went out on a nation-wide strike in 1970, they halted mail deliveries across the land for the first time in history. They were striking against the policies of the Nixon Administration and against the do-nothing policies of their union officials. But they were not striking against unionism. They hung their union president in effigy, picketed with placards calling him "rat"—his name was Rademacher—but they did not abandon their union or consider it obsolete.

The same is true of the coal miners who participated in dozens of wildcat strikes that paralyzed coal region after coal region. But these actions were meant to save their union, not destroy it. The corrupt Boyle gang had weakened it to such a point that a large portion of coal mining had become nonunion. Union miners did not want to wind up in that blind alley. In fact, some of them earlier hesitated to get into the fight against the Boyle machine because they feared the coal operators would take advantage of the inner-union dispute to destroy it completely. Actually, the union was rejuvenated.

Thus, again there is no evidence that organized workers are now turning their backs on unionism or reevaluating its viability. Good or bad, they see unions as speaking for them—not always as they would like, but as the most important barriers to employer greed. This is why unions constitute the largest, most stable mass movement of workers in this country. This is even more true, in the United States than in other developed capitalist countries. Here, the workers have no labor party of their own, or a mass political equivalent for it. They are still tied to the two parties of monopoly capitalism. The trade union movement is the only organized *mass* expression of the working class at this time.

Attendance at local union meetings is generally low and large numbers of workers are inactive, many even passive and apathetic. Yet hundreds of thousands of rank-and-file workers are extremely active. As one labor observer estimates, this is a level of participation without parallel in the nation. "Proportionately, there is probably more sustained involvement by workers in unions than by all the people in politics."[8]

Local union attendance is an important barometer of workers' concern and involvement. But it is not the only one. The nerve center of the union is in the work place. Here it must react to the stimuli of a daily class war both hidden and open. Often nerve endings become atrophied, or the center itself becomes insensitive and indifferent to workers' needs. Yet it is in the work place that grievances get aired, policy and leadership discussed, issues crystallized and demands formulated, and what appears as a passive and indifferent membership one day may be an angry and rebellious one the next. Slowdowns and work stoppages suddenly erupt and union meetings swell in attendance like rivers pregnant with angry spring waters.

This should be borne in mind in any serious assessment of the labor movement. One can recognize the existence of a deep crisis in labor's ranks without belittling the trade unions as a bona fide movement that gives millions of workers a sense of collective strength and dignity.

ONE reason for Aronowitz' one-sided view is his mistaken, erroneous estimate of contemporary capitalism. Writing in 1973, when the evidence of an impending economic crisis was already here, Aronowitz still refers to modern capitalism as a "post security society" and a "relatively successful capitalism."[9] For him "inflation, wages, or general economic conditions'' are no longer as important as heretofore and not the stuff from which class-consciousness is made. For him the issue of issues is alienation.[10]

But, as indicated previously, alienation means different things to different people. Only when seen as a clear expression of class exploitation can it lead to a greater class awareness. Aronowitz points to the militancy of the Lordstown, Ohio, General Motors workers as being induced by alienation. But the wildcat strikes would not have occurred had the production of the small-car Vega not brought with it a greatly juiced-up assembly line. The issue was not alienation in the abstract, but increased speed-up in the concrete.

ARONOWITZ is opposed to labor-management agreements. He sees them as instruments that impede workers' militancy and tie their hands. And, of course, they do in many cases. But it does not follow that the absence of collective bargaining agreements would enhance labor militancy and strengthen the workers vis-à-vis the employing class.

The South is the least organized region of the country with the fewest collective bargaining agreements. But this has not enhanced the ability of workers to combat the corporations. The South may still become the area of greatest worker militancy, but if this occurs it will be part of a great upsurge *for* unions and collective bargaining agreements, not against them.

Most union contracts place restrictions on the kind of struggles workers may conduct during the life of a contract. Strikes are usually banned or restricted to rare circumstances, and then only with the approval of the national union leadership. But even with such limitations on freedom of action, organized workers have many more opportunities than the unorganized to exert pressure. And when the going gets rough, contractual restrictions get shoved aside, as the term ''wildcat strike'' testifies.

The view that a labor-management agreement is to the sole advantage of the employer is false. It ignores the many decades of bitter conflict that finally compelled corporations to bargain with unions. It also ignores the fact that most workers have still not won that right. If these are all to the sole advantage of the employers, why don't they rush to recognize unions everywhere?

Of course, like every bargain, there are two sides; and each side gains something. Otherwise there could be no agreement, only surrender.

What the worker gains is that he no longer has to face his employer alone. When he does, the trump cards are all on the other side; one worker can be pitted against another. By compelling the corporations to bargain with the workers as a collective, the workers are able to impose certain restraints on the corporations, which no longer can reign supreme over them.

The employers also gain. They win a temporary truce that enables them to maintain uninterrupted production and with it the ability to earn profits. But this is a concession that workers cannot but grant so long as they are not in a position to end the system of so-called private enterprise.

What happens after an agreement is arrived at depends on whether it is viewed as a declaration of peace or a truce in an ongoing struggle. The ability of workers to halt production is what gives them bargaining muscle. This capability should always be in evidence. If it is signed away and the company given the feeling that it no longer is to be feared, the union becomes like Samson with his hair shorn.

It stands to reason that corporations will use every trick they know to violate agreements and to test the fighting mettle of the workers and their leaders. It is in the nature of every truce that each side continues to exert pressure on the weak flanks of the other. To expect anything less is naive. Hence, if union leaders permit corporations to get away with attempts to undermine working conditions, or if they permit a situation where workers become frustrated and infuriated by endless and fruitless red-tape grievance procedures, the fault lies with them and not with the act of signing an agreement. It is then the duty of workers to find their own way to correct the situation.

## The Nature of the Conflict

Shortly after World War II, the Management and Labor Center of Yale University conducted a study to ascertain "the basic nature of the conflict between management and unions as they face the future." Prof. E. Wight Bakke, director of the Institute, summed up its results. Labor leaders, he found, did not want to run industry and had no plans in that direction. Yet he feared that this was where the conflict was heading. He quoted one union leader as saying that the union sought to regulate the discretion of an employer "at every point where his actions affect the welfare of the men."

This covers a lot of territory, observed Bakke wryly, for "there is not a single managerial function which does not fall within that area. Where will the process stop? Where can it stop," he asks, "if the union is to fulfill its basic objective of regulating collectively all those industrial policies and practices which affect the welfare of the men?"[11]

What is most irritating to management, Bakke found, "arises from specific restrictions on such items as discipline, hiring, transfers, work assignments, promotions or demotions, lay offs, the establishment and administration of work schedules and production quotas, organizational and technological innovations, the setting up and administration of wage systems, and like matters. Particularly irritating to many managements is the denial of their freedom to reward or punish individual workers in accordance with management's estimate of their individual merit and promise."[12]

What is irritating to management is that it cannot do with its work force as it pleases.

Adding a new section to his book in 1966, 20 years later, Bakke points to a much improved atmosphere in capital-labor relations. He calls it a form of "antagonistic-cooperation." He finds the "basic issue," however, still unresolved. "In some ways it isn't as stubborn as it was then. But in other and important ways it is more stubborn."[13]

In his earlier report he indicated that labor leaders are "opportunistic and pragmatic in their policy and practice. How far they go is guided by practical needs, not by any revolutionary philosophy." Yet even if they wished to be reasonable, he found, "there's a problem. The fellow at the top means well, but the men down the line have different ideas." This is easier for management to handle in its own ranks, because the "fellow on the top" can replace "men down the line." But it is not that easy for labor leaders. Sometimes it is they who get replaced.[14]

Bakke perceives a perpetual pressure of workers to challenge management rights and prerogatives. Even the union with the most reactionary leadership must from time to time dispute employer rights to unilaterally determine wages, hours of work, safety regulations and conditions of labor. Prof. Selig Perlman was right in saying that the labor movement "from its very nature" must be an "organized campaign against the rights of private property."[15]

This is the class-struggle side of trade unionism, and it must endure as long as does capitalism. To ignore it, as Aronowitz does, is not more "radical." Rather it is to argue that workers should pursue a self-defeating strategy.

THERE is another side: bargaining is conducted within the framework of bourgeois property relations. This is so even when the absolute rights of private property are challenged; what is not being challenged is the very right to this ownership. Even the most class-conscious union must bargain with employers for the best conditions under which it will continue making profit for them. In other words, workers bargain for the best conditions of their own servitude.

This is inherent in the labor contract, whether written on parchment and legally binding, or in the form of an informal agreement between hirer and hireling, between employer and employee, whether individual or collective. The same workers who suspect their leaders of too cozy a relationship with management, and who demand more aggressive union policies, also expect their leaders to know how far to go in open frontal assault, and when, and for what, to settle for a temporary truce (agreement). This arises from the worker's lack of independent means of livelihood. Workers must sell their labor power for the best terms they can get.

In this sense and in this sense only, wrote Marx, the interests of the workers and the capitalists are *"one and the same."* [Emphasis in original.] "The worker perishes if capital does not not employ him. Capital perishes if it does not exploit labor power. . . ." In this is to be found "the much vaunted community of interests between worker and capitalist."[16]

Thus, the dilemma of the worker under capitalism is manifested. Every union is subject to two contradictory pulls—class struggle and class conciliation. It is this duality—of fighting capitalists yet accepting capitalism—that introduces elements of conservatism in all unions. This pull depends on objective conditions of the time, the level of workers' consciousness, and the character of trade union leadership.

## Glorification of Anarcho-Syndicalism

Those who, like Aronowitz, believe that workers can defend their interests better without unions, apparently think that the tendency toward conciliation would disappear once unions were eliminated. Then there would be no contracts, no agreements, no compromises; only bald, blunt class struggle.

But unions are not the cause of the dilemma, and their disappearance would not remove it. So long as workers must accept conditions of exploitation, the contradiction will exist. Individual unions may perish—they have in the past when they failed to meet new conditions of struggle—but unionism will not. This is borne out by the history of the working-class movement throughout the world.

The failure to understand the objective need for trade unions produces a great deal of radical rhetoric and empty gesturing. On the part of some, it leads to a glorification of anarchism and anarcho-syndicalism. This is expressed in a current adulation among some young leftists of the Industrial Workers of the World (IWW) as the model of what class-struggle unionism should be.

There is much in the history of the IWW that is heroic, praiseworthy, even glorious. For more than a decade, up to the end of World War I, it led scores of militant class battles at a time when AFL leaders were rocking in their swivel chairs. The IWW made a first noble effort to organize the unskilled workers in the mass-production industries and on the farms. And it was proudly and defiantly anticapitalist and revolutionary in its outlook.

The IWW was a response to the corruption and class partnership that prevailed in the AFL. It set out to build "pure" unions in which every form of compromise would be ruled out. Rejecting the duplicity of "bourgeois" politics, it also opposed political action as a matter of principle, holding that by the economic struggle alone the workers could build "One Big Union" as the prototype of the new society emerging in the shell of the old.

But the IWW was incapable of converting the human energy it helped release into a permanent, viable movement of workers. By its rejection of political struggle and labor-management negotiations and agreements, it made a permanent mass movement impossible. At a time when the corporations were refusing to grant any form of recognition to industrial unions, the IWW reciprocated by refusing to recognize the companies. When one of its locals signed an agreement with a company, it was expelled. Soon the Western Federation of Miners, its most important and most stable mass base, parted company with it. Eugene V. Debs and William Z. Foster did likewise.

Aronowitz states that the IWW has been the only radical alternative to liberal union leaders. But it was no viable alternative. In time, its inflexible purism gave opportunists and careerists the appearance of "practical" people capable of bringing at least some bacon home to workers some of the time. IWW rigidity lent credence to the view that only the liberal and conservative labor leaders were concerned with, and capable of building, a permanent on-going labor movement. Thus the radicals, unable to understand the need for compromise as a tactic, lost out to those who saw compromise as a way of life. The IWW unions disintegrated, and nothing was left of its organizing efforts.

## The Question of Compromise

There are valid reasons for fearing compromise. The history of the American labor movement is replete with acts of betrayal perpetrated in the name of compromise. Each of these carried a surface plausibility and brought tangible temporary concessions to some workers, but concealed the sacrifice of primary interests in exchange for what too often were secondary benefits.

For example, that coal miners won a welfare and retirement fund was important. But when Lewis gave the mine operators a free hand to mechanize mining, and even loaned them millions of dollars for this purpose from the union-controlled—really Lewis-controlled—bank in Washington, it was a pure and simple sell-out.

This may be the crassest example of union leadership complicity with management, but it is not the only one. In exchange for more money per hour, or for some fringe benefits, unions have signed long-term contracts containing no-strike clauses and have given corporations carte blanche to introduce radical work changes. Shop-steward systems have been weakened, plant grievances permitted to pile up, and the grievance procedure turned into a process conducive to aggravation rather than rectification.

The solution to this problem requires raising the level of workers' consciousness so that they understand their long-range class interests and judge momentary compromises from that vantage point. But to achieve this level of class consciousness is difficult. A union is not an organization of radicals united by a common ideology. It is an elementary form of working-class organization uniting workers, irrespective of ideology, so long as they agree to confront their employers collectively. As the overwhelming majority of American workers still accept capitalism as a preferred social system, this has its influence on union policies and practices. It tends to dilute clear-cut class positions.

This is complicated still further by the way bargaining is conducted in this country. In Italy and France, for example, unions are not the agencies of direct bargaining. The workers of each establishment elect a shop committee that performs this function. This committee may be composed of members of different competing unions and of no union whatever. Whether a union's position prevails in bargaining depends on its ability to win a majority of the committee for it.

Unions under Communist, Socialist and Catholic influence operate side by side. Each has a somewhat different political-ideological thrust and is part of a separate national labor federation. The problem of unity is that of achieving agreement between them.

In this country, unions do the direct bargaining. Only one union has the right to speak for the workers of a given bargaining unit. To have a say on bargaining policy and on the handling of grievances, workers must belong to the union that speaks for them. This makes more difficult the establishment of unions with an advanced left-wing ideology. It requires that the majority of workers of a given union must first be won to such views.

Lenin warned that there are no pure forms of organization or methods of struggle. He pointed out that "all, positively all methods of struggle in bourgeois society . . . if left to the spontaneous course of events, become frayed, corrupted and prostituted." Strikes, he noted, become corrupted into "agreement between employers and workers *against* the consumers." Parliaments become corrupted into "public pimps, into means of corrupting the masses, of pandering to the low instincts of the mob, and so forth and so on." The *only* thing that can prevent such corruption, Lenin stressed, "is the ennobling influence of socialist consciousness." [All emphasis as in original.][17]

THE ANSWER to conservatism in trade unions is not to be found in abandoning them, but rather in the struggle to make them more powerful and consistent class instruments. The starting point is winning internal democracy and rank-and-file control. This is something all workers want. It would enable the workers to judge for themselves between the two main contending tendencies in the labor movement—that of class struggle and that of class accommodation.

Most top union officials fear such a test. They realize that despite a lack of ideological class consciousness on the part of American workers, they have an instinctive class-struggle gut reaction to on-the-job questions. That is why the worst charge that can be made against an unpopular labor leader is to call him "company man." Even the charge of personal corruption is sometimes overlooked if the leader in question has a reputation for standing up to the companies. This is why Jimmy Hoffa was so popular among teamsters. And, conversely, the worst company man will try to appear militant to his rank and file. The struggle for union democracy is key, therefore, to any change in the labor movement.

Because unions are composed of workers of varied political and social views and thus influenced by both class-struggle and class-partnership pressures, they cannot lead the struggle for revolutionary change. They must be won for it. "Trade unions work well as centers of resistance against the encroachments of capital," observed Karl Marx, but, "they fail partially from an injudicious use of their power. They fail generally from limiting themselves to a guerrilla war against the effects of the existing system, instead of simultaneously trying to change it, instead of using their organized forces as a lever for the final emancipation of the working class, that is to say, the ultimate abolition of the wages system."[18]

To change this negative side of trade unionism; to help win workers and unions for the abolition of capitalism, a special organization of class-conscious, revolutionary-minded workers is needed. That is why Communist parties exist all over the world as well as in the United States. These are able to speak and act from a more consistent working-class and socialist point of view. They help the trade union movement in every way, point up its weaknesses and mistakes, and help convince workers that by narrowly confining the trade union movement to economic battles, "they are retarding the downward movement, but not changing its direction; that they are applying palliatives, not curing the malady."[19]

But Aronowitz, who sees only the negative side of trade unions, is even more vehemently opposed to a political, vanguard-type of workers' organization. He frowns on the need for any type of leadership. The workers, he argues, need no leaders and no vanguard. First, because they can comprehend everything themselves; second, because the Left "has no credentials" for leadership; and third, because he is against "authoritarian social relations in the workers' movement."[20]

If it is all that simple, why haven't workers comprehended everything up to now? Certainly it is not only that their leaders have been in the way, for a majority of the working class is still unorganized. Is it not rather that there is no such thing as an ideological vacuum? Whether workers realize it or not, they inhale and exhale the poisoned air of bourgeois ideology. Otherwise they would have removed phoney leaders and class partnership policies a long time ago.

To patronize workers by telling them they can comprehend everything spontaneously, is to leave them to the mercies of bourgeois ideas. It is true that workers are now better educated and can arrive at many general Marxist conclusions by their own observations and study. But even then, they cannot apply this understanding in a serious and collective fashion except through association and interaction in a disciplined way with others who think likewise. By denying the need for Left leadership, workers are really being told to stick with right-wing leaders, for a movement without leaders is like a mass of protoplasm without skeletal form.

# 14 : ORGANIZING THE UNORGANIZED

THE CHANGES in the composition of the work force, particularly the drop in the proportion of manual workers, have led some to conclude that the labor movement has passed its peak in relative size and influence and is now on an irreversible decline.[1]

This is not the first time that changes in the composition of capital and labor were given as evidence—and inside the organized labor movement as justification—for a failure to grow. At the beginning of the century when modern large-scale production superseded the small workshops, and when a new division of labor resulted in the employment of large numbers of unskilled labor, these changes were viewed as inimical to further union expansion. The huge corporations seemed to be too powerful, and the unskilled workers, largely foreign-born or Black, too heterogeneous to be organized.

This theory, seemingly so logical and plausible—and so pleasantly self-serving and smug for a conservative, lethargic craft union officialdom—was quietly laid to rest when the unionism sweep of the mid-thirties proved it to be nonsense.

The data cited in Chapter I show that the changing composition of the work force does not mean shrinkage or disappearance of the working class. It is the middle class that is eroding, not the working class. An increasing proportion of white-collar and professional people are now becoming part of an enlarged working class, even though many may think of themselves as middle class.

There is even evidence that automation does not eliminate the need for many types of unskilled labor. A study conducted over a number of years of so-called automated plants found that automation actually "reduced the skill requirements of the operating work force, and occasionally of the entire factory force including the maintenance organization." The "labor effect" of automating a job depends on what functions are automated and what degree and level of mechanization are attained.

When work processes are first automated, a great responsibility rests on the operator who must detect and correct malfunctions. But as the kinks get ironed out, and the machine begins to monitor and correct itself, "the operator literally loses the opportunity to exercise 'responsibility' even though the machine may be more complicated and costly."

The writer of this report, James R. Bright of the Harvard Graduate School of Business Administration, advises management against upgrading and more pay when automation begins, because as time goes on "the more automatic the machine, the less the operator of the machine has to do." Greater skill, he notes, is required for "conceiving, designing and building new machines," and for more sophisticated types of service repairmen, but the routine operation of the computer, "and even programming, do not require the high order of skill and training anticipated in the mid-fifties." Public high schools are now training students to program computers.[2]

Thus the popular assumption that automation will eliminate the average worker who lacks education, training and technical skill is challenged.

## Obstacles to Organizing

In addition to the automation theory, those who argue that the labor movement has peaked in size and is now on the irreversible downgrade, give as evidence the following:

1) Blue-collar workers in the large industrial establishments, with the exception of textile, chemical and mining, are now organized in the main;

2) New and rapidly expanding industries, such as electronics, chemical and petroleum, are highly capital-intensive, that is to say, they operate with a smaller work force composed of more technicians, engineers and research personnel. They are paid considerably higher salaries and are harder to organize than ordinary wageworkers;

3) Workers in small factories and workshops are also more difficult to organize, service and keep organized because they are spread over vast areas and located in thousands of separate production units;

4) Many of the newer, more modern industrial plants are in the South, or in agricultural and small town communities, less tolerant of unions;

5) In nonmanufacturing industries there are "institutional barriers" to organization—the smaller size of trade and service units, the difference in outlook of office and professional employees, and the fact that many of these are women, who are often harder to organize;

6) Federal laws are less favorable to union expansion than they were in the days of the New Deal, and the so-called right-to-work laws in 19 states are distinctly hostile to trade unionism.

Yes, there are obstacles such as these to further organizing. Obstacles have always existed, but one can use them either as a pretext for not organizing or a stimulus for doing more.

The above arguments include an assumption that because workers in large plants are better organized, most of the job of organizing industrial workers has already been done. But one-half of the workers in manufacturing, 25 percent of those in transport and communication, 29 percent of those in construction, and 53 percent of workers in mining, are still without unions.[3] Thus there is still a great deal to be done in organizing industrial workers, not to speak of millions of blue-collar workers in service occupations and government employment.

Mythology would have us believe that for the blue-collar workers in the large industrial plants unionism was "natural" and therefore they were easy to organize. This is not true. Often workers in large plants were sharply divided along racial, nationality, language and religious lines. Frequently a large plant was a cacaphony of discordant tongues, with one group of workers pitted against another in hiring and job placement. Workers also feared reprisals. Industrial towns were "company towns," owned and run by the corporation, and the mines, mills and factories were laced with Pinkerton spies. In many towns, open union meetings were impossible. During the 1919 effort to organize the steel industry, the mayor of Duquesne, Pennsylvania, proclaimed that "Jesus Christ himself could not speak in Duquesne for the AFL!" He meant it. And sheriffs, police, state troopers, and the courts, were there to back him up.[4]

It took many decades of militant struggle and countless martyrs and, of course, innumerable heartbreaking defeats, plus the important political victory which the Wagner Labor Act represented, before industrial unionism finally won out. The arguments of craft-union leaders that the unskilled could not be organized because they lacked the job leverage of skilled workers, the confidence of native-born whites, or the natural pride and solidarity of skilled craftsmen, were thus exposed as being prejudiced.

Most manual workers, of course, have a more instinctive class feeling than white-collar or professional workers. This arises from the physical nature of their labor, their more direct role in the production of material goods as against paperwork, their close cooperative association with large numbers of other workers in the work process itself, and their generally subordinate place in the bourgeois scale of social values. This holds for blue-collar workers in smaller production units as well, even if not always to the same degree.

### Smaller Unit Organizing

The argument that workers in large industrial plants are more easily organized than those in smaller ones is not necessarily true. A large corporation has far more resources with which to combat unionism should it desire to do so. It was more difficult to organize General Motors or Ford, for example, than the many smaller auto parts suppliers. Currently, the majority of NLRB elections won by unions are in units of less than 100 employees. In the decade from 1963 to 1972, unions won 58 percent of elections in work places of less than 100 employees, but only 48 percent of those in work places of over 100 employees.[5]

Historically, the first local unions on record were made up of workers scattered in dozens and even hundreds of small enterprises. This is true of the origin of nearly all craft unions. The first manufacturing workers organized were in small workshops of the garment trades, cigar-making, printing, machine shops, bakeries, shoemakers, and so on. To argue, therefore, that smaller shops and factories are a major obstacle to organizing is to find an excuse for not doing so.

Daniel Bell stresses the smaller size of units in service and trade as obstacles to their unionization. Yet he points to District 65 of the Distributive Workers as "most successful" in organizing such units because of amalgamated locals." We are not concerned at this point with the structure of organization, only with its possibility. Bell gets closer to the problem when he observes that bureaucracy is a much greater factor in the failure to organize. Labor leaders have lost their elan and "there is no will or ability any more to begin large-scale organizing drives."[6]

The same loss of social motivation is reported by Professor Irving Bernstein. He states that union representatives in both manufacturing and service informed him that their organizations could unionize many more small units if they wished. "The question is only in part whether the job can be done; more often it is whether it is worth the expenditure—the time and money in view of the potential return. In recent years the labor movement seems normally to have answered in the negative."[7]

Whether organizing is "worth the expenditure" cannot be measured in dollars-and-cents terms. Unionism is not a business, although some union officials act as if it is. It is a workers' movement, and as such it must ceaselessly seek to expand the unity and organized strength of the workers.

Of course, where unions are small and weak, with limited resources,—and this (limited resources) may sometimes be the case with large unions as well—the appropriate answer can be found by pooling resources and uniting organizing efforts. Expenditures need not be so great where unions encourage rank-and-file organizing instead of the bureaucratic top-down variety. If a new crusading spirit animated the labor movement, the workers in organized work places would be inspired to reach out and help organize nonunion shops in the vicinity. The Left-led Italian Confederation of Labor (CGIL) encourages workers from northern industrial regions to take trips to the unorganized areas of the South to talk with workers about joining the union.[8] This method is also used by the independent United Electrical Workers (UE).

During the great organizing crusade of the mid-thirties, especially after the first successes were registered, much of the organizing was done by workers themselves. James Matles and James Higgins, in their book *Them and Us–Struggles of a Rank-and-File Union,* describe the self-organizing that took place in the building of the UE. In the span of 18 months from March 1936 to September 1937, the union at the plant in Schenectady grew from 650 to 8,000 members, "but not even a single full-time staff organizer from the UE international union was assigned to the campaign."[9] This is possible only when workers feel that the unions are worth fighting for and are encouraged to move out on their own. As Matles and Higgins say, "the secret of success lies in spirit."

The same phenomenon occurred in France in the great workers' upsurge of May-June 1968. During the general strike in which some ten million workers participated, millions of unorganized workers, many of them immigrants, left their work places to march side by side with the union workers. And about two million workers joined unions for the first time.

Likewise most of the servicing can be done without the need for a large bureaucratic staff, where local unions are democratically structured and run, and where shop stewards and shop committees are democratically elected and directly responsible to the workers.

Neither does the argument about small towns hold up under scrutiny. Some localities are more difficult to organize than others. But there is no rule that says a smaller community must be more difficult than a larger one. Los Angeles, the third largest city in the country, has a relatively poor record in union organization. In the same state, much smaller communities, such as Fresno and Bakersfield, are far better organized. The three largest areas of union growth in California—the Southeast, the Santa Barbara-Ventura region, and the Sacramento Valley—contain no large cities.[10] And Cesar Chavez has shown that it is possible to organize agricultural laborers despite immense employer terror. The very fact that growers sought to replace the militant United Farm Workers with the "sweetheart contract" unionism of the Teamsters, is a tribute to the organizing successes achieved by the Chavez leadership. The size of a community, therefore, is not the main determining factor in union organizing.

## Government Employees and White Collar Organizing

Organizing office and white-collar workers does present special problems. But with more office workers becoming mere appendixes to machines, their former hostility to unionism is waning. Proof that service, professional, government and office workers can be organized in large numbers is shown by the experience of the past decade. The fastest growing unions of the AFL-CIO are those of government employees and white-collar workers. The American Federation of Government Employees grew from 70,000 in 1960 to 293,000 in 1972. The State, County and Municipal Employees increased its membership from 235,000 in 1964 to 529,000 in 1972. The Teachers Union led hundreds of militant strikes across the nation and grew from 53,000 in 1963 to

248,000 in 1972. In December 1973, a new national hospital and health care union was formed with some 80,000 members. Its parent, Local 1199 of New York, organized about 48,000 hospital workers in four years' time. The Service Employees Union has also grown rapidly, from 320,000 in 1964 to 484,000 in 1972. In 1970, the percentage of white-collar workers in AFL-CIO unions rose to 16 percent. The proportion of women members also increased, from18.6 percent in 1962 to 21.7 percent in 1972, an increase from 3.5 million to 4.5 million.[11]

## Organizing the South

These facts show that there are no insurmountable barriers to organizing where there is the will and the unity of effort to bring it about. This holds also for the greatest challenge of all—the organization of the South. This region is now the fastest growing industrial area of the country. While it is not yet possible to speak of a "new South," there is ample evidence that the old South is changing rapidly. Recent labor victories, while still modest, indicate that the time is approaching for an all-out assault on this largest open-shop bastion in the country.

The victory of the workers at the Farah Manufacturing plants in Texas is of signal importance. This strike of terribly exploited Chicano workers dragged on for nearly two years and was finally won by the combined efforts of the strikers and a nationwide boycott of Farah pants. It proved that workers' militancy when backed by labor solidarity can defeat even the most vicious strike-breaking attempts.

The victory of the Mine Workers in their bitterly fought, long-drawn-out battle with the Duke Power Corporation in Harlan, Kentucky, is also of major significance. It indicates that the miners, under their new leadership, are determined to complete the organization of the industry.

The United Electrical Workers also won an impressive victory in the Tampa, Florida, plant of the Westinghouse Corporation. The Tampa plant is relatively new, established in 1968. It has a normal work force of about 400, about 15 percent Black. The company resorted to its old tricks of red-baiting and racism. It charged the UE organizer with "communist activities" and tried to frighten white workers by saying that the Blacks "were trying to take over" and would get into "job classifications they weren't qualified for."[12] The victory of the union upset a master plan of the corporation for developing a chain of nonunion plants in the South. Even after the union won, the FBI sent a special agent into the plant to work with the company to break up the union. The FBI agent Joseph

Burton, a resident of Tampa, was given a job in the plant, told to be a "superrevolutionary," and to act both as informer and provocateur. But this maneuver also failed; the workers saw through the phoney ultra-leftism.[13]

Another telling victory took place in Andrews, South Carolina, at the Oneita Knitting Mills. The 700 workers won a six-month-old strike and with it a contract and union recognition. The strike was an inspiring display of Black-white unity. As one white worker put it, "what really made the difference was the Black people were so together and strong. They carried the strike." Ten years earlier, when the plant was all white, an eight-month strike was broken. This time, with Black workers in the lead, it was won. The leader of the strike was a Black woman, and a majority of the workers were women.[14]

The textile union also won a first victory at a mill of the J. P. Stevens Company.This took place in Roanoke Rapids, North Carolina. The Amalgamated Clothing Workers, in addition to the victory of Farah workers, also won elections in a clothing factory and in a knitting mill in Pascagoula, Mississippi. And gains in Southern organizing have been scored by other unions as well.[15]

The victories in textile are important because, with some 700,000 workers, this is the largest industry in the South. Wages are exceedingly low and a majority of the workers are women, an increasing percentage Black. The mills are scattered over many small towns in rural, backward, and politically conservative states. North Carolina, one of the worst antilabor and repressive states in the country, has more than a quarter-of-a-million textile workers. What happens in textile, therefore, can be decisive for the whole South.

From the foregoing it can be seen that organizing is taking place and with some degree of success. But this should not be exaggerated. It indicates what can be done, not necessarily what will be done. Over-all the labor movement is still stagnating. The new organizing is not even keeping pace with the growth in the size of the labor force. In 1945, 35 percent of the nonagricultural labor force was organized; by 1970 only 27 percent was organized. In industries such as construction and printing, where craft unions have operated for many decades, more and more work is being done by nonunion labor. Depressed economic conditions, with growing unemployment, may undermine unions in other industries as well.

Even where unions work energetically to organize the unorganized, only the bare surface of the problem is being scratched. In the hospital and health field, for example, about two million workers are employed in private health institutions and about one million in public ones. This is an immense challenge. Even if the entire labor movement pooled its resources it would be no easy matter to get this industry organized.

What complicates matters further is that the unions committed to organizing hospitals are in competition with each other. Hence, side by side with gains, considerable effort is duplicated and dissipated, resources wasted, and workers often alienated from all unions. At the end of 1973 an important election for bargaining agency was held at the Henry Ford General Hospital in Detroit. The approximately 2,000 employees became the concentrated focus of a number of unions each determined to win the hospital for itself. None did; the "no union" vote carried the day.

The recent federal legislation which extended to hospital workers the right to organize has encouraged more unions to seek footholds in this industry. In many ways the logical union for these workers to join is the National Union of Hospital and Health Care Employees. It specializes in this field and has done a remarkable job in raising the wages and the status of fiercely exploited workers in New York. But it is being challenged by the Service Employees Union, the Teamsters, the Laborers, and in a few places by the Carpenters and Operating Engineers. In the field of public hospitals, the American Federation of State, County and Municipal Employees (AFSCME) has the lead. But as private and public health facilities always overlap, and the AFSCME organizes voluntary (private nonprofit) hospitals where it can, there is also collision between this union and the others.

It is good, of course, that more unions want to do organizing. But it is questionable whether a major national breakthrough can be made in organizing hospital workers without the concerted, united efforts of a number of unions with the support of a large section of the labor movement.

### Preparing for a New Upsurge

Labor history demonstrates that trade union growth occurs at a modest pace for lengthy periods of time, and then in sharp spurts and on a massive scale at much shorter intervals. The slower periods of growth are influenced by the objective conditions of so-called normal times; the stormier periods of growth, when giant leaps forward are taken, are related to times of widespread, deep-seated social unrest. Usually such periods have occurred in the upswing side of a major economic crisis and during periods of war, when labor shortages and inflation prod efforts to organize.

No artificial walls separate the longer periods of slow crawl from the shorter ones of steeplechase speed. Each affects the other. What is decisive in each period is the level of organization and consciousness among worrkers and, in particular, the quality of leadership.

It is generally assumed that in normal "good times," when employment is relatively high, unions will grow—if not in a spectacular way, at least steadily. But this did not happen in the twenties. Despite the so-called permanent prosperity of the time the labor movement lost about 30 percent of its membership. Nor did growth occur during the fifties and sixties, despite two wars—Korea and Vietnam—and constantly increasing inflation. The numerical size of the labor movement increased somewhat, but its proportion of the work force declined.

Even in the great upheaval of the mid-thirties, when workers surged toward unionism, there was no automatic guarantee of permanent organization of the mass-production industries. In earlier periods, too, there had been immense opportunities to do what was finally done in the thirties, but the attempts failed. In 1918 and 1919 industrial workers were ripe for organization. But despite immense successes on the part of William Z. Foster and other trade union militants associated with him, the breakthrough made in packinghouse and steel were short-lived. The AFL bureaucracy was too venal, and labor discord too great, for permanent success.

The quality of leadership is of decisive importance. What made the difference in the thirties was not only the greater depth of economic and social crisis, but the preparatory work before the conditions of upsurge had fully matured in order to bring them to fruition. The Communists and other left-wing militants slowly and methodically began to organize. They knew that there is no plant or workers' community completely devoid of organization. There are always formal and informal groupings of workers, whether along social, cultural, nationality, racial, religious or political lines. These can become nuclei for change at times, but something must first happen to make this possible. That "something" could be a new irritant inside the plant or industry, or the coming of an "outsider" into the picture who acts as catalyst. But it is best induced— and on a mass scale covering more than one group or factory—when the workers get the feeling that something big is stirring, that there is an opportunity to make a change in their way of life, and that the time for unionism and action in its behalf has come.

Such a psychological mood can be brought about only if something big, something real and tangible is actually taking place. This requires an organizing effort so united and together, so daring and sweeping in its appeal and execution, so productive of immediate results, that the great mass of workers are caught up in its spirit and, in turn, carry it still further.

This was an important lesson of the great 1919 steel campaign. Foster's plan called for a whirlwind campaign. It had taken only nine weeks to organize the meat-packing industry. Foster believed that once the workers saw that the trade union movement meant business, the steelworkers could be organized in even less time. The plan included "huge mass meetings, noted speakers, brass bands, parades, full-page newspaper advertisements, etc., to get the masses in motion."[16]

The CIO organizing crusade of the thirties was patterned in part on the experiences of 1919, especially the need for an all-out effort, one that could capture the imagination of the workers, combat their fears and hesitations, and create something of a bandwagon psychology. One favorable factor was the changing political climate of the time. The defeat of Herbert Hoover in 1932 and the election of Franklin D. Roosevelt with his promise of a new deal for the "forgotten man," gave workers a feeling that the federal government was more "on their side." The passage of the Wagner Labor Act in 1935 gave a new great momentum to the organizing effort, which in a number of industries had already been making headway. This had a lot to do with the unionizing upsurge that followed.

Considerable credit goes to those who paved the way. By their example they proved that organization was possible, and by their policies they helped bring about the necessary unity. While the Communists were the pioneers in this effort, credit also goes to other left-wing and progressive forces and to the more conservative-minded labor leaders, such as Lewis, Murray and Hillman, who for a brief historic moment, at least, responded to the militant mood of workers and rode the tide of history.

Another labor upsurge is in the making. We live in a period of intense social unrest. Depression and inflation coexist, both preying on the living standards of workers. At a time such as this, labor upheavals can be triggered by a multiplicity of causes. The great French general strike of

May-June 1968, was the product of accumulated economic, social and political grievances.

The slow, tedious, one work-unit at a time organizing is still decisive in preparing the ground for a more massive organizing offensive somewhat later. But this requires policies that foresee and prepare for the approaching storm. The struggle for unity assumes great importance. Each union conscious of the need for organizing cannot sit back and wait, but should press ahead on its own. At the same time it should be recognized that a massive breakthrough can only be made by joint efforts, first by a few, and then by as much of the labor movement as possible.

If the printing industry is to be organized, for example, it can be only by the joint efforts of the present-day craft unions in the industry. If they don't do it, they each will pay a bitter price. The same is true of other industries. And without the great united effort of many unions the organization of the South is impossible.

## The Challenge of the South

Shortly after World War II, the CIO Executive Board launched a campaign to organize the South. Despite large sums collected for this purpose, it proved abortive. Later, when the CIO and AFL merged, talk was renewed about organizing the South. Again, without tangible results.

When the CIO began its shortlived campaign in the South, it mistakenly assumed that a strong anti-Communist stand would help it with more conservative workers in the South.[17] The unions also tried to avoid the issue of Black-white workers' unity, believing this too would help them. The opposite is true: the South cannot be organized by concessions to racism and political reaction.

Nor can it be organized by bureaucrats. It can be done only by a grass-roots effort in which the workers themselves are thoroughly involved. Discussing the experiences of the CIO in the thirties, sociologist Seymour M. Lipset notes that, "The men who are ready to take risks, must be motivated by more than a desire to make a higher salary or gain a white-collar position." John L. Lewis, he points out, "was forced to employ many young Communists as organizers for the CIO when it first started, because they were willing to take the risks involved for the low pay. Two of the three major unions of the CIO—the UAW and the United

Electrical Workers—as well as the smaller ones, were organized largely by Communists or democratic leftists.''[18]

Organizing in many areas of the South is still a risky affair for the organizers and even more so for the workers involved. It cannot be accomplished by labor ''piecards'' with high salaries and expense accounts. It can only be done by people motivated by the ideals of working class solidarity and militant, class-struggle unionism.

Whether the South gets organized depends greatly on the situation inside the labor movement. There is stagnation in trade union organizing because there is stagnation in trade union leadership.

part
# THREE

---

## 15 : THE PROCESS OF CHANGE

---

NO MATTER how dictatorial a union regime may be, it must still respond, at least minimally, to pressure from the ranks. Where it arrogantly turns its back, protests mount, lower bodies of the organization become disaffected, and sooner or later rifts appear in what had seemed a solid phalanx of leadership. If the demand for change is blocked indefinitely, and if arbitrary administrative measures and expulsions are used to shore up shattered authority, workers begin to use their economic power against the union leadership, and mass split-offs from the union become probable. It is a story repeated many times in American labor history.

Undemocratic rule must be interlaced with considerable guile and duplicity. Officials must know how far they can go and when to "give" a little. Employers understand this, too. When union leaders are accused of going to bed with management, the company will go out of its way to save the "honor" of its consorts. A. H. Raskin of the *New York Times* has noted that "some excellent agreements cover a rank and file in open rebellion against their officials. Indeed, the more signs there are that a favored union is in trouble, the better contract the employer may feel obliged to give."[1]

How solicitous corporations can be toward the welfare of labor leaders who befriend them is illustrated by an incident in the steel industry. In the fall of 1973 an advertisement paid for by U.S. Steel, appeared in *Business Week, Wall Street Journal, U.S. News and World Report*, and *Time*. The headline read, "At the invitation of United States Steel . . . I. W. Abel tells how America can become more productive."[2] Later the ad was reproduced as a poster and put on plant bulletin boards. J. Bruce Johnston, U.S. Steel vice-president, became so disturbed about this that he wrote a special memorandum dated October 15, 1973:

> During a visit to Homestead District Works on Friday morning I noticed on plant bulletin boards prominently featured a copy of I. W. Abel's productivity ad. During our discussions with Advertising and Marketing people, it was, I thought, clearly agreed that this particular poster would not be utilized in our plants. We have all feared over-exposure of I.W. Abel on this whole ENA-productivity question, and we have recognized the risk of setting him up for his political opposition by too much identity with us. He has trusted USS not to do this.[3]

Mr. Johnston was referring to the so-called Experimental National Agreement (ENA) signed by Abel, which surrendered the workers' right to strike. No wonder the U.S. Steel Corporation was worried about "setting him up for his political opposition."

One writer on labor affairs says that when a corporation executive is friendly toward the union leaders he deals with, he does not want them to "look foolish" in the eyes of the workers. When he is ready to make some concessions, he calls in the labor leaders and tells them what he is willing to do and suggests "that they 'demand' these things . . . so that they can get most of the credit from the workers for these improvements." After all, he reasons, "None of the people below me in management votes me into or out of my office: I tell them, they don't tell me. But these union fellows can get voted out if I don't let them look good."[4]

Such loving concern must be deserved. It occurs when corporations fear that things may get out of hand, that their labor "friend" may lose control. Giving a little under such circumstances saves giving a great deal more if changes in union leadership occur and a group more class-struggle-oriented takes union power.

Sometimes this creates a complex and often paradoxical situation. To "prove" its militancy, a threatened union leadership may even decide, with the understanding of employers, to propose strike action to "take the steam out" of the workers. At times union leaderships *must* collide with management whether they want to or not. Beholden to the corporations though they may be, they still have bureaucratic interests of their own to protect. Where union elections are rigged, officialdom still needs a degree of inner-union stability to maintain discipline on the job. If inner-union dissatisfaction and strife spill onto the production floor, the companies may want to dump leaders incapable of guaranteeing uninterrupted production and maintaining order in their own house.

## Longshore Rank and File

The International Longshore Association leadership is as corrupt as one can find. But because it is "a union [read: union leadership] in terror of its rank and file"—according to the *New York Times* of January 18, 1965—and because it cannot fall too far behind gains won by West Coast longshoremen, it is often compelled to heed mass pressure from the ranks.

This was confirmed once again in 1968. The rank-and-file organization of longshoremen in the port of New York learned that Tommy Gleason, the union president, was planning to give back to the shipowners millions of dollars set aside in a "royalty fund" to ameliorate dislocating effects of containerization on workers' employment and earnings. The rank-and-file's mimeographed sheet, *Dockers News*, asked: "Where is the container money?" It warned that "a big steal is in the making," and expressed amazement that "Gleason wants to give the money back to the owners."[5]

Its suspicions borne out, the *Dockers News* appeared again with a call for rank-and-file action:

> We longshoremen, who bust our asses climbing over those containers stacked two or three high on deck, and who take all the chances when they buckle, we want the money now! We have waited, we have listened . . . we are fed up!!! NOW MR. GLEASON, WE ARE TELLING YOU . . . WE WANT THAT CONTAINER MONEY NOW!!! WE WANT IT AS A CHRISTMAS BONUS!!!
> "And as a step to show we mean business, we are calling on all Rank and

File Longshoremen to STAY HOME, THURSDAY, OCTOBER 31, 1968
. . . its time we went on strike for ourselves.[6]

The next day, "to the surprise of many," the rank-and-file stoppage took place. "Gleason, nonchantly remarked, 'They'll be back tomorrow.' " As if in response, the strike tied up the port of New York for five days. It was also in violation of an 80-day Taft-Hartley injunction against striking.[7]

Frightened at the mood of the workers, the shipowners and top union brass tried to avoid conducting negotiations in the presence of 125 members of the Wage Scale Committee, composed of local and district representatives. Attempts were made to have the government arbitrator convene a small select negotiations session in Washington to escape from what was called, "the mob scene." "More importantly, perhaps, was that Gleason had little maneuverability within his own organization, was desperately looking for a way off the hook, but was in no position to make choices."[8] The result was that the longshoremen got a sizeable chunk of the "royalty fund" and other concessions as well.

Thus a rank-and-file movement wields considerable influence even when it fails to win elected posts. Were it not in existence, contracts and conditions would be much worse than they are.

The problem of changing union leaderships is complicated. Workers do not judge their union from an abstract, moral point of view. Their first criterion is protection from employers. To the extent that they receive it, they are ready to overlook the seamier side of union affairs. Workers may dislike the fact that some union leaders live like members of the upper class, but if this is accompanied by steady gains for them, too, they are likely to close their eyes to such corruption.

In the UMWA election which ousted the Boyle gang, most retired workers voted for the Boyle slate. This did not imply their approval of Boyle's union treasury raiding, his nepotism, or his sell-out deals. What motivated them was their pensions. For when Boyle took Lewis' place on the welfare fund board, one of the first things he did was push through an increase in pensions from $115 to $150 a month. This met with the approval of the 70,000 retired pensioners, and they were prompted to vote for him.

A somewhat comparable situation existed in the National Maritime Union. Many seamen who did not approve of Joseph Curran's style of leadership nonetheless voted for him. Curran propaganda led them to believe that their pensions would be jeopardized if they put men into office who had no experience in such intricate financial matters. Over one-quarter of seamen's earnings were going directly into a non-vested union fund. The workers were "doubly hesitant," explained one NMU member, "to vote for the unfamiliar."[9]

In the Teamsters, too, over-the-road drivers did not overlook the gains won under Hoffa's leadership. These loomed larger in their minds than his alleged use of union funds for private investment ventures.

Some people reproach workers for such self-centered concern. But working people are compelled to be practical; they want to be sure that the little they have is not jeopardized. In a conversation between Mayor Carl Stokes of Cleveland and Cesar Chavez, the former complained that liberals "cry out continually about principles but do nothing." To which Chavez replied that "liberals were rarely as helpful to the poor as the old-style local politicians who were corrupt and didn't care who knew it, but who worked hard for the poor because the poor get them elected."[10]

To a limited extent this holds also for labor leaders. As corrupt and coopted as many of them are, they are compelled to do things for their members if they are to remain in office. As one labor official remarked, "There is nothing that travels faster than the news of an important gain won by workers elsewhere." Every union leadership is under some pressure not to fall too far behind.

This complicates the problem of ousting a reactionary leadership. Workers do not go for promises of "pie in the sky." Most organized workers believe they do have something to lose. They want to be sure, therefore, that any change is for the better. This is not understood by middle-class liberals and ultra-Leftists, who tend to sermonize to the workers.

A further difficulty is that the great majority of workers in this country are neither class-conscious nor socialist-minded. They have an instinctive class reaction to on-the-job economic issues, but often see these from the narrower perspective of craft, occupation or industry, rather than from that of the wage-earning class as a whole. Inevitably, therefore, what they consider to be their self-interest is often in the long run self-defeating.

The decade of the sixties marked the beginning of a period of new labor unrest. This was more than the usual and normal on-the-job complaining. The unrest fanned out, involved increasing numbers, and found expression in concerted forms of action. Union memberships turned down contracts with increasing frequency. Wildcat strikes sharply increased.

Stoppages during the terms of an agreement accounted for more than one-third of all strikes. They rose from 22 percent of all strikes in 1960 to 36 percent in 1966.[11]

The discontent was often triggered by technological change affecting work assignments and job security, or by threats or fear of such change. According to Willard Wirtz, Secretary of Labor in the early sixties, increasing competition had "pushed employers to manpower economies not previously considered necessary."[12] As a consequence, work grievances escalated, and existing long-term contracts further exacerbated the dissatisfaction.

Rising inflation was also an important factor inducing unrest, and new categories of employees were compelled to seek protection in unionism for the first time. Teachers, sanitation workers and hospital workers were now proving their fighting mettle on the picket line. A number of professional associations that had previously frowned on unionism began to act more and more like unions, demonstratively removing no-strike clauses from their constitutions. West Coast Chicano farmworkers were at long last successfully building a union of their own. A network of Black caucuses dotted the labor movement. A new breed of young workers, many of them Black and Latin, entered industry for the first time, bringing with them different generational perceptions and a certain spirit of revolt. In the background was the trauma of the Vietnam War and that of "ghetto rebellions" here at home, raising before millions disturbing questions about the nature of American society.

The unrest was bound to affect the labor movement. Before the decade had ended, a number of important unions took a stand against the Vietnam War and joined the movement for peace. In a score of unions—including Steel, IUE, State, County and Municipal, Textile, Machinists, Rubber, and later, the Miners—internal eruptions dislodged old, entrenched leaderships. In each case it was preceded by a split in top ranks, with the dissident group fielding a slate of candidates in opposition to the official slate. Only in the Mine workers Union was a clean sweep made in 1972, with a rank-and-file slate of candidates winning the most important union posts.

Stirrings were felt in other unions as well. Top officials were challenged in the National Maritime Union, Retail Clerks, Postal Workers, Government Employees, and others. In the Federation of Government Employees, despite the opposition of the union's president, the no-strike clause was removed from the union's constitution by overwhelming convention majority. In New York City, the International Brotherhood of Painters ousted a long-entrenched, corrupt district council machine. Old leaders, under the gun in a number of unions, found it wise to step down. And in still other instances union constitutions were amended to compel leaders to retire by a certain age. In this general atmosphere of unrest, Walter Reuther led the UAW out of the AFL-CIO and, together with Frank Fitzsimmons, formed the short-lived Alliance for Labor Action.

## A Squall – Not Yet a Storm

Although discontent was widespread, it did not equal in intensity or dimension earlier labor upheavals. It was a squall, not yet a storm— merely an indication of sharpening class relations, of the clouds of a new labor tempest that were gathering but had not yet arrived.

One historian referred to the labor shifts as more akin to the changing of the palace guard than to a revolution. He points out that few contesting oppositions based themselves on programmatic differences. Their appeals were of a narrower range. In this respect, he believes that the insurgencies differed greatly from those of the past, and "in no way resemble the radical advocates of the 1920's."[13]

This observation is not without validity although it needs some qualification. Muffled though it often was, the issue of class struggle versus class harmony was involved in each of the inner-union conflicts. The contest between Abel and McDonald for the presidency of the powerful steel union is a case in point. It is particularly illustrative precisely because of Abel's subsequent role as chief spokesman for class collusion. Yet when he was asking steel workers to dump McDonald, he took a very different position.

Abel's literature pilloried "tuxedo unionism" and "mutual trusteeship." His basic appeal declared: "The Abel-Burke-Molony team stands for 'Union Stewardship'—not, 'Mutual trusteeship!' The union can't serve two masters—the companies can well take care of themselves—the union's leadership must look after the interests of the membership!"

In another election campaign leaflet Abel promised "to restore rank-and-file control over basic policy." He recognized the importance of local agreements and that "all too often what appears to be won in national negotiations is lost in local applications." He pledged that his stewardship would give management "no chance to miscalculate the true temper of the rank and file."

There was no mistaking this language: it appealed directly to the class feelings of steelworkers. That Abel soon forgot his words does not detract from the significance of the kind of campaign he felt compelled to wage. The cynical betrayal of election promises tells much about Abel, but the kind of pledges he made tells a great deal about the mood of the steelworkers he was wooing.

The basic issue of rank-and-file discontent arose, as in the past, from the failure of union leaderships to aggressively defend the interests of the workers. Although the "revolts" hinged often on issues of union democracy, these cannot be separated from those of militant leadership. When workers are relatively content with the way their union fights for them, the issue of inner-union democracy is, for a time, secondary. But when they are dissatisfied with the stodgy, reactionary, do-nothing leaders, and realize that the purpose of undemocratic control is to prevent them from changing policies and leadership, the issue of democracy emerges as central.

STILL it is true that the labor insurgencies of the sixties lacked some of the radical qualities of former times. Strikes no longer were the simple, direct, crude capital-labor confrontations where no quarter is asked or given. Union recognition and collective bargaining had softened labor-management relations. Times also were fairly good as compared with the past, at least for organized workers. And the first flush of the Indochina war made the economy appear deceptively healthy.

Some of the issues stirring discontent were also less amenable to pure and simple, one-employer-at-a-time, trade-union tactics. Problems of inflation, automation, taxes, racism, the military draft, to take a few examples, required united labor action and a more advanced social program, in which economic and political action were closely integrated. In turn, this needed a clearer conceptualization of the social system in which we live, the nature of its crisis, and a readiness to project more radical solutions to the challenge of the times. Lacking these, the unrest of the sixties could not accomplish more than it did. It shook things up in a number of unions and replaced many top leaders, but it could not guarantee a change in basic direction.

## The Continuing Effects of Anti-Communism

The massive bloodletting of the cold war had a devastating effect on the labor movement. The anti-Communist purge left labor a weak, flabby and anemic giant, deprived of that indispensable substance which supplied class perspective and fighting élan. The history of the labor movement indicates that whenever new breakthroughs were made, they were conceived, inspired and spearheaded by class-conscious, socialist-minded workers. In the twenties also, when anticommunism and anti-radicalism took over, dormancy and stagnation were the consequence. When the greater vision and militancy of the Left, particularly the Communists, came to the fore in the thirties, the labor movement made its greatest breakthrough.

Insufficient time had elapsed in the sixties to make up for the casualties of the previous decade. The atmosphere was beginning to change, but slowly and hesitantly. It is doubtful whether the advances that were made could have occurred had anticommunism not worn somewhat thinner. It had become more difficult to crush union oppositions by painting them with a red brush. By 1972, when Tony Boyle charged Arnold Miller with receiving aid from the Communist *Daily World*, it no longer intimidated the coal miners.

The longer-range crippling effects of anticommunism still persist. Communists are no longer sent to prison for holding union office. That law was finally declared unconstitutional, after the damage was done, and the high court assumed that the "threat" of communism was no longer great. But anticommunist provisions in union constitutions still remain in effect.

George Meany's policies continue to be motivated by his uncontrollable hatred for socialism and all socialist countries. Even when important sectors of capital seek more trade with the socialist countries, and when this could mean jobs for American workers, Meany remains adamantly opposed. He acts as if he would even sanction atomic war, so intense and unreasoned is his hostility to the Soviet Union.

Anticommunism, even if not of this virulent kind, lingers on in other sections of the labor movement, often where labor leaders know better but still feel intimidated by the issue. This can be seen by what transpired at the most important and most democratic union convention held in decades, that of the UMWA, following the victory of its rank-and-file slate. Held for two weeks in December 1973, in Pittsburgh, not in some swanky resort area, the convention discussed and debated questions fully and openly in an atmosphere devoid of manipulation or intimidation. The union's constitution was overhauled article by article and transformed into a refreshingly democratic document, in many ways an example to other unions.

There's one major exception: the clause excluding Communists was carried over without change from the older version. Surprisingly, not a single delegate rose to speak either for or against this provision, as if the convention was embarrassed to face the issue at all. Even this great and historic convention could not shake off the stultifying effects of the cold war and the influence of those who seek to banish the ideals of socialism from American workers.

It cannot be argued successfully that it is not socialism that is being banished, only communism. The labor leaders who once spoke for socialism, no longer do so. They may say they still believe socialism is the only basic solution to the crisis of capitalism, but they rarely say this inside the labor movement. In a climate in which every progressive and radical idea is branded as "communistic" by a labor bureaucracy more pro-capitalist than many capitalists, to speak of socialism is considered sinful. At a time when capitalism is being challenged and socialism is being considered by increasing numbers of people outside of organized labor, socialism is still a forbidden subject within the labor movement. Those in labor who believe in socialism mute their views. This is what anticommunism has also accomplished.

Some recent changes are evident. A few leaders have publicly associated themselves with Michael Harrington's Democratic Socialist Organizing Committee.* But unless they join the fight to end anticommunism within the trade union movement, they will fail in making socialism a legitimate issue for discussion and action. While it is less possible to wage an anticommunist crusade in the name of an increasingly discredited "free enterprise" system, there are some, ironically, who would like to revive anticommunism in the name of socialism. This has been the tendency of Michael Harrington, although he has recently broken from the extreme anticommunism of the Meanys and Shankers. Those who try to win so-called support for socialism by "proving" their anticommunism, will only find themselves in the sorry position of defending capitalism, whether or not that is their intention.

People need not approve of the Communist Party or its policies, or of one or all of the present socialist countries, but they must agree to permit *all* tendencies to be discussed and debated on their merits, without bans or taboos of any kind. Trade union democracy is a sham if it permits a discussion of only minor, trivial differences, while prohibiting the dis-

---

* Patrick Gorman of the Amalgamated Meat-Cutters, David Selden of the Teachers, Victor Gottbaum of the State, County and Municipal Employees, Victor Reuther of the Auto Workers and a number of others.

cussion of more fundamental ones. Workers should have the right to decide for themselves between the policies of the two inherently contesting currents within organized labor—that of class struggle versus that of class partnership in ideology and practice. Without a readiness to discuss these policies, without a fearless search for more basic answers to new, more complex and challenging problems, the labor movement is doomed to sterility.

## The Need for a Basic Change in Outlook

The solution to the crisis of organized labor is far more complicated than the mere replacing of "bad" leaders with "good" ones. Unless the labor movement is seen as an antagonist of capital; unless its working-class character is understood and underlined, an atmosphere is bred in which so-called good leaders easily become bad ones.

Even when changes as important as those in the miners' union take place, there is no guarantee that things will not revert to where they were in the past. They may not return to the Boyle-type gangsterism, but they could go back to the kind of policies that made this possible. Honest and dedicated leaders may not remain so, if they wear miners' headgear when handling workers' grievances and bankers' top hats when dealing with huge welfare and pension funds. Even if union funds are no longer invested in mining corporations, so long as the union leadership is faced with the problem of where to invest its money with the aim of the highest returns, it cannot help developing a capitalist outlook and interest.

One militant labor leader noted that in his own union there were younger lower-level leaders who were highly critical of, and dissatisfied with, those holding the key union posts. But these younger officials have no clearer perceptions of what kind of labor movement they would like and where to start in making some meaningful change. They too are part of the bureaucracy and share in the perquisites of union office, although to a lesser degree. They know of no other unionism than the one they now have. If and when they take over, there will be no assurance of a different kind of unionism. Once they feel secure in their union berths, build their own personal political machines, they too may become entangled in the dilemma of wearing two different class hats at the same time. Individual actors may leave the stage, but the same play goes on. It is necessary to change the script, not merely the cast.

Some progressive labor leaders hope that things will change for the better when George Meany passes from the scene. They believe that members of the Executive Council who disagree with his policies will then find the courage to speak and fight for their views. But before George Meany there was William Green, and before him, Samuel Gompers. Only when the ranks began to move in a massive way, as they did in the mid-thirties, did changes at the top have more than a momentary significance. And then only to the extent that within labor there was a conscious Left force fighting for basic trade union principles, rooted in rank-and-file democracy and class-struggle policies.

The reshuffling of leadership in a number of unions this past decade was a product of the growing discontent of the workers. But when the turbulence subsided somewhat, the class-partnership policies tended to take over again, even if not with the same individuals.

The high rate of contract rejections and strikes that marked the sixties receded for a few years in the early seventies. Contract settlements generally approximated government guidelines without militant opposition. This period of lull saw I. W. Abel of the steel union gradually assume the role formerly played by David McDonald as U.S. Steel's favorite consort. But in 1973-4, with the cost of living completely out of control, a new strike wave began. In 1975, faced with a deep economic crisis and mass unemployment (on a scale unknown since the thirties), union leaders began to talk more militantly and mass marches of workers to Washington were organized. Behind the scenes, however, many union leaders, including some of those using more militant rhetoric, were quietly giving way to corporation pressures for undercutting wages and working conditions.

In this period of greater mass discontent and at the same time more subtle leadership betrayal, Ed Sadlowski, steelworker, ran against Abel's candidate for district director of District 31, the largest in the union, and beat him two to one—40,000 to 20,000 votes. Sadlowski's winning slogan was, "Return the union to the rank and file!"

Hence, there is always dissatisfaction among workers, which smolders for periods of time and then suddenly flares up, depending upon circumstances and the level of awareness of what can be done. But even when unrest is at a seething point, there is no assurance that meaningful change will result. It depends upon what is done to bring this about.

# 16 : DEMOCRATIC ADVANCES

THE CHANGES that took place in the labor movement during the sixties and early seventies were significant. They broke the grip of old bureaucratic machines and, temporarily at least, pried open the doors for a freer discussion of issues and problems. The victory in the United Mine Workers was of the greatest importance. When a rank-and-file slate can overthrow a union dictatorship as entrenched as that in the miners' union, it is an example not lost on workers elsewhere. It wasn't lost on Ed Sadlowski of the steelworkers' union, who consciously patterned his fight for union democracy after the miners' model. It is therefore important to know how and why they won.

## How the Miners Won

There was great dissatisfaction in the miners' union long before the Boyle gang was finally ousted. Attempts were made at union conventions to challenge the officialdom, but things were rigged against change. The other path open to the miners was the referendum election of officers. Finding a candidate to run against Boyle was not easy. When Ralph Nader suggested to Jock Yablonski, a member of the union's executive board, that he run for president, Yablonski reportedly said, "If I do run, Ralph, they'll try to kill me." "They wouldn't dare," responded Nader, "you'll be in a goldfish bowl."[1] Yablonski knew better than Nader the nature of those with whom he was dealing.

Election odds were heavily on the side of the union machine. Boyle controlled the means of communication with the locals and membership. In one issue of the *UMW Journal*, 30 photos of Boyle appeared but not a single mention of Yablonski. Hundreds of full-time staff workers and organizers, all of them Boyle appointees, worked overtime for his reelection. The union constitution also permitted retired miners to vote, which made the "bogie locals" perfect set-ups for bogus returns.

The Boyle machine had political pull. The leaders of both major parties were on its side. When irregularities, such as the printing of 50,000 extra ballots, began to mount, Yablonski's attorney appealed to Republican George Schultz, Secretary of Labor, to investigate and intervene. He did neither.[2] The attitude of the Democratic party establishment can be summed up in the remarks of Hubert Humphrey, its Presidential candidate, when he addressed the 1968 UMWA Convention: "I am mighty glad to rub shoulders with this fellow Tony Boyle. He has been giving me advice and counsel for a long time."[3] And George Meany sneeringly referred to Yablonski's attempt to oust Boyle, as "just one of the boys in the kitchen trying to move into the living room."[4]

When the votes were in, Boyle was declared the winner—81,000 votes to 46,000. Yablonski charged that the election was stolen "by fraud, coercion and intimidation." He claimed evidence of "200 separate irregularities in the balloting," and demanded a postelection investigation. In one district Boyle was given 273 votes to only one for Yablonski.[5] Frightened by the imminence of further disclosures and of seething turbulence in the ranks, Boyle decided to "solve" the problem in a way that would foreclose an election probe and teach a lesson to any future would-be challenger.

On New Year's Eve, a few weeks after the 1969 election, three men jimmied their way into the Yablonski home. Jock, his wife Margaret, and their 22-year old daughter, Charlotte, were murdered in their beds.

In a country in which political assassinations had become commonplace, this wholesale cold-blooded murder of three members of a family, two of them women, shocked the nation and outraged the miners. This time, the Secretary of Labor was compelled to act. Tony Boyle had gone too far. Within 48 hours, 230 investigators were dispatched to the coal fields.[6] The sordid tale began to unravel. A court order set aside the election results. A new election was ordered for 1972, to be closely supervised. Arnold Miller, a coal miner never on a union payroll or even a delegate to a convention, was elected union president.

THERE is more to the story. Why did Yablonski, a long-time member of the mine union's executive board, decide to run against Boyle? He was earning $30,000 a year, with a no-questions-asked expense account.[7] He lived in a large fieldstone house on a 365-acre farm near Clarksville, Pennsylvania. It is said that he suffered pangs of conscience about what was happening to the union, that he opposed the Vietnam War, supported Senator Eugene McCarthy at the 1968 Democratic Convention, and that his daughter and sons were a liberal influence on him.

Yet Yablonski was frequently called upon to introduce Boyle at miners' rallies, at which he used his forensic skill to laud Boyle, "even as he was privately expressing his contempt for him."[8] Later, when a *New York Times* reporter asked him why he had eulogized Boyle, he replied by quoting John L. Lewis: "When ye be an anvil, lay ye still; when ye be a hammer, strike with all thy will."[9] But why had the servile anvil decided to become a sledgehammer?

Something new was happening. A group of three courageous doctors—I. E. Buff, Donald L. Rasmussen and Hawey A. Wells—had conducted a vigorous enlightenment campaign about what they called "black-lung" disease. This ailment maimed and killed miners by the tens of thousands, yet was unrecognized as a special disease by the orthodox medical profession and by workers' compensation laws.

## The Birth of the Black Lung Association

One Saturday morning, in the first weeks of January 1969, a group of miners, headed by Woodrow Mullins, a disabled miner, went to Charleston to enlist the help of a liberal lawyer in drafting a "black-lung" compensation bill for the West Virginia legislature. Paul Kaufman, the lawyer, agreed to do this; also to become the group's lobbyist. He asked for $2,000 to get things started.

The next day a somewhat larger group of miners met to discuss a plan of action. There was disagreement, for some feared being accused of "dual unionism," especially as the UMW had promised to introduce its own bill. Brit Humes, whose book *Death in the Mines* describes what happened, explains why the "dual union" charge was to be feared:

> One of the most serious accusations in organized labor, and one which had often been made against dissidents in the UMW, was participating in a "dual"

movement. The UMW Constitution provided that a member could be expelled for joining any organization deemed "dual" to the UMW. Loss of membership meant loss of job and of pension and hospital benefits. It was a punishment few members were willing to risk.[10]

After a few of the men most worried about a possible "dual union" charge had left the meeting, Ernest Riddle, a miner at the Allied Chemical Company's Harewood mine, "solved" the dilemma. He proposed the formation of a loose "association," which could not be construed as a dual union because it would have but one objective—the enactment of an effective "black-lung" compensation bill. It was agreed to form the Black Lung Association (BLA). Charles Brooks, one of their number, a Black miner, and president of the local at the Carbon Fuel Company mine at Winifrede, was chosen the BLA's first president. Later that night, Lyman Calhoun, a charter member of the new association, called his friend, Arnold Miller, president of the local at the Bethlehem Steel Company's mine at Kayford, for help in raising money. Within a few days Miller raised $1,000 from his own local and $550 from two others. Calhoun's local also contributed $1,000 and Mullins' and Brooks' local did likewise. "The Black Lung Association was off to a good start."[11]

On January 29, the director of District 17 of the union sent a letter instructing support for the UMWA-sponsored bill: "Therefore, your local union has no authority to donate money from the treasury, to some unknown group which, in my opinion, is dual to the UMWA, to be used for any purpose they see fit." .

It was too late. Things had moved so swiftly and so many miners had enlisted in the cause that, as many put it, "They can't kick us all out."[12]

The difference between the BLA's bill and the UMW's was great. The Association's bill included a "presumptive clause." This specified that any miner who had worked underground for a number of years and suffered from the symptoms of "black-lung" disease could be presumed to have it and to have contracted it by working in the mines. This was meant to defeat the strategy of the coal operators and their doctors who claimed that there was no "proof" of such a disease or that the symptoms suffered were occupationally caused. The UMW's bill, supported also by the AFL-CIO, merely proposed that the old silicosis board be renamed and given jurisdiction over "black-lung" cases.

After hearings were held by the House Judiciary Committee, the miners were promised the prompt reporting out of a bill. When this did not happen, and the day for session adjournment drew closer, the miners became more and more impatient. The impasse was broken when 500 miners at the Eastgulf mine near Beckley went out on wildcat strike over what appeared to be a minor dispute. But they refused to return until a "black-lung" compensation bill had been passed. In a few days, 12,000 miners were out.[13]

This created a momentary crisis in the ranks of the miners and among their supporters. Some feared that the strike was premature and would produce a blacklash. But at a mass rally the following Sunday near Beckley, the words of Charles Brooks helped consolidate the ranks:

> This is the first time that the coal miner has ever come out and asked for anything. . . . But this time the coal miner is asking for something for himself. So, . . . if it takes pressure to get this done, put pressure where it belongs. Now as president of my local union, I can't tell my men to strike. You know that. But if it takes pressure, put it where it belongs. Now if you men want to go on vacation, I'm with you 100 percent. Every man in my local union can tell you that. If you're wrong and you think you're right, I'm still with you.[14]

The strike lasted three weeks and involved 45,000 miners. It was "the first ever started by miners for purely political purposes." With the industry shut tight, the state legislature was under great pressure to act. A veteran labor reporter describes the scene:

> I watched miners filling the State capitol building in Charleston day by day, and filling it tight. The capitol building lobby was a sea of miners' hats with Black Lung emblems. Miners occupied every seat in the legislative galleries. They told legislators that they were staying until a bill to compensate their sick and dying brothers was enacted.[15]

A final bill was adopted only a few minutes before the session adjourned. It was not everything the miners asked, but much closer to their version than that of the UMW's. It was the most progressive workers' compensation law in the country. Even then the miners would not relax their vigilance. They feared a last minute double-cross; that if they returned to work the governor would let the measure die without signing it into law. The strike continued until the bill was signed.

This militant political strike of the West Virginia miners also influenced Congress to adopt the Federal Coal Mine Health and Safety Act of 1969.* The great significance of the West Virginia victory was dealt with by Brit Humes:

---

*By October 1974, 483,000 miners had collected benefits under this federal law.

More important than what the crusade might have taught the politicians, however, was what it taught the miners themselves, about politics, their own potential strength, and their union leadership. The taste of triumph had led many of them to ask themselves, ''If we can do this, why did we have to put up with things as they were for so long.''[16]

It also taught something to Jock Yablonski. He saw rank-and-file miners build a movement and win an important victory against the combined opposition of the coal operators, reactionary politicians, and the officialdom of the UMW and state AFL-CIO. He began to realize that the days of the Boyle machine were numbered; that he belonged on the side of the miners and could win.

## Miners for Democracy

The murder of Yablonski did not intimidate the miners. Immediately following the funeral in Clarksville, before departing for their homes, they met to lay out future plans. From this meeting was born a new organization, Miners for Democracy (MFD), whose open purpose was to end the Boyle dictatorship and bring democracy to the union. In addition to the MFD, two other militant rank-and-file organizations were pledged to the fight—the Black Lung Association, now spread throughout the coal fields, and the Disabled Miners and Widows Organization, whose president was Robert Payne, a Black disabled mine worker.

On May 1, 1972, a U.S. District Court in Washington, D.C., set aside the fraudulent Boyle election. On the 28th of May a rank-and-file convention of 463 miners was held in Wheeling, West Virginia, to choose a slate of candidates and a platform for the new election. Arnold Miller, himself a sufferer from ''black lung'' and a former mine repairman and electrician, with 24 years in the mines, was chosen to head the slate. Mike Trbovich, a mine shuttle-car operator with 25 years' mine work experience, was the vice-presidential candidate; and Harry Patrick, a mine mechanic with 18 years in the mines, was chosen for the secretary-treasurer spot.

The MFD platform called for many reforms—the election of district officials and executive board members; the rank-and-file ratification of contracts; no firings for refusal to work in unsafe conditions; a mine committeeman at each shaft of each mine; a full-time safety committeeman in each mine; national and district union support of local disputes; no discrimination in hiring and firing; the uniform enforcement of contract—with no exceptions; an increase in pensions for retired miners; and the responsible management of welfare funds. It also pledged to reduce the salaries of top officials and to cut the president's from $50,000 to $35,000 a year.[17]

When the votes were counted, Miller won over Boyle by a margin of 70,000 to 56,000. The rank-and-file slate had gotten its greatest support from working miners, especially from the young and the Black workers. A year later Miller told his union's convention: "It is not enough to write the words 'Rank and File' on the banner at the front of the hall. Those words must be etched into our Constitution so deep that they can never be erased."[18]

## The Sadlowski Victory

The victory in District 31 of the steel union also didn't just happen. It came after a long period of struggle, of deep-seated grievances, dedicated commitment to bring change, constant close contact with the workers, and intelligent, careful planning and organization. As in the case of the miners, despotic control on top could not prevent organized bases of rank-and-file influence and strength at the bottom. Miller had been the president of his mine local; Sadlowski had been elected to every important post in Local 65 of the steel union. A caucus had functioned in the local for eight years, made up of white, Black and Latin workers. When Sadlowski stepped down as local president, for example, he supported a Black worker for that post.

There was also some rank-and-file organization elsewhere in the district. The National Ad Hoc Committee of Concerned Steelworkers was one of the largest Black caucus movements in the country and had its strongest base in the district. Formed in 1964, it fought for greater Black representation on all levels of the union. Although 30 percent Black, the steel union had no Black district director, international officer, or member of the executive board. The Ad Hoc Committee sought unity "with other steelworkers' caucuses that are ready to join with us to achieve our goals, such as the Steelworkers National Rank and File Caucus; RAFT (Rank and File Team); Chicano groups. . . and many other caucus groups."[19]

Over the years, steelworkers' grievances had mounted. Gains in wages and fringe benefits were more than paid for by murderous speed-up. The 1971 contract had called for active cooperation with management to increase productivity still further. In 1973, a company-union sponsored movie, "Where's Joe?" was shown. This set out to portray the

steelworkers of other countries—Germany, Japan, etc.—as the enemies.
As one rank-and-file steel worker put it, the movie was telling them,
"you've got to help your good ol' U. S. Steel, Bethlehem, and so on to
beat these guys. And the way to do it is to work your ass off and not go out
on strike because this will just screw up the whole works."[20]

A number of additional factors led to 1973 as the year of showdown.
Joe Germano, the old district director, was retiring. Abel had chosen Sam
Evett, a union staff hack, who had never worked a day in a steel mill, as
his candidate to replace Germano. And in the wings, a young, more
militant steelworker—Ed Sadlowski—was anxious and ready to challenge the machine. Sadlowski had worked in a mill for 15 years, had been
elected as local president twice, and had served a spell as a staff representative.

Faced with the threat of losing control over the largest and most
important district of the union, the Abel machine threw in large sums of
money, a large full-time staff, and its own interpretation of the union
constitution. It also had the full cooperation of the steel corporations.
Evett had easy access to the plants, could walk in, distribute his material,
and talk with workers. "When Sadlowski's rank and filers came along,
they were thrown out of parking lots and constantly pushed outside the
gates where they couldn't get at the people."[21]

Sadlowski asked Walter Burke, the union's secretary-treasurer, for the
location of the 400-odd plants in the district. Burke refused to give the
information, citing the lack of a constitutional provision covering this
request. Sadlowski also asked for the time and place of local union
nominating meetings, so as to obtain the local endorsements he needed to
be on the ballot. This, too, was turned down on the same grounds. Thus
the problem of how to locate the 290-odd local unions, scattered over
hundreds of miles of the district, remained with the campaign committee
to the end.

These obstacles were partly overcome because the Sadlowski campaign started early, the district was divided into subdivisions, and rank-
and-file campaigners learned to establish their own information
grapevine:

> We got the information we were seeking by knowing a guy who knew a guy or
> knowing a saloon someone drank in, or having a pal that worked in another
> plant.[22]

In many ways this was the most effective method of all, but still many locals could not be reached. In some cases, Sadlowski campaigners were prevented from reaching locals because of misinformation given by union staff representatives.

Lack of complete information was a double handicap in guaranteeing an honest count. Sadlowski appealed to the International for specific facts regarding where, and between what hours, elections were to take place in each local. "I needed types of information like that," Sadlowski explained, "in order to place observers. I got the same stock standard letter from Burke that those provisions weren't provided for in the constitution. They wouldn't even let me know where the polling places were going to be. They wouldn't let me know what time locals were going to be voting."[23]

Commenting on this later in an interview with Jim Williams of *Labor Today*, Sadlowski recognized that the "crummy clauses" in the constitution "didn't just drop out of the sky. There were a lot of son-of-a-bitches sitting in a back room somewhere figuring out how to shaft people . . . if you don't have any intention of running an honest, decent election, then that constitution will provide you with a lot of areas where you can get around an honest election."[24]

When the returns began coming in on the night of February 13, 1973, Sadlowski was sweeping all the large locals. He went to bed with what looked like a safe 4,000 vote lead; he awoke next morning to find himself 2,000 votes behind.

The rank-and-file grapevine began to collect the facts. Workers appeared voluntarily to give examples of locals that had cast more votes than they had members, of members who had gone to vote only to find that their names had already been checked off. In downstate Illinois, 50 locals of the old UMW Amalgamated District 50, recently absorbed by the steel union, were counted as voting 100 per cent for Evett. And in one Hammond local the totals for Sadlowski and Evett had reportedly been switched.[25]

Sadlowski filed a protest with the International Executive Board. After months of stalling, the International upheld the official returns. On June 25, having exausted all avenues of redress within the union, Sadlowski filed charges with the Department of Labor. It was soon discovered that there had been massive fraud, misuse of funds and forgery. In 62 locals alone, more than 4,000 votes had been stolen. In the spring of 1974 a federal judge demanded all the records. Evett backed down and agreed to a new election. It was ordered to start on November 16 and to run four days. This time, Sadlowski could not be counted out; he won 39,000 to 20,000. In his opinion it was the first honest election in the district.

As in the miners' election, the support was greatest from the young and the Black, Chicano and Puerto Rican workers. A Sadlowski campaigner reported, ''I can't think of one Black worker who even mentioned Evett's name, let alone voted for him. So I can see this thing carrying over. We're together now, and it will broaden. . . .''[26]

The central issue in the Sadlowski campaign was union democracy — returning the union to the rank and file. Sadlowski's program for the union was not as concrete or specific as Miller's in the mine union. Sadlowski spoke of conditions in the plants, criticized Abel's concern with productivity, and opposed giving up the strike weapon.

But what stood out above all other issues was the stress on a new style of leadership. The union belonged to the workers and leaders should work for them, not the other way around. As long as elections can be ''won'' by stuffing ballot boxes, just so long will bureaucrats get away with selling out workers and depriving them of their due.

The Sadlowski inauguration ceremony was conducted in the spirit of this theme. Instead of being presided over by International officers, rank and filers from each of the five subdistricts, including Black, Chicanos and women, administered the oath of office. Sadlowski told the over 1,000 assembled steelworkers that they had ''sent a message to Pittsburgh'' — the headquarters of the International — and hoped there would be many such messages. He was cheered as he said, ''If you don't let race hatred break you up, if you don't let name-calling break you up . . . you'll make it!''

# 17 : THE YOUNG AND THE OLD

SPEAKING to a class of shop stewards and local union officers in November 1968, James Matles of UE discussed the new challenge of the young. "The young people in the shops," he told the group, "are involved in a revolt of their own, which is growing day by day. It is not based on ideology. It is not political in character. It expresses itself today solely in economic terms, but as it develops it is bound to have far-reaching political consequences."

Matles gave examples of the revolt. Young workers ignore company rules, drive foremen mad, come to work when they like and leave at the drop of a hat. They are the most militant on the picket line, spark work stoppages over grievances, and often make union leaderships wring their hands and denounce "the stoppages as wild cat, unauthorized and illegal." He saw the revolt as directed at the "company Establishment" but also a challenge to "the union Establishment as well."[1]

So serious was this problem considered by both auto company and UAW officials that they commiserated with each other about it. During the 1970 Ford negotiations, for example, a full day was spent discussing the "new and serious problem, caused by a new breed of factory worker whom both the union and the company are trying to understand."[2] Sidney McKenna, chief of Ford's negotiating team blamed high rates of absenteeism on the "younger employee whose environment and social background is so different from a generation ago." And GM complained that such absences of newer workers included "all races and types of people," who "often take one or even two days off every week."[3]

In 1966 Walter Reuther told a Steelworkers' Convention that the younger members "don't know where we came from. They don't know where we're going. They don't know what the American labor movement is about. They think the American labor movement is a kind of slot machine—you join in January, you put your dollar in the slot in February, and you hit the jackpot in March."[4]

The sharp division between younger and older workers was dealt with at some length in the *Aliquippa Steelworker,* the publication of Local 1211 of the steel union. This read in part:

> The young man is in disagreement with most of the things the older men accept and understand about the union and because of it a barrier exists between the young man in the union and the older men. . . .
>
> The older men can't understand why the young men are griping, especially since the young man gets all the benefits and never has to sweat a thing except a 60 day waiting period. The young man doesn't appreciate the struggle that he, the older man, took part in to get this union organized. . . .
>
> The young man in the union is faced with a situation that looks hopeless to him. As a rule he gets the lowest paying jobs. . . . He doesn't like paying five dollars a month. . . . He feels he's being held down on the job, that it takes too long to advance up the line to get a good paying job, that the seniority system is unfair because it protects the older man only, that the contract isn't protection enough for him, that the majority of union representatives don't want to hear his complaints, they give him the brush-off, and he feels he doesn't get enough vacations and what he does get he has to take when he doesn't want it. And that for the next ten years this won't change.
>
> His feeling about belonging to the union is one of having to, to keep his job. After all, how can he take pride in it when he feels that it isn't doing enough for him and his disenchantment toward the union, his dissatisfaction and dislike is channeled toward the older man, because the older man represents the union and all the things he, as a worker, would like to have right now.
>
> The biggest thing about the young man is his impatience; he doesn't seem to care about 20 years from now, he is only concerned with today. And the worst thing about the problem is the older man resents and fears the younger man as a threat to his job. . . .[5]

An older worker in a bar off Cadillac Square, Detroit, argues: "These kids have a different outlook on life. They've never been broke the way we were, and they've got a hell of a lot of more schooling. You want to know something— they don't even know how to take the crap we took!"[6]

Undoubtedly many young workers who entered industry in the late sixties and early seventies did not know what it meant to be as broke as their fathers had been. Nor did they have the continuous and extended bouts with joblessness of an earlier generation. But this cannot be the full explanation for the difference in generational outlook. Black youth have known and do know what it means to be broke and jobless. Yet they have been among the most militant of the new workers. One white young worker put it, "I'll tell you something, a lot of those Black guys won't take any crap from the company. I don't mind working with them at all."[7]

Many white youth, particularly those in the 16-to-21 age bracket out of school, also faced a disproportionately high rate of unemployment. In October 1969, this was 10.6 percent—more than double the rate for the labor force as a whole.[8] Hence "good times" was not the only explanation for the difference in generational outlook.

Young workers were being influenced by the same factors as were causing restlessness in their entire generation. If they appeared to be more concerned with the moment than with the future, this was often deceptive. The overconcentration on "living today" was itself a form of running away from a future that seemed uninviting and even fearful. From their ranks came those who were being drafted to fight and die in Vietnam. The young were better educated in a formal sense and more knowledgeable, sophisticated and worldly. They were more aware of the racial injustice and inequality in American life. Also they had fewer illusions about the "American way of life," its institutions, and leadership, and about union leadership as well. Nor were they thankful for what many older workers considered higher wages. Their measuring rod was different, they were more aware of the immense wealth of the nation, the huge profits of the giant corporations, and of the revolution in science and technology that made it possible to live and work in an entirely new way.

Thus the revolt was both economic and also political and ideological, in a confused sort of way. Its more conscious expression was that of youth identity, rather than class identity. The antagonist seemed to be the older worker, not the ruling class. The young workers' greater education and sophistication, and their general abhorrence of authoritarian rule, pitted them in constant battle against conditions of labor that sought to turn them into automatons. Assigned generally to the less desirable jobs, they felt more sharply the lash of speed-up that came with the new technology. In 1971, three years before Ed Sadlowski was elected as District 31 director of the steelworkers union, he described the situation in his local union. "In 1965— get this!—only a few hundred disciplines were issued to the guys in the Southworks [Local 65]. Guess how many the company gave out last year?. . .3,400 disciplines in 1970—for coming late, for not coming at all, for swearing, arguing, drinking."[9]

A tough-minded company man in Pittsburgh mused that "maybe some big doses of economic trouble will shape these kids up," but hurriedly added, "I'd hate to see too much of this breed out on the streets without jobs. I just don't think it'd be healthy."[10] An assembly group leader in a Hartford, Conn. plant, said that he prefers to get them "when they're just married, especially the male," because then they don't want to lose their jobs.[11] And when they get older and have a few kids, "everything'll probably settle down."[12]

## A Major Demographic Change

The age division of a few years ago has narrowed somewhat, although it has not disappeared. One of the most important reasons for this is that the older generation, those who worked in the thirties and forties, is now largely out of industry. Already in 1966, the UAW found that 45 percent of its members had joined in the previous three years and one out of three working for the big corporations had less than five years seniority. The Communication Workers reported in 1967 that almost 50 percent if its members were under 30, a jump of 20 percent in only few years.[13]

The first two decades immediately following World War II had a much larger proportion of older workers and a relative scarcity of younger ones. This was due to the lower birth rates of the depression and war years. When the GIs returned home the postwar baby boom began. "Thus from 1947 to 1963 there was a general aging of both population and labor force." In this period the under-45 male population increased by 11.3 percent—but the over-45 male population increased by 31.3 percent—a disparity a little less than 3 to 1. Among women it was even greater— better than 4 to 1.[14]

In the period 1963 to 1969, however, this trend was reversed. Those born in the years following the war were now entering the labor force. The younger male group increased by 11.1 percent, the older male group by only 7.2 percent. In this same six-year period, the older male worker increased by five percent, the younger male worker by 9.4 percent. The new trend will continue through the seventies. It is estimated that from 1970 to 1975 the older group increase was only 1.2 percent compared with a 15.6 percent increase for the younger group. In the 1975-80 period the younger male group is expected to increase more then ten times as fast as the older one. The 1970s, therefore, loom "as the retirement decade."[15]

It can be seen therefore that one aspect of the revolt of the young in the sixties was the unconscious recognition of a major demographic change taking place. Young people sensed their increasing numbers and potential strength. They were a numerical force to be reckoned with and were also better educated. The older generation, with its more conservative and conventional ways, seemed to refuse to recognize this. It is as if youth were saying, "Look, here, old man, you've had your turn. Now make room for us." And one must admit that the young left their mark on many things—from taste in music, clothes and hair styles, to the more important matters of attitudes toward the Vietnam War, racism, sexism, and new ideas in general.

Those who fought so hard to be heard in the sixties are now no longer the younger members of the youth group. They are either in the old age of their youth or in the youth of their middle years. Together with a still newer generation they constitute the decisive majority in most industries and professions. They do not yet occupy the towering heights of leadership and authority, but they no longer are corralled in the valley.

With increasing participation has come a certain bridging of the age gap. Increased family responsibilities make it more difficult to take off one or more days a week from work to escape the plant's stifling, deadening pace and monotony. Changed economic conditions make the chance of finding a better job—or any job—slim. Slowly, there is recognition that the main problem is not one of age—neither of young against old nor old against young—but of something more basically common to both.

Three years after the rebellion of young workers at the GM Lordstown plant against the murderous speed and monotony of the fastest and most automated assembly line in the world, a reporter from the *New York Times* visited the factory. He found that "the line runs just as fast as it ran in 1972—at the top speed of 100 cars an hour—and in the same manner." The average age of the plant's workers was now over 30, "and attitudes have aged accordingly." The issues are the same; "the workers continue to simmer," but they are more tempered. "It changes your outlook quite a bit," said Marlin (Whitey) Ford, the 33-year old president of Local 1112 of the UAW, "when you have those mortgage payments, car payments and kids to feed.'' There is a greater awareness that the changes they still want will take longer to achieve than they previously thought. ''We're here to do a day's work,'' added Whitey Ford, ''but we're not here to be anybody's slave.''[16]

Younger workers are now learning the hard way lessons that older ones learned a long time ago. In one plant young workers found that by teaming up and working faster they could finish their daily chores in less than the alloted eight hours. They felt that the time gained belonged to them—to chat and relax. But management insisted it belonged to the company and upped production quotas accordingly. It was then they learned why older workers carefully paced themselves to keep the employer from knowing how much they could really produce, well aware that he would then make them do as much and more.

While the age gap still exists and will continue, it is no longer as sharp and divisive as it was some years back. Youth consciousness is slowly giving way to a more general social-and-class consciousness. While younger workers learn from older ones, the latter are also learning to respect the militancy of the young, their desire for change, and their general irreverence toward company big-wigs, top-union brass, and things as they are.

## Workers in Retirement

The increasing number of younger workers entering industry is matched by an increasing number of older workers in retirement. The percentage of older workers is declining, not only relative to youth, but to any period of the past. In 1890, nearly 67 percent of all men aged 65 and over were still in the labor force. By 1969, it was only 27 percent.[17] There are two explanations for this: the sharp reduction in farm population; and the existence of a system of social security and private pensions which enables people to retire at an earlier age. The man on the farm ceased to work only when he could no longer do anything more, but most industrial workers are compelled to quit when they no longer can keep up with the grind. Corporations pay bonuses to workers to get them to leave before they reach 65, so as to reduce the total size of the work force and to remove those whom the years have slowed down.

Projections for the years ahead indicate that by 1980 only 23 percent of men and 8.7 percent of women age 65 and over will remain in the labor force. It is expected that by that year there will be some 34 million men and women in retirement.[18] These figures may be an understatement.

Increased automation and mass unemployment exert mounting pressure upon older workers to leave.

After giving a lifetime of productive labor to society, workers should have the opportunity to retire and to live out their years in relative security. This should not mean retirement into a state of permanent hibernation, or semi-death, or poverty. Doing something useful is as important to life as eating or breathing. The older worker should not have to work to earn a living, but to feel free to do the work he/she would like to do. For this, society owes them enough to live decently. Yet 40 years after the Social Security Act was first adopted, it is becoming less and less possible for an older worker to live on Social Security without becoming the victim of humiliating deprivation and destitution. This shameful state of affairs has become one of the nation's most urgent social problems.

The Social Security system never fully met the problem of the retired worker. When it was adopted it represented a major reform, a bridgehead from which new advances could be made. From the outset, workers who earned little when employed were penalized to live on even less when retired. As the system provided only a portion of former earnings, the unskilled, marginal or part-time worker was condemned to live on less than a living income. But the percentage of Black people over 65 living in poverty is twice what it is for white.[19] The percentage of those in the 65-and-over group is more than twice as large for whites as it is for Blacks.

The inflation which started with World War II and has since become consistently worse has undermined the Social Security Act disastrously. The declining purchasing power of the dollar, plus the fact that benefits are based on past earnings and not on current wage levels, has continuously widened the breach between benefits received and the mounting cost of living. Workers' savings, carefully husbanded over the years, have also been reduced by inflation.

When this trend became apparent a few years after World War II, a massive movement should have been built to bring the Social Security Act in line with the new conditions. Instead, a number of unions seized upon private pension plans as the answer. The steelworkers' and autoworkers' unions led the way. In 1950, when the Korean War began, the Wage Stabilization Board made known its preference for so-called fringe benefits in lieu of wage increases, as a way of postponing increased costs. The rush for private pension plans began.[20]

Private pensions were not a new idea. In the early years of the century a number of corporations favored them as a paternalistic effort to tie workers closer to the company, to reduce their mobility, and to check their militancy and desire for unionism. In some cases, as in the railroad industry, private pension plans were jointly sponsored by employers and unions. But during the economic crisis of the thirties most of these plans went bankrupt. Down the drain, too, went the union banks built around them.

The Social Security Act was, in part, an answer to this failure. Workers saw in it the foundation for a federal system of social benefits to meet their needs. In fact, when the private pension route was taken once again, some labor leaders argued that it would compel employers to "press for higher Social Security benefits in order to reduce the cost of private pension plans." It did nothing of the kind. It only helped reduce the pressure of workers in that direction in the "expectation of another source of income for retired people."[21]

Employers' preferred pension plans, as in the past, to reduce labor mobility, to get older workers off the payroll when no longer as productive, and to weaken workers' militancy by threatening loss of pension rights. Also employers can make tax deductions for the amounts they contribute to such plans, although what workers contribute is not similarly tax deductible.[22]

Once a number of the largest unions had won pensions, other unions had no choice but to follow suit. In this way, the fight for a vastly improved Social Security system was abandoned. Each union moved to obtain the best possible deal for its own members. The net result was that some workers, in the strongest unions, received the promise of pensions ranging from a low of $50 a month to a high of $700 a month. But the great mass of unorganized workers, those unskilled and marginal, largely of racial minorities, were condemned to subsist on the shrinking benefits of the Social Security system. While benefits have been increased somewhat in the past few years, they continue to lag far behind the rise in the cost of living, like a snail racing with a hare.

## The Private Pension Scandal

Those who thought that private pensions were the answer were in for a rude awakening. So scandalous did the pension situation become that a United States Senate subcommittee spent endless months trying to unravel the mess and develop pension reform legislation. A bill was finally signed into law in September 1974. Senator Jacob Javits, who sponsored the new legislation, estimated that only one in 12, at most one in 10 persons covered by pension plans, benefit from them. And Professor of Law Merton C. Bernstein testifying before hearings, compared private pensions to a race track — many bet, but only a few win.[23]

For one thing, a worker's vesting rights — i.e., the point at which he can collect benefits upon retirement — began only after he first served a specified number of years of steady employment with a single employer. Even then, he had to reach a certain age to qualify. If he was laid off, changed jobs, became disabled, or worked only 29 out of, say, a stipulated 30 years, he could end up getting nothing. There are many thousands of such examples. In one case cited by Ralph Nader, a glass worker was employed by a concern for 32 years before he was forced to quit because of a stroke. Just short of age 50, he was therefore declared ineligible.[24]

Workers lost their pension rights when they changed work assignments and transferred from one union to another, although employed by the same company. In numerous instances, pensions were lost when a firm went out of business, changed hands, or merged with other firms. In 1964 the Studebaker Corporation shut its South Bend, Indiana, plant. Only workers who had reached 60 years of age and had 10 years of service received full benefits. Those between age 40 and 49 with 10 years of service received 15 percent of their promised benefits; the rest got nothing.[25]

Mergers and business failures are far from few. Even before the economic depression which began in 1973-4, "the annual number of business failures varied from 11,000 to 17,000." And more than 250,000 firms change hands yearly. Often a conglomerate will buy up a firm, with no intention of keeping it going, but for tax write-off purposes.[26]

Senator Javits has charged that the $150 billion dollars in pension funds represent "the largest concentration of wealth with the least regulation in the country." More than 73 percent of the workers covered by UAW pension plans that terminated between 1959 and 1968 received no benefits at all, or reduced benefits, because the plans had insufficient funds.[27] In numerous instances, the funds have been used to bolster the financial position of a firm by investment in its own stocks or real estate, or for speculative purposes. *Fortune* notes that one reason for the popularity of pension plans in the fifties and sixties was the "bull market." It was possible to gamble with greater possibility of success. The greater the risk the greater the possible returns, so both employers and unions were tempted to gamble with the pension funds in their trust.[28]

The Pension Reform Act of 1974 established some controls, but did not basically alter the situation. The 23 million workers covered by private industry plans still have no assurance that they will collect on the promises made. The worker who leaves company "A" for company "B" can now take his accumulated benefit rights with him, but only if both companies approve. Part-time workers are now eligible for pension rights, but only if they average at least 20 hours of work per week during the year. Workers employed by companies with pension plans must be given vesting rights, "but exactly what the rights are has been left to the option of the individual employer."[29] Three options are possible. The most important new feature is that a worker is entitled to full pension rights after 15 years of continuous service. But the so-called job hopper, or the worker who faces repeated layoffs, may pay into pension plans all his working life and still end up with no benefits whatever.

Another important new feature of the Act is the establishment of a government agency, the Pension Benefit Guarantee Corporation. This is modeled after the Federal Deposit Insurance Corporation. It has the purpose of ensuring benefit payments to workers should their plans collapse. It is empowered to pay up to $750 a month to individual workers whose plans have failed.

This represents improvement. But it would be a mistake to assume that the pension crisis is now over. Rather, it has just begun. The new agency can plug a hole in the pension dike as long as it is small enough to be plugged. But should numerous failures occur, one on top of the other, the agency does not have the resources to hold back the floodwaters for long. Its funds are to come from annual premium payments amounting to from 50¢ to $1.00 per worker on pension. It will take a long time therefore to amass a fund large enough to cope with a major crisis. This is recognized in the Act itself, for some of its provisions will not apply immediately. They are staggered to Jan. 1, 1981.

The danger of multiple breakdowns is real. Many plans are already in arrears. *Fortune* states, "Unfunded obligations represent one-quarter to one-third of the net worth of scores of companies, and the proportion sometimes runs higher still." This is 53 percent at Bethlehem Steel "and an astounding 86 percent at Uniroyal." Four years ago Ford owed its pension fund about one-half billion dollars; by 1974 it was $2.7 billion.[30]

The catastrophic stock market decline has also "shrunk the value of most pension funds." By how much is not yet publicly known. Should the market continue to fall, more pension funds will be wiped out.[31]

Demographic changes, unemployment and automation are bringing about a more rapid increase in the number of workers leaving industry for retirement. The drain on pension funds will therefore increase, this being "the retirement decade."

More important than any of these factors is that pension benefits, like Social Security benefits, are being eroded by constant inflation. Thus, there is a growing demand for cost-of-living "escalators" to maintain the purchasing power of pensions during the years of retirement. Already the first contracts with such provisions have been signed.

This combination of pressures may cave in the roof on the entire pension structure. An Alcoa executive vice-president is quoted as saying that the prospect of meeting these commitments is "frightening." And Professor Bernstein has stated that, lacking the fuel of a bull market, he doubts "whether prefunded pensions are viable in a period of double-digit inflation."[32]

Without doubt pension plans are in trouble, which means that the workers dependent upon them are in greater trouble. The *Fortune* article believes that no matter what happens, pension costs are going to be much higher and that this is "apt to exert some downward pressure on wages as well as profits." That employers will attempt to place the entire burden of these extra costs on the backs of the workers is a foregone conclusion. This will affect both wages and working conditions.


IN RESPECT to retirement needs, workers are at a crossroads. Should private pension plans collapse as they did in the thirties, workers will be hurting badly. This is already happening to a number of public pension plans. But should the plans remain as they are, without cost-of-living escalators, their value to workers will greatly diminish. The time has come for a renewed, major struggle for a social security system that can protect workers fully — from unemployment, medical and hospital costs, and from a retirement of insecurity and deprivation. The funds for this should come from general revenues. The socialist countries have attained this. Other capitalist countries have social security systems far in advance · of our own. The time has come for young and old to pick up the cudgels where they were dropped a generation ago.

# 18 : CLASS AND RACE

AMERICAN capitalism has been racist from its inception. It was founded on the genocidal slaughter of Indians, the robbery, pillage and oppression of Mexicans, and the brutal enslavement of Blacks. To the extent that white workers have accepted the holding down of other races in the belief that it benefits them, they have been trapped in a dilemma. They dilute and distort class awareness by finding common racial ground with the very class that is their antagonist.

This has been, and remains, the chief obstacle to greater class consciousness and a wider workers' and peoples' unity. It is the meaning of Marx's trenchant observation that labor in the white skin can never be free as long as labor in the black skin is branded.

Black workers have always been ready to unite with white workers on a basis of equality. They have shown this on numerous occasions. Yet time and time again their hopes have been dashed. So all-encompassing is the effect of racism on their lives that some find it difficult to identify with white workers as members of a common class, fighting a common foe for common ends.

## .Black Workers Came Early to Unionism

No sooner did slavery end than Black workers began to find their way to trade unionism and class struggle. Although the great majority of

216

Blacks tilled the soil, a considerable number were engaged in industrial pursuits. It is estimated that there were 100,000 Black mechanics in the South when the Civil War ended, as compared with some 20,000 white mechanics. Large numbers of Black workers were employed in tobacco, brick-making, ship-caulking, railroad construction, house-building, and on the docks.[1]

In 1867 a strike on the Mobile levee spread rapidly, "resulting in some of the most stirring mass demonstrations in Southern history." In Charleston, the Black longshoremen formed their own Protective Union and won a strike for higher wages. The dockworkers of Savannah, Georgia, nearly all Black, won a strike to repeal a city tax of $10 on all persons employed on the wharves. By 1869 Black labor organizations had mushroomed so rapidly that central labor bodies became necessary and the National Colored Labor Union was formed.

So impressed was William Sylvis, the leader of the National Labor Union, with what he saw while on a tour of the South that he believed "a vigorous campaign [could] unite the whole laboring population of the South, white and black, upon our platform. If we succeed in convincing these people that it is in their interest to make common cause with us," he wrote from Wilmington, North Carolina, "we will have a power in this part of the country that will shake Wall Street to its boots."[2]

It can be seen, therefore, that Black workers were not slow in coming to unionism. Nor did they wait for whites to organize them. They organized themselves, but their objective was not separate unions. Isaac Myers, president of the National Colored Labor Union, made this clear when he said, in a speech in Norfolk, Virginia, in April 1870, "We are organized for the interest of the workingmen, white and colored, and to do this, let the officers be composed of both white and colored men."[3]

The white-Black unity that Sylvis envisioned would "shake Wall Street to its boots" did not materialize. Wall Street determined to prevent this. It gave more and more concessions to the former slave-owning and still propertied class. It closed its eyes to the mounting Klan terror aimed at crushing the rising democratic movement for land, free public education, higher wages and full equality. The final act of betrayal came in 1877. Speaking for Northern capital, the Republican Party agreed to end Southern Reconstruction and permit the class defeated in the Civil War to regain power in the South again. In return, the Southern Democrats agreed to throw the electoral votes of a few states to the Republican presidential candidate. The right to vote was replaced by poll-tax and other restrictive electoral measures, and one Southern state after another imposed Jim Crow segregation laws. Black organizations were smashed and the right of workers to organize ended. The chain gang and the lyncher's noose became the symbols of Southern justice. Thus, Southern Reconstruction, which held such hope for making the South the nation's democratic bastion, was replaced with policies which made it the worst cesspool of racist violence, obscurantism and exploitation.

## Racism Prevents Unity

Organized labor did little to prevent this. Prejudice and discrimination were widespread within its own ranks. The call for the founding of the National Colored Labor Union in 1869 gave as a reason the fact that "colored men are excluded from workshops on account of their color."[4] Even some of the more class-conscious white trade union leaders lacked understanding of the *special* nature of Black oppression. Like Sylvis, they believed that with slavery ended, Black oppression would also end automatically. Sylvis, therefore, was critical of Southern Reconstruction, supporting those who called for letting the South solve its own problems. This meant, in effect, leaving Blacks to the tender mercies of the racist white land- and property-owning class. Nor did these labor leaders conduct a struggle within the labor movement against racial discrimination and for the right of Black workers to belong to unions and to have equality in job opportunities. Even the son of nationally famous Frederick Douglass was denied membership in the Typographical Union although he was a qualified printer.[5]

In this critical juncture of their history — and of the nation's history — Black people were left largely on their own resources. The labor movement which should have been their staunchest ally did not come to their aid. They were deprived of the gains they had won in the Civil War and during Reconstruction were driven back; and the foul stench of racism was permitted to penetrate deeper into the organized labor movement.

THE SITUATION has changed immensely, yet the effects of the betrayal of 1877 are still with us a century later. Black people are not "free and equal," and discrimination is still the American way of life. One need but mention the largely unorganized state of labor both white and Black in the South, to recognize that even though the prime victims have been Black, white workers, too, have paid for this. Had the South been organized, as it was well on the way to becoming, there would be no runaway shops from the North to areas of the South where wages are low and unionism absent.

The situation today is more than a consequence, or continuation, of the past. Inequality and discrimination have been reinforced by the rise and dominance of monopoly capital.* Highly developed capitalism needs cheap labor markets from which to draw unskilled and semiskilled labor reserves. This was noted by Lenin in his classic work on imperialism. "In the United States," he wrote, "immigrants from Eastern and Southern Europe are engaged in the most poorly paid jobs, while American [white] workers provide the highest percentage of overseers or of the better paid workers."[6]

There has been some change since then. Europe is no longer this country's main source of cheap labor. The great majority of low-paid workers have been migrants from the rural South to both Northern and Southern industrial areas, and immigrants from the colony of Puerto Rico and the peasantry of Mexico. Smaller numbers have come from other Latin American countries and the Caribbean, as well as from Asia. Many are so-called illegals, often permitted to "slip" into the country to be transformed into the cheapest of cheap labor sources. As most of these people have darker skins, white racist views and practices have been reinforced.

The tendency to import cheap labor from less developed countries and regions is not limited to the United States. It is seen in every developed capitalist country. More than 12 million foreign workers are employed in West Germany, France, Britain, Sweden, the Netherlands, and a few other European countries. Many of these lower paid workers return home after awhile, and newcomers arrive; so the turnover of cheap foreign labor involves many millions more. They come from Italy, Spain, Portugal, Greece, Yugoslavia, and from former colonial countries such as India, Pakistan, West Indies, Algeria, Morocco, and other Asian and African states. Israel, too, is increasingly dependent upon cheap Arab labor to do its hard, dirty work, while Japan brings workers from neighboring poorer states, particularly South Korea.

No matter how developed a capitalist country may be, the need

---

* A well-documented study of how the U.S. Steel Corporation deliberately fostered racism as part of its labor policies for over a half-century, is the subject of a paper presented by Edward Greer to the American Political Science Association Convention, Chicago, 1974. It is a section of a forthcoming book, *Big Steel; Little Steal: Limits of Black Reform in Gary, Indiana.*

remains for untapped sources of cheap labor. Such a reserve is needed to fill unskilled and "marginal" jobs and "to deter unionized workers from asking too much."[7]

## Blacks and Latins – Mainly Workers

Black workers are no longer mainly Southern and rural. They live now in the North and West as well, concentrated in the inner cities of the huge metropolitan areas. This is true of the Puerto Ricans in the United States as well, and somewhat less so of the Chicano people. All three of these minority peoples are predominantly working class. About 40 percent of Black workers are employed in basic industry,[8] and from 1966 to 1973 those employed in enterprises of 100 or more workers increased by more than 50 percent.[9]

Generally speaking, Black, Puerto Rican and Chicano workers find employment in greater numbers in industries where work is seasonal or irregular. Even in auto and steel, two basic industries employing large numbers of minority workers, employment levels tend to be erratic. When times are good, job opportunities expand: but when times are bad, minority workers are the first to go. This is reflected in Black income. The median Black family's earnings in 1969 was only 60.9 percent of the median white family's. But no sooner did production fall, than the median Black family income fell to 57.7 percent of white in 1973.[10]

Exceedingly significant is the fact that a larger proportion of Black workers is organized than white. Black workers make up from 10 to 12 percent of the employed labor force, but the three million Black trade unionists represent about 15 percent of trade union membership. This is explained by a number of factors: A larger percentage of Blacks are manual and blue-collar workers in industries that are more highly organized. Despite continued discriminatory practices, Black workers have seen unions as necessary in defense of their interests as workers. Studies have shown that inequality is consistently less "in labor markets organized by industrial unions," manufacturing industries organized by such unions "have been one of the few sources of high wage employment for black workers."[11] Where workers are unorganized, or organized by craft unions, wage and job inequality is greatest.

The rise in Black consciousness and militancy in the past two decades also stimulated more Blacks to seek trade union organization. The civil rights and freedom movement has spilled over, therefore, into the class arena, to the benefit of the labor movement. The recognition of the potentiality involved in the great civil rights upsurge first gave the leadership of the small New York City drug and hospital union, Local 1199, the idea that it could go out and organize the important and growing hospital and health-care field. The success achieved in the building of a rapidly expanding hospital and health care national union is a testimonial to the validity of this estimate. Immense headway in organizing could have been made by other unions had they understood the great opportunities offered by the Black people's upsurge.

While their record is better, job discrimination is widespread in industrial unions as well. In nine high-pay industries in which Black workers held 9 percent of the jobs in 1970, they had only 1 percent of the high pay jobs, but 20 percent of the lower-pay ones.[12] There is less discrimination in federal employ than in the private sector, but here, too, minority workers held 20 percent of all jobs in 1973, but only 3.5 percent of the higher-pay jobs.[13]

Discrimination is so pervasive and so customary that it is often taken as a matter of course by whites. Everyone knows, for example, that train porters are Black and train brakemen, white. Yet they both do similar work, except that "porters receive less pay and segregated status." In many steel mills, the millwright is white, but his helper, who often does most of the work, is usually Black or Spanish-speaking.[14]

These examples could be multiplied by similar ones from many other industries. Frequently they are the result of outright collusion between union officials and management to segregate Blacks, Chicanos and Puerto Ricans in the hardest, dirtiest, most hazardous and least paying jobs. This is particularly true of the steel industry. The steel union has been notorious for permitting discriminatory job classifications and seniority provisions. By means of departmental and job-category seniority, rather than plant-wide seniority, minority workers have been prevented from climbing out of the hell pits in which they are segregated. Until recently, a Black worker employed in the coke plant or foundry had little chance of moving up into other more skilled departments. When he did, it was at the expense of his accumulated years of seniority. He had to start all over again from scratch. Despite decades of protest and militant struggle by minority workers against this discrimination, it has persisted.

At the end of 1973 an historic federal court decision brought the beginnings of a change. In response to a suit against the U.S.Steel Corporation at Fairfield, Alabama, under Title VII of the 1964 Civil Rights Act, the court ordered the establishment of a system of plant-wide seniority which would allow workers to transfer from job or department without loss of earnings or seniority. It decided that workers who had lost considerable pay over the years due to discrimination had a right to special compensation. To guarantee that at least 25 percent of trade and craft positions would be held by minority workers, it ordered that one Black apprentice be chosen for each white until this ratio was reached. The same procedure was to be used to guarantee that at least 20 percent of office, technical and supervisory personnel are Black. And a court-appointed committee of three—one each from the company, the union, and the minority workers—would oversee the implementation of the decision.[15]

This court order had far-reaching effects, going beyond the particular plant and industry. But the companies and the union leadership were not disposed to abide by it. With the approval of the federal Equal Employment Opportunity Commission in early 1974, they entered into a "Consent Decree" which nullified, in essence, much of the spirit and specific proposals of the Fairfield decision. Instead of granting victimized workers the pay they lost, the Decree offered them $400 to $600 as total settlement which, according to Herbert Hill of the NAACP, represents about 5 percent of the average actual wages lost. In addition workers were expected to sign a waiver, yielding their rights to sue the company. They were told the government would enter the case on the side of management if they refused to waive their rights. Most important of all, the principal issue of plant-wide seniority was so obfuscated that it was left essentially up to voluntary compliance.[16]

A petition jointly presented by the Steelworkers Rank and File Committee, the NAACP and the National Organization of Women asked the court to set aside the consent decree. The judge ruled that the decree could stand, but without final status. Appeals could be made to vacate or modify it, and individuals could enter the court with private suits.[17] The final outcome is not yet certain. But this case illustrates how tenacious the grip of racism is in an industry and union in which over 30 percent of the workers are Black, Chicano and Puerto Rican.

## Racism and Seniority

Another complicated seniority problem has surfaced since the large-scale layoffs hit industry in 1974-75. The accumulated seniority of many workers who had found employment since Title VII of the Civil Rights

Act was adopted in 1964, has not been enough to keep them from being laid off first. A possible consequence can be seen in what happened at the Continental Can Company plant in Harvey, Louisiana. Of its 50 Black employees, 48 got their jobs as a result of Title VII. All 48 were laid off. A suit was filed in federal court in their behalf. The judge ruled that, "The company's history of racial discrimination in hiring makes it impossible now for blacks (other than the original two) to have sufficient seniority to withstand layoffs. In this situation," said the court, "the selection of employees for layoffs on the basis of seniority unlawfully perpetuates the effect of past discrimination."[18]

William E. Pollard, civil rights director for the AFL-CIO, has said that "Seniority is one of the most highly prized possessions of any employee." He believes it should not be tampered with.[19] Yet he does not answer the question of what is to be done to prevent minority workers from carrying the burden of layoffs. Certainly they cannot be told that Title VII applies only when employment is high.

There is grave danger that worsening economic conditions and protracted large-scale unemployment may exacerbate race relations over the job issue. No simple or foolproof answer to this problem has been given that is in the interest of class unity and that jeopardizes neither the interests of minority workers nor an effective seniority system.

This knotty problem can be answered only when white workers are won to the battle against every form of discrimination as a matter of principle. In some cases the institution of plant-wide seniority, rather than only job and department seniority, can provide a part of the answer. In other instances the approach of the Steelworkers Rank and File Committee can be considered. It proposes that "voluntary inverse seniority be applied," allowing older workers with longer seniority to get supplemental unemployment benefits (SUB), and younger workers who are not entitled to these to continue working.[20] In some places older workers agreed to such a switch, but it can be applied only where SUB exists and for as long as it lasts.[21] Where workers understand the need for unity, it is possible to modify seniority rules by agreeing that the proportion of minority and women workers should not be reduced. This is more equitable than having the full burden of lay-offs fall on the minority and women workers, but it is still no solution.

The answer lies in the determined struggle of the workers as a class to win a shorter workweek without reduction in weekly earnings, the earlier voluntary retirement of older workers at full social security and private-pension benefits,* and in compelling the government to accept responsibility for full employment.

## Albert Shanker and the Building Trades Unions

The greatest discrimination is to be found in the construction trades. This is so conspicuous, so blatant, so long-standing that it seems unnecessary to validate the charge further. Yet a defense of the building trades record on this score has come from a curious source, Albert Shanker of the United Federation of Teachers. Shanker insists that "considerable progress has been made in integrating the building trades during the past several years." The general public is unaware of this, he claims, because "the press continues to play up restrictive practices of the past rather than the integration efforts of the present."[22]

Can Shanker really mean it when he says that restrictive practices are only "of the past?" He mentions the skilled building trades locals in New York City as examples of such progress. He mentions the plumbers union. But in June 1973, four months after Shanker's optimistic estimate appeared in his paid weekly column in the *New York Times,* Federal Judge Dudley B. Bonsal arrived at an opposite conclusion about New York Local 638 of the Plumbers and Steamfitters International. He found that only 4.5 percent of the local's membership was Black and Puerto Rican. And even these were discriminated against. The local had an "A" branch of highly paid construction workers in which there were but 191 Blacks and Puerto Ricans, out of 4,198 members, and a "B" branch of lower paid workers in which there were 500 Blacks and Puerto Ricans out of 3,362 members. In other words, nearly three-quarters of the minority workers in the local were in the lower-pay category.[23]

To Shanker, this may represent great progress, but Judge Bonsal thought otherwise. He ordered the local to upgrade all qualified "B" branch members into the "A" division. He also stipulated that 30 percent of the local's membership be Black and Puerto Rican by July 1, 1977.

Local 638 is not alone in this kind of "progress." The other skilled construction crafts have a similarly dismal record. Shanker points to a somewhat higher number of minority workers on apprenticeship. But this is by no means true of all building trades unions. He also ignores the fact

* Retirement at 65 years of age is meaningless for many workers in the United States. The life expectancy of white men was only 68.1 years in 1970; for nonwhite men, only 60.5 years.

that the entire apprenticeship system is now archaic and meant more to prevent minority workers from entering the crafts as full-fledged workers than to help them reach this status. About three-quarters of skilled construction workers never went through apprenticeships. They were trained right on the job.[24] As anyone experienced in the building trades knows, white officials and members regularly bring sons and friends on to the job and into the union without their going through the slow apprenticeship mill first. They learn as they go.

There appear to be two reasons for Shanker's concern with the reputation of the building trades bureaucrats. First, he shares with them the racist view that if the percentage of minority workers is low, whether in the building trades or in teaching, it is because they lack the necessary qualifications.

A second explanation is that behind the scenes of the AFL-CIO high command a struggle is being waged to determine the successor to the aged George Meany. The building trades unions do not want this post to fall into the hands of the more liberal elements on the Executive Council. They fear the greater susceptibility to more progressive policies of the larger industrial unions with their sizeable minority memberships. Meany, who speaks for this building trades grouping, wants to make sure that the labor movement continues reactionary foreign policies. But the weight of the building trades unions in the AFL-CIO is insufficient. They need allies. Shanker, as the head of the Teachers Union, is such an ally. He agrees with them on policies and has the ambition of replacing Meany. But he must prove his loyalty.

Shanker and his building trades cronies may outsmart themselves. The situation has changed. Teachers now face both job and salary reductions. Building trades workers face mass unemployment with no immediate prospect of the industry returning to normal. They mistakenly believed that by keeping Blacks out of construction jobs they could safeguard their own. Now whites, too, are unemployed. Sooner or later the truth must dawn that as long as the Pentagon gets the bulk of federal spending, it will be impossible to mount a massive public-housing program. Thus the members of these unions may move in directions quite different from those their present-day leaders have planned for them.

## The Issue of "Quotas"

Shanker's major obsession has become the issue of "quotas." He is opposed to their use in the struggle for equality, whether in the labor movement, the Democratic Party, or anywhere else. Shanker charges that quotas are a form of "reverse discrimination," because, according to him, they mean choosing inferior, unqualified people solely for their dark skin color.

Once again Shanker conceals something. He is very concerned lest unqualified Blacks be chosen rather than qualified whites. But he is not disturbed at all that less qualified whites have been chosen over the years instead of more qualified Blacks. The practice in education, Shanker's own field, has been to choose people without regard to qualification merely because of their white skin color. In many of the larger cities a majority of public school children are now from racial minorities. But the great majority of school teachers remains white. If this is because they are better qualified it should be measurable in some way—the greater school attendance of children, greater student involvement and discipline and, above all, quality education. But everyone knows the reverse is true. Hence, an important aspect of teacher qualification must be the ability to communicate with, have empathy for, and be accepted by, minority children. If this is lacking, all other qualifications become meaningless. And in the building trades, the argument of lack of qualifications used against Blacks is a smokescreen for denying them equal treatment.

Shanker asks: Why quotas? Why pin things down to arbitrary mechanical numbers? These questions might have validity if everything else were equal, that is, if *real* efforts were made to end discrimination. But as wolves cannot be trusted to guard sheep, neither can racists be trusted to end racist practices. This is why Judge Bonsal felt compelled to rule that the steamfitters local must guarantee that at least 30 percent of its membership be from minority groups by a specified date. A U.S district Court upheld the so-called Lindsay Plan for New York City for the same reason. The plan calls for the hiring of one minority construction worker for every four workers on a project. This fixed quota of one to four was imposed by the court despite the stubborn protest of Peter Brennan, then Secretary of Labor, and his brethren in the building trades hierarchy.[25]

The fight against discrimination is not new. Fair employment practice legislation has been on the law books for over 30 years, but it is still being violated shamelessly. The time has come to end reliance on the voluntary compliance of people who have no intention to comply. Only by imposing concrete, tangible goals, to be realized in fixed specified periods, can measurable results replace hypocritical promises.

In recent years Black workers have become an increasingly significant force in the labor movement. Approximately three million Black unionists are concentrated in large numbers in just about every important industrial and public-employee union in the country. Black workers comprise 20 percent or more of Auto, Steel, Meat Cutters, Garment, Men's Clothing, Building Service, Hospital, Transit, Laundry, State, County and Muncipal, Letter Carriers, Postal Clerks, Teachers, and many others. In 1973, 53 UAW Locals had Black presidents, of which 26 were in the Detroit area.[26] Many of the largest UAW locals now have Black majorities. Even more significant is the fact that locals with white majorities also elect Blacks to top posts, including that of local president. This change of attitude of many white workers is not limited to auto. A young white shipyard worker in Pascagoula, Mississippi, put it in these words: "White against Black is just not as strong in this state as it used to be. Before, Black and white couldn't get together. . . . But I told my friend here (gesturing to a Black officer in his local) I might not know what it is to be Black. But I sure know how it is to be treated like a nigger by management. And Blacks can see that whites are getting the same old shaft Blacks get. We fought each other for a long time, with the company egging us on. But now we are—some of us—fighting together."[27]

This growing strength and influence of Black workers at the lower levels of union leadership, is not yet reflected in the middle and top bodies. William Lucy, secretary-treasurer of the State, County and Municipal Employees and the president of the Coalition of Black Trade Unionists, has said that "Blacks are nearly as rare in the policy-making bodies of most major unions as they are in the executive suites of major corporations." Out of 35 members of the AFL-CIO Executive Council, only two are Black—both from small unions "with little clout." "If labor unions are the movement of Black working people," asks Lucy, "why are there so few Black labor leaders in this country?"[28]

The reason is obvious. Racism is still deeply imbedded in the thinking and policies of many union officialdoms. How else can one explain the situation in unions like steel, ladies' garment, men's clothing, machinists, and the craft unions. So intolerable did the situation become that the Steelworkers Ad Hoc Committee, a movement of Black steelworkers, picketed its own union's 1968 convention in Chicago. It demanded Blacks on the executive board, full integration at all levels of union leadership and policy-making, and the reorganization of the union's civil rights department. Yet, seven years later, there was still not a single Black member on the union's executive board.

Chicano workers have also won a considerable number of positions in local unions, especially in the Southwest, but not in top leadership. They founded and lead the United Farm Workers and are influential in western metal mining and in the laborers union. Puerto Ricans hold very few leadership posts even on the local level. As more recent immigrants with language problems, they feel less at home and many hope to return some day to their island; so they participate less in union affairs. In turn, this situation is utilized by employers and racist union officials to exploit them further.

### Minorities Organize Within Unions

The general rise of Black consciousness and militancy, plus the increasing weight of Black workers in industry and unions, have intensified the search for special organizational instruments with which to wage the fight for full equality. A myriad of organizational forms have emerged, not as separate Black unions, but as groupings aimed at changing the situation in existing unions. During the past decade many Black caucuses have come and gone; a few remain on a semiofficial basis. These relate to specific conditions of a given union or industry, although they are also identified with the more general movement in the country for Black freedom. Whether a Black caucus continues to exist or not depends on how acute the specific injustices are, the nature of internal union developments, and the degree to which white workers join in the common battle. For a period of time, so-called revolutionary Black organizations arose in various plants of the Detroit area. These soon disappeared when they projected programs out of line with reality.

Attempts have also been made to tie together Black trade unionists across union lines. The Negro American Labor Council existed for several years, but never recovered from the explusion of its Left-led branches during the anti-Communist witch-hunt. In Detroit, the Trade Union Leadership Committee came into existence at the height of the civil rights movement and has played the role of prodding white officialdom. More recently a Black Labor Leaders Committee took shape in Chicago as part of the Jesse Jackson-led community-based People United to Save Humanity (PUSH) movement. But most promising of all has been the formation of the national Coalition of Black Trade Unionists (CBTU).

The Coalition held its founding convention in Chicago, in September 1972. At the outset it made clear that it was not a separatist organization.

Its statement of purpose said: the CBTU "will work within the framework of the trade union movement. It will attempt to maximize the strength and influence of Black workers in organized labor . . . [and] as Black trade unionists, it is our challenge to make the labor movement more relevant to the needs and aspirations of Black and poor workers. The CBTU will insist that Black union officials become full partners in the leadership and decision-making of the American labor movement."[29]

The CBTU has since held three annual conventions—in Washington, D.C., Detroit, Michigan, and Atlanta, Georgia. As many as 2,000 delegates from some 70 unions attended. The CBTU has the endorsement of a number of powerful unions. Leonard Woodcock, president of the UAW, and Jerry Wurf, president of the AFSCME, addressed the Detroit convention in 1974 and recognized CBTU as a new force that was enhancing the strength of organized labor.

In his opening remarks to the convention, William Lucy reiterated the demand that Blacks be included in all decision-making processes, and noted, "Those who've got the power will not give it up. It will not come by petition."[30] In this spirit the convention resolved to "aggressively forge ahead for a more representative voice in all policy-making bodies of the AFL-CIO." It condemned lily-white union leaderships and urged the CBTU to identify and expose those who refused to modify their positions.

The 1974 convention supported the struggle for women's rights and endorsed the newly formed Coalition of Labor Union Women. Thus, in spirit at least, were joined the two new currents in the labor movement which, if they learn to consult and act together, can affect policies and give hope for progressive change. The CBTU can also form alliances with Chicano and Puerto Rican trade unionists, encouraging them to form their own corresponding trade union agencies.

The resolution adopted on organizing the unorganized is of greatest importance. It calls "on all sectors of the labor movement, AFL-CIO and Independents, to pool their latent and financial resources, in a mass effort to complete the task of organizing the unorganized without regard to crafts, skills, or jurisdictions; and help workers in these various industries to build unions upon which they can rely, and control, and unions which will adhere to the basic principles of militant, progressive, democratic trade unions."[31]

Large numbers of Black workers remain outside of unions, but not by choice. Experience has shown that they are most responsive to unionism if it offers them equality. Black working women, for example, now have more than one-third of their number employed in clerical jobs. They could lead the way to a general organization of clerical workers, but only if they see a trade union movement ready to respond to their needs and in which Blacks are the equal of whites and women the equal of men.

The CBTU can play a vital role in helping to change the situation in the labor movement if it avoids the trap of interunion rivalry, consciously builds a mass base, does not permit the CBTU to become just a movement of, or for, full-time Black officials, and functions in a democratic way.

William Lucy; Charles Hayes, vice-president of the Meat Cutters; and Cleveland Robinson, vice-president of the Distributive Workers Union —the three key officers of the CBTU—have militant records. They can succeed in making it a powerful force, if it is rooted in the rank and file.

## 19 : WOMEN WHO WORK

WE LIVE in the midst of a women's awakening greater and more profound than any in history. Vast changes are occurring in male-female relations and the process is only beginning. The revolution in technology has drawn more and more women out of the restrictive confines of the home into the expanding world of production, equalizing the work capacity of the sexes, making possible the emancipation of women from household drudgery and subordination by males. Just as marriage and parenthood do not transform a man into a "house-husband," neither should they make a woman a "house-wife."

The awakening is also a response to the advancing technology of birth control and the winning, at last, of the right to abortion. These give women greater command over their own bodies and reproductive functions. And there is, no less, a response to the revolutionary spirit of the age, which questions old norms and customs, and reshapes the clay of human relations into more liberating forms.

This is not the first epoch of women's rebellion. But it is the first to embrace the great majority of women and affect every aspect of social life. Its over-all impact on working-class struggles and the labor movement is bound to be immense.

When the "women's liberation movement" first made its appearance in the 1960s, it was mainly middle class in origin and conception. This was true of earlier women's movements as well— the Women's Rights

Convention at Seneca Falls, N.Y., in 1848; the National Women's Suffrage Association of the post-Civil War period; and the reborn suffrage movement in the early 1900s. Yet each of these movements became linked in time with the cause of Black freedom and the struggle of the working class.

Frederick Douglass was a featured speaker at the Seneca Falls convention; and William Sylvis, militant head of the National Labor Union, was likewise a staunch supporter of the women's movement. In turn, the women's movement supported the abolitionist cause, and suffragist leader Elizabeth Cady Stanton participated in the second convention of the labor federation, in 1868. This convention made history by adopting a resolution which, for the first time in labor history, called for equal pay for equal work for women.

Karl Marx was so elated with this development that he wrote a friend contrasting the American attitude with the "spirit of narrow-mindedness" of the English and French. He added that anyone who knows anything about history knows that "great social changes are impossible without the feminine ferment." Social progress, he wrote, "can be measured exactly" by the social position of women.[1]

Thus there has been a deep historical linkage between the women's movement, the labor movement, the movement for Black freedom, and that for socialism. But there has also been a gap separating middle-class feminists from their working-class sisters.

Feminists have frequently seen things in non-class terms. They have been correct in stressing that all women feel "put down" by men. This is a social issue not limited to the working class, affecting the women of all classes in varying degrees. But feminists have been wrong in thinking that working-class women have more in common with their so-called sisters of the ruling class than with working-class men, sexist though they be. Yet the women's movement has played a significant role in heightening the consciousness of all women of their subordinate position in society, and in forcefully projecting the issue of women's status on the order of the day. That issue in now worldwide.

Its repercussions in the labor movement are already being felt. Women's caucuses have sprung up in trade unions, resolutions concerning women have been introduced at union conventions, more women have run for union office, and those unions "with the vision to understand what is happening among women have started to address themselves to women's issues," and to upgrade women in union staff positions.[2] Most important of all, union women have begun to organize a movement of their own inside the trade unions to advance their struggle. In March 1974, in Chicago, a spirited national conference of over 3,000 women trade union delegates, from 58 separate unions, established the Coalition of Labor Union Women (CLUW). The conference pledged to improve ⟵ the lives of working women by activating them around women's needs within their own unions. The conference set a number of objectives for the new organization:

To encourage unions to be more aggressive in efforts to organize unorganized women;

To strengthen the participation of women in union policy-making positions;

To encourage unions to act against sex discrimination in pay, hiring, job classification and promotion;

To support legislation for adequate child-care facilities, a "liveable" minimum wage, improved maternity and pension benefits, and improved health and safety laws;

To work for ratification of the Equal Rights Amendment and for legislation to provide both sexes the protection of statutes originally aimed at protecting women.

Instead of making male workers, and men in union leadership, the main target, the conference concentrated its fire on the employers. In the words of Olga Madar, vice-president of the UAW and the elected president of CLUW, "It is to the advantage of the employer not to give equal pay, not to follow the contract clauses that provide equality in upgrading, not to provide maternity benefits."

Ms. Madar gave credit to the women's movement for getting things started. It "gave an impetus to our moving ahead," she told the conference. While trade union women do not agree with everything these women's organizations have done, she continued, they helped make "union women and blue-collar wives aware that there was blatant discrimination against women just because they were females."[3]

Two reasons explain the relative restraint with which the conference dealt with the union leadership's share of responsibility for the "blatant discrimination." First, union women recognize that unions have done a great deal for them despite the dominant male supremacist practices. Addie Wyatt, director of Women's Affairs in the Amalgamated Meat Cutters Union and vice-president of CLUW, has told women around the country of her personal experience. "I went to work at an early age because I had to," she relates. "I originally applied for a typist job, but because I am Black, they sent me to work in the packing plant." There she found she could earn $24.80 a week at a time when typists in the office were getting only $12 to $15 a week. She preferred to stay in the plant. The difference was the union.[4]

A second factor in CLUW's hesitation to sharply challenge union leadership has to do with how the conference came into being. The prime initiators and leaders of the new coalition are women union officials. They do not want to come into collision with their own leaders. They do not want their effort to be labeled a "sex opposition." This may hinder the way the new coalition functions, but it also has some advantages. The fact that the dominant male leaderships did not oppose the conference indicates that at least some of them are becoming aware of the growing ferment among women and its immense potentialities for unions.

Thus, a new force has appeared on the labor scene. It symbolizes the new working women's awareness of their own status and needs and of their latent power.

CLUW can become the medium through which an alliance is consummated between the labor movement and the women's movement. Should this take root and flower, it can help bring into being a new period of rapid growth and vitality for trade unions. History shows that women have played critically decisive roles in all crucial labor struggles of the past. As strikers, they have time and again fought valiantly for "bread and roses too." As wives of strikers they have courageously walked the picket lines to face policemen's clubs and troopers' guns. Recently this was shown again in the Harlan miners' strike and is now being displayed in the heroic struggle of Chicano farm workers in behalf of their union. Dolores Huerta, vice-president of the United Farm Workers and herself a symbol of women's courage and leadership ability, has pointed to the decisive role played by women in the farm worker's long and extremely difficult fight against conditions of shameful exploitation. Her conclusion is that, once aroused and engaged in battle, "women are stronger than men."

But to arouse and commit women to the fight requires a major effort by unions to overcome the "blatant discrimination" against women as workers and as trade unionists. CLUW cannot serve its purpose if it covers up the true state of affairs in the labor movement itself.

The proportion of women in the civilian labor force has risen constantly — from 23 percent in 1920, to 31 percent in 1952, to 38 percent in

1973.[5] In 1968, 30 percent of men in the civilian labor force were in unions, compared with only 12.6 percent of women. Further, the ratio of women in unions to women employed is declining. The organization of women workers lags far behind that of men.

One reason for this is that fewer women are employed in the industrial plants, where unions are strongest. In 1950, BLS statistics listed 22 percent of women in the labor force as nonfarm and nonservice blue-collar workers. By 1974 this had fallen to 15 percent. On the other hand, the proportion of women has increased from 30 to 36 percent for clerical workers and 15 to 20 percent for service workers.[6] These categories are not only the least organized, but frequently the lowest paid.

Women employed in factory jobs are concentrated in the most techni-cally backward industries, which employ large numbers of low-paid, low-skilled workers. About half of women factory workers are concen-trated in clothing, food and textile, and about another half-million women are in footwear, plastics, toys, costume jewelry and notions.[7]

Even in these so-called female industries, men get the more highly skilled, better-paid jobs. In union shops of the women's apparel industry, for example, the men work as cutters, markers, pressers and on custodial and maintenance jobs; the women are mainly sewing machine operators.

It was a full century ago that Marx congratulated the National Labor Union for its resolution calling for equal pay for equal work for women. And still this demand is unmet. BLS statistics indicate that men usually receive higher rates of pay than women for the same work performed. This varies between industries, occupations, types of establishment and regions.

Where men and women are employed together the wage differential is considerably less than where women alone are employed. The difference in pay between male and female class-A accounting clerks, in establish-ments where both sexes were employed was 12 percent; where only women were employed they received 23 percent below the wage male clerks received elsewhere. The largest differential was for elevator operators in the North Central region—a difference of some 53 percent between men and women. This was largely due to the different industries for which men and women worked. Nearly 40 percent of the women worked in retail establishments and hotels, where wages are generally low. But 50 percent of the men worked in office buildings, and a much smaller proportion in retail establishments and hotels. In the South, however, where men and women elevator operators — mainly Black —

tended to work in the same kind of establishments, the differential was small.[8]

## Sex Discrimination

In July 1973, the Joint Economic Committee of Congress held hearings on the economics of sex discrimination. Herbert Stein, chairman of the President's Council of Economic Advisers, testified that women on an average earned only 80 percent as much as men, and that this was "simply because they are women." Barbara R. Bergman, professor of economics at the University of Maryland, challenged Stein's figure. She told the committee that of seven separate studies of this question only one showed a differential as low as 20 percent. This was the one which Stein chose to use.

The Joint Economic Committee heard six days of expert testimony about sex discrimination in virtually every aspect of women's economic lives — jobs, pay, education, taxation, insurance, credit, unemployment compensation, social security and private pensions.[9]

The gap in pay scales between men and women working together on similar jobs is narrowing. Yet, as such gaps close, women lose ground in job opportunities, particularly in the professions. Women's professional employment has grown more slowly than that for men. There was a time when nursing and teaching were considered "female professions," but no longer. Men in teaching rose from 25 to 28 percent; male social and welfare workers went from 30 to 36 percent; male librarians, from 11 to 14 percent. Only among medical technicians did the proportion of women grow from 57 to 63 percent. Women social scientists declined from 33 to 25 percent; women designers from 27 to 18 percent; and women technicians, other than medical, from 21 to 13 percent. Thus, although employment of professional women has increased, it is only because of expansion in the fields in which they were concentrated. But in proportion to men, they have been losing ground.[10]

The trend in the employment of women depends almost exclusively on the growth rate of the industries they are in. Should there be stagnation or should employment shrink, as it has in 1974 and 1975, the prospect of more jobs for women, especially in the higher-pay categories, is "not a cheering one."[11]

Black women have traditionally had a higher percentage in the active labor force than white women. Unemployment is so great among Black men, and their wages so low, that Black women have been compelled to take whatever work they could find in order to make ends meet. This is why so many of them worked in private household service, where the work is menial and the pay exceedingly low. Recently, there has been some improvement. White-collar employment among Black females, according to the BLS, increased from eight percent in 1950 to 42 percent in 1974. Private household employment declined from 41 percent in 1950 to 10 percent in 1974.* Blue-collar factory jobs also showed an increase of about 3 percent.[12] But the gains made can easily be wiped away under depressed economic conditions.

In 1971, for the first time, more than half the married women in the United States were working on paid jobs at least some part of the year. If there had been more jobs available, the proportion would have been higher. It is difficult for many working-class families to get along with only one breadwinner. Census Bureau statistics show that the great majority of married women who work have husbands earning less than $7,000 a year.[13] New needs, such as more schooling for children, and new manipulated needs, such as constant changes in style — plus permanent price inflation — make a second employed worker increasingly necessary. New household appliances and services also make it easier to stay away from the home part of the day. And women need to escape from the narrow confines of the home and domestic drudgery.

At one time, when European immigration was at its peak, an estimated 23 percent of blue-collar and clerical workers' families added to family income by taking in boarders and roomers. This accounted for an average of 8 percent of family incomes. Working children brought in another 9 percent.[14] Both of these sources of income have shrunk greatly.

Of course, married women who work outside the home are far from free of household chores. A survey made in Syracuse, N.Y., showed that wives who worked 30 hours or more a week on a paying job, spent an additional average of 34 hours a week on household tasks.[15] This is "moonlighting" on a grand scale — and without pay. From this point of view, women are apparently the stronger sex.

A recent theory developed by some in the women's movement holds that the answer to women's enslavement is not her emancipation from household drudgery, but her full and adequate payment for it. This being a commodity-producing society, it is argued, women should be paid in

---

* Bearing in mind that government figures tend to list many manual jobs as white collar, the extent of this increase may be exaggerated.

full for "producing" the original commodity of all — living labor. "Most incredible of all," writes one proponent of this theory, "the women who produce this most essential of all commodities for the capitalist, living labor, are not even recognized or acknowledged as a class of workers producing a critical commodity!" The answer, therefore, is "that all women involved in the production of this 'commodity,' living labor, be paid a wage commensurate with the most skilled workers, a wage to be financed directly from the profits of industry, and paid to the women themselves, A radical demand? Yes, but one flowing directly from the analysis of the camouflaged and hidden role of women in the productive process itself."[16]

The trouble with this theory and this demand is not that they are "radical," but simplistic. They confuse biological reproduction, necessary for the procreation of all living species, and material production. They further confuse a worker's laboring-power, which is bought by capitalists on the labor market as a commodity, and the worker as a human being, who is not a commodity. Wage slavery is not chattel slavery.

Suppose women did get paid directly for their "production" of living labor from the fount of corporate profits. What would be the source of these profits? Not living labor in and by itself, but only living labor engaged in material production and in the creation of surplus value. In other words, we still would have to go to the world of labor for the means of payment. If the mere "production" of human beings created material wealth, India would be one of the richest countries in the world.

Thinking that direct remuneration to women for motherhood is the answer to women's oppression leads to completely erroneous and reactionary conclusions. It tends to reinforce the view that women's prime role is that of a reproductive organism — a "body." Certainly, society has the responsibility to provide a living income for every human being and family. Where there are no nurseries and child-care centers or jobs at decent wages for women, society must assume the burden of giving such families the means with which to live. This is nothing new. There are many countries in the world today where governments pay stipends to families with a number of children. But even were such stipends to be increased and called "wages," it would not change the subordinate position of women in society. It would tend to reinforce it.

In the United States today we face the problem of millions of women who are on welfare and receive aid commensurate with the size of their family. Obviously these women should receive enough to maintain their families at a decent standard of living instead of at the shameful present poverty level. But even if the demands of welfare mothers for increased allotments were won, it would not mean their emancipation.

Marriage and motherhood should not make of a woman a one-dimensional human as embodied in the word, "housewife." She should be mother, worker, artist, writer, doctor, scientist, professor, political leader, and/or government official. She should have the desire, and the ability to implement it, to reach for the stars. This can come only when men, too, are free, and when capitalism has been superseded by a collectivist, socialist society. In this sense, women in socialist lands, even though not yet fully emancipated from the hangovers of male prejudice, capitalist mentality, and economic difficulties, are a thousand times freer than women under capitalism. They have a right to work or stay at home, and are guaranteed free medical and hospital care, maternity leave with pay, child care centers, and opportunities to perfect their talents and abilities for their own greater happiness and the benefit of society.

## The Equal Rights Amendment

Disagreement also exists on the proposed Equal Rights Amendment (ERA) to the Constitution. This Amendment was passed by Congress in 1972 and since then attempts are being made to get ratification by two-thirds of the states to become effective. There are differences having to do with the possible effects of this Amendment on state protective labor laws for women won over long decades of struggle.

Those who argue for ERA believe that its embodiment into the Constitution would have a profound effect on the moral and legal status of women and on their ability to win full equality.

Critics of the Amendment within the women's and labor movement agree with its principles, but fear these may prove empty generalities if they are not tied down to specifics, and that they may even have harmful consequences.

They cite the existence of laws in a number of states that protect women workers from excessively long hours of work, heavy weight-lifting, night work, and so forth. They also point to the situation in the state of California where for years the state minimum wage for women was somewhat higher than the federal minimum wage. They fear this would mean a cut in wages for California working women. "Other protections that [the California] state laws provide are: time-and-a-half pay after eight hours of work per day, as opposed to the federal law of after 40 hours a week; and rest periods every four hours, as opposed to no federal provisions for rest periods. The protective orders for women also include some 50 'health, welfare, and safety' measures covering lighting, ventilation, seats on the job, elevator services, toilets,'' and many others.[17]

Some trade unionists and working women fear that these gains will be wiped away if ERA is ratified. Myra Wolfgang, militant vice-president of the Hotel, Motel and Restaurant Employees Union, and the secretary-treasurer of Local 705 in Detroit, is for women's equality but opposed to the Equal Rights Amendment. It ''is the wrong instrument,'' she claims. Responding to the pro-Amendment argument that 78 percent of doctors in the Soviet Union are women, as compared with only 9 percent here, she answers: ''The reason so many women were able to become doctors was that the government by legal decrees established legislation which made it tenable for them to become doctors. The legislation was designed specifically for women, it gave them special benefits.''

She points out that, ''when a woman is interning to become a doctor in Russia, the hospital is not permitted to let her work on Sundays, on holidays, or on any days her children are not in school. But this is a recognition of the role of the mother, and, incidentally, special protective legislation that would be outlawed with an Equal Rights Amendment.''[18]

On the other hand, many women, including trade unionists, believe that the special protective laws for women are themselves discriminatory. They prevent women from working longer hours where they can, and thus permit men to accumulate overtime pay. In some industries and occupations this may mean double and triple time for Sundays and holidays, and time-and-a-half for general overtime. It is also argued that the special protective laws for women are already unenforceable because of Title VII of the 1964 Civil Rights Act, which outlawed, among other things, discrimination in employment because of sex.

Unions have interpreted this Act as extending to one sex beneficial laws affecting the other, not driving both down to the lowest common denominator. The corporations and the courts interpret the Act another way — as removing protective laws for women. Some companies hesitated to take away these protections until ERA entered the picture, but now such actions have been increasing.

In California, a special measure was carried by both houses of the state legislature extending existing protective laws to men as well. Governor

Ronald Reagan vetoed it . . Then a district court knocked down the state law requiring overtime pay for women after eight hours of work a day. Thus the concern of some that they would lose benefits of laws on minimum wages, rest hours and safety requirements, "represented valid fears," according to a recent report. The report believes there should have been an active campaign to insure "the continuation of these protections for all workers."[19]

Be that as it may, it is now too late to backtrack. With only a few more states needed for ratification, the important thing is to end this source of division and unite the women's and labor movements for the struggle to gain full equality for women without the loss of whatever real protections were previously attained. This is the essence of the changed position of the AFL-CIO on ERA, adopted at its 1973 Convention. Noting that state protective laws were being scuttled under Title VII of the Civil Rights Act, it called for the ratification of ERA as a necessary "symbol" of commitment to women's equality. This, too, was the position of the women's trade union conference which called for work to ratify ERA and to gain "legislation to provide both sexes with the protection of statutes originally aimed at protecting women."

Deteriorating economic conditions and mass unemployment have already hit women hard. Employers have been taking advantage of a buyers' labor market to further undermine women's job opportunities, wages, and working conditions. The extent to which this succeeds will depend increasingly on the state of the labor movement and women's allegiance to it.

## Sex Bias Inside Unions

Most sections of organized labor are ill prepared to take advantage of the rising tide of women's awareness and militancy. At a time when women are especially conscious of their subordinate place in society, and are winning more and more elective posts in government, a glance at the situation in the House of Labor is not likely to inspire them. The august Executive Council of the AFL-CIO is an exclusive men's club. Not one woman sits among its 35 men. Women make up at least half the membership of 26 unions, but represent only 4.7 percent of union leadership posts.[20] In 1970, 45 unions with a combined membership of 2.2 million workers reported no women members at all.[21] The Ladies Garment Workers, with an 80-percent women membership, has one lone woman among its 20 vice-presidents. The Amalgamated Clothing Workers, with a 75-percent women membership, also has only one woman among 28 vice-presidents.

In 1952, only 30 women held 31 elective and appointive national union posts. Two decades later this had risen to 33 women in 37 positions. Even this slight increase may be illusiory, for legal, legislative and public relations posts were not considered in the 1952 survey. Out of 177 unions reporting, the 1972 survey showed 15 elected national union offices occupied by women. Appointed posts were: three research directors, three educational directors, six heads of social insurance departments, three editors, one in legal activities, and three each in legislative and public relations work.[23] The percentage of women in official posts is somewhat better in employee associations.

Thus, even when women are given posts of responsibility, these tend to be in peripheral areas, not in the actual leadership of the union. There are some exceptions. Dolores Huerta, vice-president of the United Farm Workers was responsible for negotiating the very first union contracts and was in charge of negotiations for five years. She believes that women are good negotiators because they have patience, tenacity, and "no big ego trips to overcome." It also "unnerves the growers" to negotiate with women because they dislike treating women as equals, and because women bring in ethical questions "like how our kids live."[23] Dolores Huerta is also involved in every other aspect of union activity. Another exception is Doris Turner, secretary of the National Health and Hospital Union. How many other unions entrust women with leading responsibilities?

A GREAT deal of change is needed if the labor movement is to be responsive to the new awareness of women and the new opportunities this presents. More than 80 percent of working women are not in unions. To begin to tap this huge reservoir of energy and latent power is one of the greatest challenges confronting organized labor.

CLUW represents an important new development. It is being threatened by attempts of certain unions to dominate it, and of small ultra-Left sects to take over local chapters for their own purposes. It can succeed only to the extent that it becomes a mass democratic expression of trade union women and compels the entire labor movement to face up to the issue of women's equality in an entirely new way.

IN 1963, Eugene Varga, Hungarian-born Soviet economist, considered the majority of American industrial workers to be a labor aristocracy in comparison with workers of other capitalist countries. He recognized the existence of widespread poverty, greater unemployment and far lower wages for minority and casual workers. Yet he calculated that the wages of West European workers were approximately "only a half or a third of those of their American counterparts." In comparison with workers in underdeveloped countries, he wrote, "U.S. workers earn in a week as much as workers in neighboring Mexico earn in a month, and as much as African workers earn in two or three months." From these facts Varga concluded that "the layer of the labor aristocracy is wider in the United States today than it was in Britain even during the period of its highest prosperity."[1]

Varga was referring to the period in Britain from 1850 to 1890, when traces of the earlier militant Chartist movement had vanished, and socialism had disappeared as a significant trend among the workers. Speaking of the corruption in British labor circles at the time, Engels wrote to Marx in 1858 that this "was indeed connected with the fact that the British proletariat is becoming more and more bourgeoisified." This, he added, was more or less natural "for a nation that exploits the whole world."[2] Later, in 1882, Engels replied to a query about British working-class views with the caustic comment that the worker thinks about colonial policy and politics generally "as does the bourgeoisie" and "daily shares the feast of England's monopoly of the world market and the colonies."[3]

This has been true of the American working class to a certain extent. Britain, an island power, always depended more on foreign trade than does the United States, with its vast continental expanse. British capitalism earned immense superprofits from its monopoly over world markets and colonial possessions. This was the source of the money which bought greater domestic working-class docility.

American capitalism has never held a similar monopolistic position in world markets and colonies, although since World War II it has occupied a commanding position in the world capitalist economy. U.S. foreign investments exceed those of all other countries, and its multinational giants have their claws in every region of the nonsocialist world, drawing from these immense tribute. Varga aptly observes, however, that the direct returns from these investments, vast though they be, are insufficient to explain the traditionally higher standard of living of American workers. In his view, the principal source of higher wages is "the rapid growth of labor productivity which is not accompanied by a corresponding shortening of the working time."[4] He cites official government statistics which show that labor productivity increased some 40 percent from 1947 to 1960. But in the same period the workweek remained the same and consumer prices rose by more than 25 percent. In other words, according to Varga, the main source of the higher wages paid in this country was a considerable rise in the rate of labor exploitation of American workers.

It would be a mistake, however, to minimize the significance of foreign investments and trade to the national economy. The direct tribute from foreign investments not only helps raise the general rate of profit for American corporations, but is based upon control over vast foreign sources of essential raw materials. The United States is endowed with immense natural riches, but these are insufficient to meet current needs. Domestic resources have been squandered and depleted at an ever accelerating pace. This was already evident a quarter-century ago when the Paley Commission made its report to the President. It showed that only about one-third of the hundred-odd essential minerals was fully supplied by our own resources. Another third came almost entirely from abroad, and the remaining third came partly from abroad and partly from domestic output. "Of 72 'strategic and critical' materials," said the report, "the United States imported all of its supplies in more than 40, and part of its supplies in all the rest."[5] The problem has become far more aggravated since then. One observation of the commission deserves repeating: "The United States appetite for material is gargantuan — and so far, insatiable."

The ability of U.S. corporations to obtain and control foreign sources of raw materials relates to much more than the direct superprofits earned from these investments. Without such imports much of domestic industrial production would be brought to a halt. The ability to exploit these resources abroad, and at the least possible cost, has much to do with the ability of U.S. concerns to maximize their profits and, from these, to pay somewhat higher wages to workers.

## European Labor Gaining

Eugene Varga was undoubtedly correct in estimating that the average wage of American workers was considerably higher than in Western Europe. Yet, the extent of the disparity may be somewhat exaggerated.

Labor movements in Europe have never depended exclusively on economic struggles and pure trade union tactics to obtain results. They have always combined economic with political action. Many strikes have been frankly political, in support of one or another legislative demand. Italian workers have conducted general stoppages over issues of social security, housing, regional pay differentials, etc. As a consequence, European workers have won some rights American workers do not possess. In most European countries, for example, employers do not have the unilateral power to lay off or discharge workers. They have a moral and legal obligation to maximize employment. Health and hospital insurance is universal; pensions and retirement plans are governmental, not private; and the multibillion dollar private pension funds in this country find limited counterparts elsewhere.

In a study of the world's labor movements, Everett Kassalow notes that the various fringe benefits won by unions in this country are a reflection "of labor's inability to make a big enough breakthrough on the legislative front. Indeed, when supplementary pensions were first won in the mass-production industries of the United States in the late 1940s, some key labor leaders believed that this was but a prelude, a tool to break down obstacles to an improved *legislated* social security system."[6] [Emphasis in original.]

As we now know; it did not turn out this way. Yet in 1956 in France, when the Renault workers won three weeks' vacation with pay — a week longer than that provided by law—legislation soon followed making this universal for all workers. By 1966, French workers were entitled to 24 work days of vacation with pay for all employees with one year of service. In several European countries employers are compelled by law to grant workers an additional week's pay as a vacation bonus, over and above their regular wages for the time off.[7] Compare this with the United States. According to the Department of Labor, only 25 percent of blue-collar workers and 26 percent of office workers with at least *fifteen years of service* received four weeks vacation with pay in 1971-2. And only 64 percent of blue collar workers with twenty five years of service received four weeks vacation with pay.[8]

According to the International Labor Office, the percentage of gross national income going to social security benefits in 1963 was more than twice as high in the countries of Western Europe as in the United States. It was 6.2 percent in the United States, but 14.6 percent, for example, in France. In Canada, just across the border, it was 50 percent higher than in this country.[9]

In 1969, 93 percent of the independent nations of the world had social security programs. Some of these offered "maternity and work-injury payments and family allowances for care of children," in addition to unemployment, disability, old-age and survivors' insurance, and medicare. Sixty-eight nations — including all European countries — had sickness and maternity programs. Cash sick benefits in most countries are about 50 to 75 percent of average earnings, and working mothers receive wage payments for periods just prior to and after childbirth.[10] In France, pregnant women workers get 90 percent of their wages for 14 weeks of maternity leave.

Even in respect to direct wage earnings, the American worker has been slipping, in comparison with workers in other capitalist countries. It is extremely difficult to measure earning capacity by a mere conversion of currencies. As the recent devaluations of the dollar showed, it had been pegged in world markets far above its real value. Thus, by the summer of 1973, the value of the dollar had plummeted 30 percent in relation to the French franc, 34 percent to the Japanese yen, and 53 percent to the West German mark.

The difficulty of measuring living standards just by converting foreign currencies into dollars, can be seen by the example of Japan. Exchanging yen for dollar equivalents in 1965, the average Japanese worker earned only 17 percent of the hourly wage of an American worker. Yet in the ownership of durable goods, the disparity was not nearly as great. Fully one-half of Japanese wage-earning families owned their own homes. In the United States, 62 percent of *all* families owned them. In Japan, 90 percent of the nonagricultural households had televisions; in the United States it was 92 percent of all homes. In Japan, 70 percent of the families had electric washing machines; in this country, it was 72 percent. In Japan, 60 percent had electric refrigerators; in this country, it was 85 percent.[11] Only in respect to automobile ownership was the disparity great.

The present trend shows unmistakeably that the workers of other capitalist countries are rapidly gaining on their American cousins. According to the Bureau of Labor Statistics, real hourly earnings of manufacturing workers for the period 1960 to 1971 rose more slowly in the United States than in any other country listed. The average annual increase in this country was 1.3 percent. In Britain, it was 3.4 percent; France, 4.4 percent; West Germany, 5.9 percent; Italy, 6.8 percent. Japan topped the list with an average yearly rise of 7.7 percent.[12]*

Since then, real income for workers in the United States has been declining steadily. Average wage gains are now considerably below yearly price rises. This was true even before the economic crisis began in 1974. With unemployment doubling, and many additional millions working only part time, real purchasing power has been dropping precipitously.

Two conclusions stand out. First, despite a historically higher standard of living which continued to rise for most of the post-World War II period, American workers are now falling behind the advances made by workers in other countries. Secondly, for the first time since the thirties, the purchasing power of the average American worker is declining absolutely as compared with yesterday, and relatively as compared with workers elsewhere.

Both of these trends are new. Both arise from an entirely new situation, quite different from that which followed World War II and lasted a full

* How rapidly the United States is falling behind can be seen in comparing real hourly earnings from 1967 to 1973. Taking the year 1967 as 100, the increases were as follows: Austria, 31 percent; Belgium, 48 per cent; Britain, 30 percent; Canada, 23 percent; Denmark, 45 percent; France, 47 percent; West Germany, 35 percent; Italy, 65 percent; Japan, 84 percent; Netherlands, 36 percent; Norway, 24 percent; Sweden, 27 percent; Switzerland, 30 percent, but the United States only 8 percent.[13]

quarter of a century. Both will have a great deal to do with the development of the class struggle and working class consciousness in the United States.

## Influence of Socialist States on Western Europe

A number of interrelated factors explain the more rapid rise of living standards in Western Europe. The level of working-class organization, consciousness and struggle is higher. And West European capitalism is in an improved competitive position vis-a-vis the United States. There is another important, although frequently overlooked, factor — the geographic proximity of Eastern Europe and the influence of the socialist states on events in Western Europe.

Wolfgang Abendroth, a professor of politics at the University of Marburg in West Germany, discusses this in his recent book, *A Short History of the European Working Class*. Abendroth believes that it is impossible to discuss postwar working-class developments in Western Europe without taking into account the influence of Eastern Europe. He writes:

> The current standard of living of the working class, which is much higher than in earlier periods, could not have been attained in any of the European countries without the rival existence of socialist states. After the Second World War the capitalist classes were convinced that the only way to retain the loyalty of the working classes and prevent them from being influenced by the policies of socialist countries was to grant them concessions. This also accounts for the extent of democratic rights still enjoyed by the working class movement in many countries. The October Revolution and the other Socialist revolutions which arose in the wake of the Second World War thus remain a vital factor in the struggle of the working class, although this is seldom realized by the reformists.

Abendroth amplifies this theme further:

> In particular the fate of the workers' struggles in the capitalist West is strongly interconnected with the fate of socialism in the East. To begin with, the mere existence of a non-capitalist zone in Europe is a factor of crucial significance for the class struggle in the capitalist countries. It induces caution in the ruling class of the capitalist half of Europe and sets certain limits on their prosecution of the class war. The working class parties in the West have a direct interest, even from the point of view of the reformist wing, in the continued existence of the socialist states in the world; anything that weakens these states also

gravely weakens the position of the workers inside every capitalist country.[14]

This is more evident in Western Europe where, historically, the working class has been socialist-minded and where the socialist countries are literally next door. It is also evident in the underdeveloped and former colonial lands, for whom the socialist countries are concrete examples of national liberation and economic development free of imperialist domination. But socialism in power also has an influence on the struggle in the United States, not only in the anti-Communist hysteria whipped up by the ruling class, but in the positive compelling of concessions which otherwise would not be granted.

When the United States Attorney General filed his brief with the Supreme Court in the famous 1954 school desegregation case, he employed a political argument in asking for a favorable ruling. He told the Court that "racial discrimination furnishes grist for the Communist propaganda mills," and that "other peoples cannot understand how such practice can exist in a country which professes to be a staunch supporter of freedom, justice and democracy." Supreme Court Justice Earl Warren, addressing the American Bar Association in 1955, emphasized the same point:

> We are living in a world of ideas and are going through a war of ideas. Everywhere there is a contest for the hearts and minds of men. Every political concept is under scrutiny. Our American system like all others is on trial at home and abroad. The way it works; the manner in which it solves the problems of our day . . . will in the long run do more to make it both secure and the object of adulation than the number of hydrogen bombs we stockpile.

We are entering a period in which the growing stability and increasing prosperity of socialist states will have an even more profound effect on the struggle in capitalist countries, including the United States. The contrast between a rising socialist system, and the decline and decay of the strongest capitalist imperial power, beset by inflation, mass unemployment and a breakdown in public services, will begin to make the ideas of socialism more meaningful to large numbers of the American workers. Conversely, the fear of the influence of such ideas will make sections of capital more amenable to further concessions, even while they seek to discredit the socialist states by exaggerating and distorting mistakes. Concessions have already been extracted by the workers in capitalist states that would not have been won except for the tremendous accomplishments of the socialist lands in the short historic period of their existence. Starting from economic bases much lower than those in the West, and compelled to pull themselves up by their own efforts, they have accomplished for working people what capitalism — even in countries of relatively high living standards — has not and could not attain.

In no socialist country are there the extremes of poverty and wealth to be found in this country. Completely absent also is the degrading poverty of our urban ghettos and rural slums. True, relatively few own cars. But there is cheap and efficient public transit; no one goes hungry; every person has free medical and hospital care; unemployment is unknown; men may retire with full pensions at age 60 and women at age 55; education is free from grade school through university; and students in higher institutions receive monthly government grants to meet the expenses of living. Thus there is less fear of tomorrow or of sickness or old age. And the workers know that as long as there is peace, living standards will move steadily upward.

Often American journalists make invidious comparisons between what an American and a Soviet worker earns in wage or salary. One fact is usually omitted. Workers' income in socialist countries comes from two separate funds. Wages and salaries are paid from the individual consumption fund. And social benefits, which accrue to *all* workers irrespective of their individual earnings, come from the social consumption fund. A portion of this fund goes to workers in monetary form, by way of pensions, student grants, illness and disability allowances, and other forms of social insurance. The largest portion goes in special services unknown in this country — workers' sanitoria and vacation resorts; summer camps for children (Soviet children usually leave the cities for the summer); health protection; subsidized rents (the average worker's family rent is never higher than 10 percent of income); subsidized sports and cultural activities, and the institutions and facilities that make these available to the public.

In the Soviet Union, for example, a pregnant working woman is entitled to 56 days off before child birth and 56 days off after birth *with full pay*. Should there be complications, her postnatal leave is extended to seventy days. If she prefers to stay home with her child, she is given a leave of absence from her job with a right to return within one year. When and if she returns to work, her baby is cared for in a nursery adjacent to the workplace. If she nurses the child, she is given a half-hour with pay every three hours for that purpose. When the child grows older, the mother can place it during working hours in a day-care center or kindergarten.[15]

Social welfare in socialist countries begins with the cradle and continues all through one's life.

## Differences in Labor Organizations

Variations can be found in the way different labor movements are organized and function. In Japan, unions are still influenced by pre-capitalist, paternal management relations. The basic bargaining unit is neither craft nor industrial, but "unity of workers of the same employer." In large firms, "regular employees" cannot be laid off or fired; their jobs are secure until retirement. The size of the work force is regulated by increasing or decreasing the number of "temporary workers," many of whom are immigrants, or the number of the employees of smaller subcontractors. There is a "spring offensive" each year in which all unions simultaneously begin collective bargaining or, if necessary, go out on strike. Building trades workers are the most poorly organized, the Left is strongest among the workers in the state sector, which is also often the most militant.[16]

The German labor movement arose, as did a number of others on the European continent, at a time of excess labor supply and when the bourgeois revolution had not yet been consummated. This combination of factors placed greater emphasis on political movement and struggle than on workers' economic bargaining strength. "It is a fact of history that the first stable organizations of the German labor movement were political parties, which later often initiated the founding of trade unions."[17] As a consequence, trade unions tended to be neglected and treated as an appendix "to the political branch of labor." Frederick Engels criticized the draft of the 1875 Gotha Program of the German Social Democratic Party for this neglect. He complained to August Bebel, a leader of the German party, that "there is not a word about the organization of the working class as a class by means of the trade unions. And this is a very essential point, for this is the real class organization of the proletariat, in which it carries on its daily struggles with capital, in which it trains itself, and which nowadays even amid the worst reaction . . . can simply no longer be smashed."[18] Since World War II, the West German labor movement has undergone change. As a result of the acute labor shortage that has persisted until recently, greater emphasis has been placed on collective bargaining. Meanwhile, the Social-Democratic Party gave up socialism as an objective.

In Italy and France, the workers are split into different federations influenced and led by different political-ideological blocs. In both countries, the strongest federations are led by the Left, which, however, would prefer to see a single united federation in each country in which leadership is shared between representatives of varying tendencies in accord with their actual support in the rank and file. This concept is embodied in the founding document of the Italian General Confederation of Labor (CGIL), adopted in June 1944. The care with which minority views are protected is to be seen in the following section:

a) The CGIL is founded on the principle of the fullest internal democracy. All the posts, therefore, on every level of the organization, shall be filled by election from below, respectively by the general assembly of the local union or by the assembly of regularly elected delegates. In every leadership body, from top to bottom, the proportional participation of minorities shall be assured.

b) In all the organizations of the CGIL maximum freedom of expression must be assured to all members and reciprocal respect of every political opinion and religious faith practiced.

c) The CGIL is independent of all political parties. It shall associate itself, whenever it is regarded as desirable, with the action of the democratic parties which are the expression of the working masses, both for the safeguarding and development of the people's liberties and for the defense of specific interests of the workers and the country.[19]

A striking example of the same concern for democracy and the representation of all political tendencies in the leadership, was seen in the Chilean United Confederation of Labor (CUT). Prior to the military-fascist coup that overthrew the democratic prosocialist administration of President Salvadore Allende, CUT's election of executive council members was conducted in a way that would guarantee no domination by any single political tendency. If the Communists won the presidency, as they did, the second highest post went to the Socialists, since its candidate ran second in votes received. Proportional representation was accorded to other tendencies in the labor movement, depending on their support in the ranks. The officers and the executive council were not elected by a convention of the hand-picked top brass of the various affiliated unions, as is true of AFL-CIO Conventions.* They were elected by the direct vote

* In France, for example, the conventions of the CGT are composed primarily of working delegates. At its 39th Congress, in 1975, 81 percent of the delegates came from the shop floor and only 19 percent were trade union officials at various levels. Over 25 percent of the delegates were women and over 15 percent under twenty years of age.

of the membership in the locals of every union affiliated to CUT. These elections were held on a number of specified days and took place where the maximum number of workers could attend, often in the workplace itself. It is as if the workers of all the unions affiliated to the AFL-CIO had the opportunity to vote directly for the AFL-CIO president and executive council. In this way the leadership would probably be a lot different, and far more attuned to the thinking and the needs of the membership.

There are still other differences between foreign and American unions. The dues "check-off" is generally unknown in most other countries, although some officialdoms seek to impose it. In the Soviet Union, dues are voluntary and collected by stewards who sell stamps that serve as proof of payment.[20]

In most European capitalist countries, union-employer agreements are regional or national in character, and frequently general in their specifications. Local plant bargaining is conducted by plant councils whose rights are often established by law and are not generally part of a union structure. Thus, tightly organized workplace unions that characterize the labor scene in this country tend to be absent in Western Europe. In this respect, many European union leaderships look with envious eyes on the strong workplace structure of unionism in the United States.

The closed union shop is also unknown abroad, where membership in trade unions is strictly voluntary. This is true in socialist countries as well. According to a report of the International Labor Office, about 93 percent of the workers in the Soviet Union are members of trade unions. Such membership "is not a condition for obtaining employment." The high percentage of union membership is due to the fact that Soviet trade unions perform many functions for their members in addition to representing them in collective bargaining. "Trade union contributions are relatively low and the welfare and other facilities controlled or provided by the unions are so extensive that few workers see any advantage in refusing to join."[21]

In the Soviet Union the shop form of trade union organization is primary. The most important body in the plant is the factory trade union committee. This committee is elected by secret ballot directly by the workers, and every candidate must receive more than 50 percent of the votes cast to be considered elected. A quorum of at least two-thirds of the members is necessary for an election to take place.[22]

One feature of trade unionism in this country generally unknown elsewhere is the so-called International character of unions. This does not mean that they are international in outlook — quite the contrary — but that they have members and claim jurisdiction outside the United States; specifically, in Canada, Puerto Rico and Panama. While the logic of such organizational extension flows from the extensions of capital, its net effect is to place the labor movements of these two neighboring countries under the domination of leaderships which, in the main, support the aggressive and exploitative aims of U.S. imperialism.

"Those international unions which provide the greatest degree of autonomy for the Canadian membership tend to be the progressive led unions. Conversely, those international unions which refuse autonomy tend to be the more reactionary unions."[23] The UE for example, has been virtually autonomous in Canada since it was founded. "In 1956, this autonomy was given constitutional recognition by the UE international convention." The ILWU took similar action in the late 1950s. And the Mine, Mill and Smelter Workers Union, before it merged with the steel union, amended its constitution "to provide for its existence in Canada as a distinct Canadian entity." "It is noteworthy that all three unions linked these decisions to the struggle for Canadian independence from US imperialism, the common struggle of Canadian and US workers against their common foe."[24]

An example of how reactionary unions react to the growing demand for Canadian autonomy is to be seen in the textile industry. By the efforts of Canadians alone, the United Textile Workers (UTWA) grew in Canada to some 12,000 members. They pressed aggressively for Canadian autonomy within the International. But in 1950 the leadership of the textile union "moved to destroy the Canadian district's autonomy." In 1952, while the union was locked in a bitter battle with the Dominion Textile Company in Quebec, "the international headquarters decided its time had come. It moved in on the Canadian organization and dismissed the entire staff." The Canadian section responded by severing its links with the International and establishing itself as a "sovereign Canadian union in the textile industry."[25]

Canadian corporations are ambivalent about workers seeking union autonomy, fearing that such unions may be more radical than those ruled from across the border. When the Canadian Confederation of National Trade Unions (CNTU) was organizing the workers of the Canadian Celanese Company in the mid-fifties, the company would have nothing to do with it. Instead, it sought to do business with the United Textile Workers. But in other instances Canadian-based corporations preferred conservative-led *Canadian* unions to more progressive U.S.-based unions.

Puerto Rico's situation is even more complicated and onerous. Puerto Rico is not a developed, independent capitalist country as is Canada, but an island nation completely subjugated by the United States. This is graphically exemplified by the disparity in wages between workers in the United States and Puerto Rico. According to the U.S. Department of Labor, the average weekly earnings of a production worker in the United States in 1972 was $150. The average wage of a production worker in Puerto Rico for the same year was only $70.[27]*

"Trade Union Colonialism," as it is aptly called in Puerto Rico, has a long history, starting shortly after the U.S. occupation of the island in 1898. But its greatest expansion came a half-century later, when Puerto Rico's colonial status was reaffirmed under the prettified seal of "Commonwealth." It was then that a distorted form of industrialization began, the object of which was not the economic development of the island, but its greater use as a cheap labor base for U.S. companies.

The women's garment industry was organized in the late fifties. Many of the plants were organized "over the top," that is, "in conference in New York with the leaders of the women's garment industry." "This technique," explains a writer for the daily *San Juan Star,* "meant that garment workers in Puerto Rico obtained the protection of a union contract painlessly, with no risk and little effort. ILGWU contracts, in turn, were for years notably painless for management."[28]

Most of the "internationals" — as U.S.-based unions are known in Puerto Rico — are of the union-conglomerate type. They organize whomever and wherever they can without regard to jurisdiction. The Seamen's International Union (SIU), in 1970, represented more than 20,000 workers in over 1,500 different job classifications in 82 separate industries. The Teamsters, another conglomerate union, including in its ranks telephone operators, hotel, brewery and soft drink workers, croupiers in gambling casinos, motion picture operators, construction and other industrial workers and, of course, teamsters.

Recently an important change has taken place. Some of the 35 "internationals" operating in Puerto Rico are on the defensive, facing a

---

* An ad of the Puerto Rican government in the *Wall Street Journal* of May 1, 1975 states that "Puerto Rican workers are unsurpassed in productivity. A worker in Puerto Rico returns $4.03 in value for every dollar earned . . ."

growing challenge from what are known as "local unions." "Wrapped within this rivalry," says the *San Juan Star,* "is local resentment for the 'trade union colonialism' practiced by some internationals, and the dislike and distrust of almost all the internationals for the Marxism espoused by some local leaders." It concludes, "Local unions are on the rise to the probable chagrin of the Commonwealth government, the alarm of some industrialists, and the satisfaction of most persons working for the independence of Puerto Rico."[29]

The change is not limited to "local unions." Larger numbers of workers have been swept into the movement for Puerto Rican independence; and the success of socialist Cuba has spurred socialist thinking. Some of the "internationals" also made use of *independentistas* with the aim of winning credibility with Puerto Rican workers. As a consequence there is radical influence and leaders in some of the "internationals" as well.

It is to the advantage of U.S. workers to support the movement for Puerto Rican independence, as well as to end every form of trade union colonialism whether in Puerto Rico, Panama, Canada, or anywhere else. Only when workers of each country have complete autonomous control of their unions can they conduct the kind of effective struggle that puts an end to cheap labor competition and raises the living standards of all workers. It is the responsibility of progressive workers of this country to oppose every manifestation of trade union colonialism in their own unions. Canadian delegates to conventions of "internationals" in this country have given examples of solidarity in leading the fight against anti-Communist constitutional provisions and for more progressive policies. Now that an important trade union Left is arising in Puerto Rico, it is important that there be unity in the common fight.

SOCIOLOGISTS have made much of the fact that some workers list themselves as middle class when interviewed about their class identity. This is seen as evidence that workers are being homogenized into one great middle-class society. But when the question is placed more concretely, by listing the working class among alternative choices, many switch their replies to working class. In one such survey, one-third to a half of the respondents did that.[1]

Much depends also on where and when the questions are asked. The same workers who say they are "middle class" in the more relaxed air of their homes, may reply "working class," in the turbulence of the workplace. "If you go to a man in the evening and ask about the neighbors, he will think about status symbols and styles of life — consumption, house, car, leisure uses; if you talk to him on the job and ask about the people there, he will think of authority — the authority of bosses, of skill and expertise. The average American is a Veblenian at home; a modified Marxist at work."[2]

This variance in worktime and leisure-time response is seen in Britain as well. When some British workers were asked to explain the contradiction, their answers were revealing: "I am working class only in the works, but outside I'm like anyone else." "Here I am a worker, but outside I'm a human being." "Outside I mix with all classes." And, "Class distinctions seem to be stronger in the works than outside."

This duality betrays a recognition of the stigma which bourgeois society places on those who are blue-collar workers. The same self-consciousness showed itself among those who listed themselves as working class from the outset. One explained, "It would be snobbish if I said otherwise." Another, "I regard myself as working class, while others would take me for middle class."[3] These reactions are not surprising in societies where bourgeois values are touted and manual workers are considered to be Archie Bunkers.

## Individualism Versus Solidarity

Hope to escape the working class by entry into the middle class was a viable dream for many in the past. It no longer is — and most workers know this. A distinctive difference between working-class and middle-class mentality relates to the approach to social goals. The worker's quest tends to be for security; the middle-class search tends to be for personal advancement. This difference has long been noted by sociologists.

A study of class structure and class mobility in the 19th century found that even then, with the greater opportunities provided by an open frontier, most workers sought "maximum security rather than mobility out of the working class." One expression of this was the stress on the importance of savings, rather than on "sending children to higher learning and thus increasing their mobility."[4]

Selig Perlman's classic work on the theory of the labor movement, written in the twenties, dealt with this phenomenon. Comparing the psychology of the bourgeois and petty-bourgeois mind with that of the manual worker, he concluded that the business person is basically an individualist, "a competitor, par excellence." The manual worker on the other hand, because his or her opportunities are restricted, is also compelled to seek restriction of the power over him. But he cannot do this by himself in competition with others. It requires collective, group effort. "A collective disposal of opportunity," Perlman wrote, "is as natural to the manual group as laissez-faire to the business man."[5]

From this he surmised that the worker's concern is narrowly focused on attaining "job security"; that is, group control over limited job opportunities. This he considered to be the distinctive, "homegrown," "practical and empirical" ideology of American trade unionism. He saw it as a rejection of the more radical and socialist ideology of European labor and of intellectuals. Perlman credited socialism with "correctly grasping a part of the psychology of the worker — his desire for solidarity," but he believed that it overlooked the worker's "unwillingness to become completely merged with his own class."[6]

The worker has not yet become completely merged with his own class. The ideology of business unionism bases itself on the need to achieve security for a more privileged group of workers, even at the expense of others and the class as a whole. Yet Perlman, too, recognized a difference between the individualist strivings of the average middle-class person and the "desire for solidarity" on the part of the worker.

## "Getting By" Rather Than "Getting Ahead"

In a study of recent changes in the working class, Professor Kassalow finds no evidence of workers evolving into a middle-class style of life or toward middle-class values. Unlike the middle class, manual workers still place a greater premium on security than on promotion. They are not less money-minded or less desirous of accumulating appliances and gadgetry, but the emphasis is on "getting by" rather than "getting ahead." He cites a survey in which "a majority of manual workers thought it more important for the government to guarantee every person a decent and steady standard of living than to make certain that there are good opportunities for each person to get ahead on his own." Business, professional and white-collar groups demurred; "they rated 'opportunities' much higher."[7]

Kassalow refers to other studies which found "that manual workers generally showed little interest in advancement, even to the position of foreman." He also mentions a discussion about college education he held with a group of officers of a steelworker's local. Several of them remarked that five or ten years ago they would have been indifferent to the idea of a college education for their children. Now, with radical job changes taking place, they had become convinced that a college education was important if their children were "to make good money." This more positive attitude toward education is not really middle class, Kassalow says for, "In a typical middle-class family the emphasis would be as much on the higher social status a college degree confers, as on the kind of a job a college degree can lead to."[8]

This evidence of a difference in outlook between manual workers and middle-class people never occurs in pure form in real life. A worker is never just a worker, period. He and she are also other things, influenced partly by sex, age, race, nationality, religion, upbringing, education, craft, skill, and so forth. In a capitalist society, for example, no one is immune to its ideology. Workers still accept the superiority nostrums and racial prejudices of American imperialism. Workers also display individualistic traits and ambitions, and a desire to climb out of their class up the social ladder. And conversely, professional and white-collar workers who may still identify with middle-class values, often begin to opt for solidarity and unity. The growth of white-collar and professional unionism attests to this.

The working-class search for security through solidarity is weakened and dissipated by the influence of other tendencies. Yet it constantly reasserts itself on an ever expanding scale, fed by the conditions of a society in which insecurity for workers is endemic. It contains the germ of the idea of socialism — of a society of cooperation rather than one in which the advancement of some is at the expense of the advancement of all.

PERLMAN wrote that American labor's "big problem" has been that of "staying organized." No other labor movement, he pointed out, has been so fragile. This was due to a "lack of class consciousness" or of "spontaneous class solidarity" which "weakened class cohesiveness." He explained the "ruthless suppression" of dual unions and outlaw strikes on the part of existing unions as arising from the need for "self protection against an environment aimed at undermining internal solidarity." He contrasted this with the situation in Britain, where "workers act together in strikes."

"The cause of this lack of psychological cohesiveness in American labor," wrote Perlman, "is the absence, by and large, of a completely 'settled' wage earning class." Greater class fluidity and ethnic, linguistic, religious and cultural heterogeneity operated against class solidarity.[9] But, less than a decade after this explanation of the historic fragility of the labor movement, labor made its greatest breakthroughs. The many millions of workers organized during that upsurge, and since, have remained organized.

At the time of writing, Perlman had reason for his pessimism. The twenties witnessed an open-shop employer's drive that wiped out two-fifths of organized labor. Many people believed the period of "Coolidge prosperity" would be permanent. Perlman states that the "abundance created" by the "new Industrial Revolution" "appears to have reconciled, at least for the time being, the conflicting interests of profits and wages."[10]

Illusions of the same kind reappeared after World War II, but with one important difference. This time the labor movement was not demolished. It has been in a crisis of stagnation, but not of organizational fragility.

## New Levels of Awareness

This difference is more than numerical. It has carried with it a corresponding rise in trade union consciousness. This is not yet class consciousness in the Marxist sense, yet it is a level of consciousness considerably higher than in earlier periods. It also reflects a new level of social and political awareness.

One of the principle issues fought out in the thirties was whether the government had the responsibility for the economic welfare of the people. This battle was won. Workers no longer accept insecurity and bad times as "natural" disasters. They expect the government to assume responsibility. The days are long gone when a labor leader could argue, as did the AFL bureaucracy in the first years of the Great Depression, that unemployment compensation and social security were humiliating "doles" to workers, challenging their sense of independence and native "rugged individualism." Workers now judge political institutions and the system itself by how these provide a livelihood and a modicum of security.

Michael Harrington, the author and socialist, concludes that organized labor's support for what he calls, "social Keynesianism . . . is the result, not of instinct or intuition, but of class position." He believes "there is a working class 'for itself' with a political consciousness that goes far beyond 'job consciousness' and expresses itself in social reformism toward the society as a whole."[11]

Harrington is right when he points to greater social and political consciousness arising from class position and not merely from instinct. But he errs when he reads into this the existence of a working class "for itself." This phrase, borrowed from Marx, was meant to describe a working class conscious of its position in society, its relationship to other classes, its own class interests, and its historic role. To say this is where the labor movement is today is wishful thinking. It confuses a greater consciousness of the need for social reforms with a consciousness of the need to replace the capitalist system. This also raises the question of what Harrington means by socialism, and whether he does not limit this to mere reforms within the system.

Unfortunately and inescapably, the increase in political and social awareness on the part of the workers has not yet resulted in a greater class "for itself" consciousness. And to confuse these things does not help. Harrington has set himself the goal of making socialism a legitimate issue once again in the labor movement. The time for this is long overdue. But one should not pass off social reforms as socialism. Social reforms are needed and can be won on the road to socialism, but a socialist society can only result from a revolutionary replacement of capitalism.

At one time the issue of socialism played an important role in the labor movement. In 1912, Max Hayes of the Typographical Union, an open advocate of socialism and a member of the Socialist Party, ran for the presidency of the AFL against Gompers. He received 30 percent of the AFL convention's votes. This was a period of sharp, confrontational class relations, in which the government's open role as strikebreaker was as revealing and convincing as the bayonet on a state trooper's gun.

But when the corporations were compelled to accept organized labor and collective bargaining, which resulted in substantial gains for workers, illusions developed, and radical thinking about class relations seemed out of place, a throwback to the past.

The cold war and the anti-Communist witch-hunt of the fifties also played their part. With United States imperialism becoming the counterrevolutionary opponent of socialism everywhere, the defense of socialism at home became suspect — a dangerous foreign "ism" from which Americans had to be immunized. Unlike the days prior to the Russian Revolution, the victory of socialism in the Soviet Union and other countries now meant that socialist ideas were no longer utopian dreams to be tolerated by the ruling class. They were embodied in state form, and in substantial achievements, an ideological-political threat that the ruling class sought to extirpate. And because there is always a difference between utopia and reality, the new socialist states, with their problems of underdevelopment, military and diplomatic siege, their difficulties and often serious mistakes, seemed not as appealing to some as was the abstract dream.

These factors played their part in holding back a greater class consciousness, and reinforced a general consensus in support of the status quo. But it would be a mistake to exaggerate the depth of this consensus.

Strongly rooted among some, it is only tissue-paper thin among others.

Political participation for most people is largely formal and passive, argues Norman Birnbaum in a book on the crisis of industrial society. People are so enmeshed in personal problems, "above all in the struggle for material existence," that their politics are limited to acts of compliance, indistinguishable from an acceptance of routine. . . . Briefly, most persons do what they have to do without reflecting upon it. The degree of conscious political consent required of the modern working class, in other words, is not necessarily very large; routine may be counted upon to do what is needed."[12]

This is as true of internal union affairs as of political life generally. Misery and poverty are not sufficient to shake this lethargy. Where so much energy is consumed in just keeping alive, and where there does not seem to be a viable, political alternative, people tend to just "go along." Frustration, despair and cynicism take over. Workers may even get used to adverse conditions. What is needed to arouse them to break with routine and inertia, is some event, some impulse that breaks through and compels action. This may be some "small" event which acts as a spark setting off a mass of accumulated tinder. Such was the simple act of a Black woman in Montgomery, Alabama, in refusing to give up her bus seat to a white person. Or it can be a major event affecting the lives of many, like the Vietnam War, which aroused a whole generation of youth. Or it can be a major depression, such as occurred in the thirties, which brought millions of people into action.

For while hardship and suffering can become commonplace, a sudden drastic worsening of conditions can set off a chain reaction that can alter a situation from apparent consensus to widespread, militant challenge. Then, workers with even relatively high living standards can rise to new levels of militancy and consciousness. A worker that earns more may also have more to lose. Statistics show that the greater the worker's income, the greater the indebtedness. Hence, "Every threat to his standard of living, which has been raised so considerably, he views with great concern."[13]

Studies indicate that individual upward mobility tends to reinforce a lack of class consciousness. But where individuals slip to a lower rung it does not necessarily result in greater class consciousness. It oftens results in personal embitterment. Many such persons rallied around McCarthyism in the fifties, supported Barry Goldwater in 1964 and George Wallace since. But where "an entire stratum, craft or profession," or a class, "is declining," or being pushed down, "there is more chance of unity in misery and a collective . . . lashing out against the symbols of oppression."[14]

Where increased education does not lead to greater opportunities and income, this also becomes a source of mass discontent. And often where class grievances are combined with racial or religious-ethnic oppression, "we find Marxist 'class' consciousness in its most intense forms."[15]

There is nothing spontaneous or automatic about any of this. To lash out at "symbols of oppression" is not always the same as striking against the real sources of oppression. A symbol can be false; it can represent a distorted view of reality, and it can be consciously induced to manipulate and mislead public opinion. Such was the anti-Semitism of the Nazis; such is racism and anticommunism in the United States.

Whether class consciousness develops on a mass scale in the period ahead depends, therefore, on multiple factors. The intensified crisis of world capitalism, the crisis and decline of U.S. capitalism, the rise of socialism as a world force, provide the objective basis for large numbers of people to recognize that what is wrong is not something isolated, but integral to a social system whose day has passed. But the ability of the ruling class to project false symbols is not to be underestimated.

## Manipulating Public Opinion

We have witnessed a vast technological revolution in communications and mass media. News nowadays travels on electromagnetic airwaves and instant interpretation comes packaged with it. Daily newspaper circulation reached a total of 62 million in 1971,[16] but it is no longer the main medium for spot news. Radio and television have preempted first place. Nearly every person has a radio and every family a television.

This has both plus and minus aspects. People know more about the world, and more rapidly, than ever before. Airwaves have also pierced provincial insularity and narrow-mindedness. An isolated hermit in the snow-covered Rockies can listen to the same broadcast as a family in a teeming tenement in Manhattan. A single major TV show may be watched by upward of 50 million people. This is "not only something new under the sun, but something our ancestors could not even have imagined."[17]

Never before were so many dependent upon so few for their information and its interpretation. "Never before could the citizen be smothered and submerged in mass communications. Now an indeterminately large measure of what he sees, hears, learns and knows — as well as many of his attitudes and values — is presented to him by mass media.'' Television produces ''greater proximity — and less intimacy — than had ever previously existed.''[18]

In past generations religious superstition and church influence were powerful holds on peoples' thinking and action. With the greater dissemination of scientific knowledge this has waned. Organized religion itself is rent by the social convulsions of our time. But today a handful of powerful communication networks manipulate public opinion so adroitly that the lie is concealed in the half-truth. A survey conducted in December 1974 showed that over 750 radio and TV stations were owned directly by newspaper and magazine corporations.[19] The freedom to know, for the great majority, is the freedom to know what the media chains think they should know.

Only when divisions arise in the upper crust of society that compel one or another ruling group to appeal to public opinion does a greater part of the truth leak out. But when sharp class issues emerge which seem to threaten the system itself, the media becomes superclass-conscious. This explains the treatment of socialism and the socialist countries. The so-called socialism of the social-democratic parties of Europe, which does not disturb the economic foundations of capitalist rule, is tolerated, but any real attempts to introduce public ownership of the monopoly corporations is fiercely attacked. When it serves foreign policy, the dagger of hatred for socialism is sheathed somewhat, but the people are never told the truth about why more and more of the world is going socialist.

The rapid growth of mass class consciousness among American workers is not something that can be taken for granted. It will not come by itself. A great deal depends upon the ability of those with class and socialist consciousness to closely link up with the workers' movement, actively participate in its battles, and help workers draw more generalized conclusions from their experiences. Two things are paramount: the nonsectarian ability to work with others in a broader movement, and the readiness to project socialist-Communist convictions in an open and forthright manner.

THE WORKING class and labor movement can no longer meet their problems in old ways. It is this which underlines the need for a new labor radicalism.

The tendency of workers to seek security through common action with other workers will now manifest itself in more than narrow group, craft, occupational or single-union lines. Workers will be required to act together on a wider front if they are to be successful. Narrow group and sectional interests will still play their part, for there is no such thing as a "pure" tendency or movement, but events now press toward a more inclusive type of unity.

Construction workers, for example, will probably continue to demand jobs only for themselves. But with mass unemployment all about them, they need to join with others to compel the government to shift from military spending to spending for housing. In such a fight the racial minorities would be their staunchest allies, for their housing needs are greatest. This may not be sufficient to dispel the racial prejudices of white construction workers, but if it does not, all workers stand to lose.

Even when depression conditions are over, things will not return to where they were. A sluggish economy of stagnation and inflation will be with us. Mass unemployment and lowered living standards are the new reality. These are consequences of economic forces operating over many years. U.S. capitalism is now in decline, challenged increasingly in world capitalist markets by other capitalist rivals. The power and influence of the socialist world have also grown immensely, and with it the national liberation movement of former colonial and semicolonial states. The ability of U.S. capital to control and exploit foreign sources of cheap raw materials has therefore greatly diminished.

The very measures taken to counter depression have added to the toll of the unemployed. The *New York Times* reports speculation in business circles that "a sustained period of high unemployment might bring real change for the better in American work habits." Absentecism may even be reduced, it opines, "if employers can always find someone to take the job."[1] Capital hence believes that the time has come to squeeze workers harder — to rationalize production methods further, increase work norms, undermine union standards, and depress wages. Direct wage cuts, dispensed with largely in postwar years in favor of indirect cuts through inflation, are now ominously reappearing.*

Nor is inflation ending, for monopoly price-fixing continues, as does government military spending. The drop in the percentage of production workers was previously countered by a tendency toward greater public service employment. Now this is shrinking rapidly, as city, state and federal employees get laid off.

The responsibility now resting on organized labor is truly enormous, but it is ill prepared. The task is nothing less than to help reverse the course of the nation.

## Multinationals and Foreign Policy

Top labor support for a reactionary foreign policy was predicated on the cynical assumption that what was good for American empire was also good for the better organized and more skilled workers of this country. It was based on the belief that they, too, would share from the immense superprofits earned from imperialist exploitation abroad. This was the ideological premise for support of every military adventure, as well as for the cold war and the Vietnam War. But the crisis of U.S. imperialism is now also leading to a crisis in this ideology. Empire-building is no longer as cheap and easy as it once was. The world has greatly changed. Today, the cost of empire often outweighs the gains of empire. But those who

* The *Wall Street Journal*, of August 25, 1975, reports that the Bethlehem Steel Company threatens to shut down a number of its fabricating mills unless labor costs are reduced.

make the gains don't usually pay the costs; most workers do. It is their sons who died in the jungles of Vietnam, and the huge sums spent on militarism are largely paid for by payroll taxes and higher prices. Likewise, the tens of billions that go into the multinational corporations come from corporate profits produced by American workers.

Fear of the multinationals has grown in labor's ranks. Union after union has demanded an end to tax incentives that make the export of capital so profitable. But the bulk of the labor movement has not faced up to the interrelationship between multinationals, huge military spending, and a reactionary imperialist foreign policy.

The need for a large military budget was accepted by many workers in the belief that it would stimulate the national economy and help avoid depression. But we've now had the deepest depression since the thirties, with military spending at an all-time peak. Albert Fitzgerald, president of the United Electrical Workers, was therefore justified in telling a labor peace conference in 1972, "You can't have guns and butter at the same time." He urged the building of hospitals, the revitalization of our cities, and the building of a railroad system to get from city to city "rather than spending billions to get men to the moon."[2]

Reducing military expenditures is imperative for the sake of the nation's economy as well as for world peace. There are powerful military-industrial interests who would use our piled-up arms in an even more aggressive foreign policy. They oppose detente with the Soviet Union and the other socialist states and even dream of reversing the tide of revolutionary change. Some of them would even gamble with fascism and thermonuclear war in order to attain world supremacy. This danger is real. The United States is the only country that used the atom bomb in war — against two highly populated Japanese cities. And Washington has refused to this very day to reassure the world that it will not be the first to use nuclear weapons again, even if this time it results in a nuclear holocaust.

There are some sections of the labor movement that understand the importance of detente despite George Meany's fulminations against it. Abe Feinglass, vice-president of the Amalgamated Meat Cutters and Butcher Workmen, publicly took issue with Meany. "Detente," he wrote, "represents a joint agreement to avoid the escalation of differences into a world confrontation. In spite of differences in ideology and social purpose, there is an over-riding need to normalize relationships among the world's leading nations."[3]

Unfortunately, this is not yet the position of most trade unions.

## Basic Structural Reforms

The roots of what is wrong in domestic and foreign policy lie in the exploitative nature of the capitalist system. The accumulation of great wealth at one polar extreme is always at the expense of the accumulation of great misery at the other end. To change this situation in a meaningful way requires policies which hit hard precisely at ruling class exploitive powers. To reshuffle the same deck of marked cards is worse than meaningless. The Ford Administration, for example, initiated tax rebates for the year 1975 in order to increase mass purchasing power somewhat. But at the very time this was done, it increased the price of gasoline and fuel oil, thereby increasing the price of just about everything.

Government policies are based on the assumption that if more is given to whose who have more, more will somehow trickle down to those who have less. Thus government policies accelerate the inherent tendency of capital to concentrate ever greater wealth and productive power in fewer and fewer hands. For four decades lavish government subsidies went to giant agri-business, to reduce, not increase, farm acreage and output. As a consequence, food prices soared even higher and small farmers were driven from the land.

The same reactionary policies are seen in the huge government hand-outs to corporations "in trouble," and in the treatment of the so-called energy crisis. If there were a real energy shortage, the logical answer would be democratic rationing, strict price control, and a crash program to build mass public transit. Instead, the oil industry, with the highest of all profit yields, is allowed to boost prices continually.*

Basic democratic structural reforms are needed to put the nation back to work, reverse the regressive tax structure, establish free medical and hospital care for all, end government anti-social spending, enforce equal rights for minority people and women, build a national system of cheap rapid public transit, remove all shackles upon labor's right to organize and strike, conduct a real war on poverty, and begin a policy of public ownership of the giant monopolies.

Mass unemployment is problem number one. The AFL-CIO has urged a huge federal appropriation to create new jobs. This is an important demand and would be helpful, but it overlooks the need for simultane-

* From 1973 to 1975 the price of gasoline doubled.

ously combating inflation. Apparently the AFL-CIO high command does not consider inflation to be a continuing major problem. This is why it does not propose a drastic shift in government spending from armaments, which is based on highly concentrated and capital-intensive production, to housing, health and education, which are all labor-intensive fields. A serious fight against inflation also requires a radical revision in a tax structure which benefits only the rich and super-rich, not the people. And it requires a mass movement to impose effective price controls, and to make it a crime punishable by expropriation and/or prison sentences for those engaged in monopoly price-fixing practices. A program of this kind would heighten mass purchasing power and also lessen the need for deficit financing.

## The Shorter Workweek

But the problem of unemployment will require an even more radical approach. Many unions over the years have called for a shorter workweek, but nothing was done to implement the demand. The 1973 miners' convention, greatly concerned with mine safety, reiterated the need for a six-hour workday. One miner argued eloquently, "Our safety requires it."[4] But the demand was quickly lost sight of when contract negotiations began.

A plan to put America back to work has been drafted by Ernest DeMaio, retired vice-president of the United Electrical Workers and representative of the World Federation of Trade Unions at the United Nations. The plan calls for a 35-hour workweek, "with wages equal to those now paid for 40 hours work." This, it is estimated, would create nine million more jobs. Federal, state, and local government would save approximately $25 billion in unemployment compensation and welfare and food stamps costs. The additional buying power of the nine million new workers would also help stimulate the economy. With a reduced welfare load, those who cannot work would find it easier to get more adequate aid.[5]

Since the mass layoffs in the auto industry, a rank-and-file movement has arisen for a shorter workweek. Many of those who formerly led the successful movement for earlier retirement have formed a nationwide committee for this purpose. The committee demands that its proposal for a 10 percent reduction in working hours get top priority in 1976 contract talks. Experience indicates that in addition to separate industry struggles for a shorter workweek, it will become necessary to launch a serious movement for federal legislation incorporating this demand into law. This was how the 40-hour week was won some 40 years ago, and it is the only guarantee that the *entire* class will be included in such a reform.

## The Issue of Nationalization

The ever increasing power and arrogance of the corporate monopolies over the economy and entire life of the nation is, undoubtedly, the most challenging issue of all. Anti-big-business sentiment has been steadily growing in recent years. The constant rise in consumer prices due to unconscionable price-gouging, the greater public awareness of how the giant corporations buy politicians, from the President down, the exposure of ITT plotting in Chile and all over the globe, and especially, the constant hikes in gasoline and fuel oil prices and utility rates, have aroused bitter public indignation. Most unions, and many other organizations, have adopted strong condemnatory resolutions. There is also a growing demand for some form of public control over these corporations, but most unions have hesitated to call for the outright nationalization of the energy and utility industries.

The Oil, Chemical and Atomic Workers Union, for example, placed a full-page ad in the *New York Times,* headed, "THEY CAN'T ROB US BLIND IF WE OPEN OUR EYES." It blasted the shameless profiteering of the oil companies — $17 billion in 1974 alone; showed that the rise in oil prices is unrelated to labor costs per barrel of oil, since these have been declining; that "the seven largest oil companies have been paying federal taxes at a rate of about five cents on the dollar," and that "if they paid their full share of taxes, it would help balance the federal budget and would help ease inflation."

This devastating indictment was followed by neither a demand for nationalization nor for public control over the industry. Instead, the ad ended with the weak admonition, "If we open our eyes, they can't rob us blind." This was the sum and substance of what was proposed!

Arnold Miller, the head of the miners' union, likewise shied away from recommending nationalization. In an interview with Jim Williams in *Labor Today,* Miller said that he sometimes baits coal operators with the threat that maybe they ought to be nationalized. This "shuts them up, because they know they're making profits and yet they try to come out and tell the public that they're not." But Miller was not sure that nationalization was the answer. He preferred the establishment of a commission "to have the authority to direct the fuel energy program."[6]

Harry Bridges believes that nationalization may seem to be the answer but "is not very feasible." Industries in the United States "are not nationalized easily," and even then the nationalization was not very real, for "the same management remained in control." He therefore advocates workers "withholding their labor power" as the effective means by which to stop oil companies' machinations.[7]

This reluctance to see nationalization as a necessary and inevitable step is more prevalent in this country, but it was not always this way. At the turn of the century there was a strong movement for nationalization, with many unions involved. It is now frowned upon for a number of reasons. First, nationalization is consciously misrepresented as synonymous with socialism. But most capitalist governments, for example, own and operate the railways of their countries. Service and efficiency on these are nearly everywhere superior to that on U.S. railroads. The capitalists of other countries favored state ownership of rail transport because it guaranteed them cheaper and more efficient freight services, with the government picking up the tab for whatever operating loss was entailed. In the United States the government also subsidizes the railroads, but in order to preserve private ownership and private profit

Urban transit lines are publicly owned in many parts of the country. This usually took place after private owners had pocketed every last drop of profit without spending money to renew or modernize rolling stock. Pressure then mounted to reconvert street-car lines to bus lines, to the great benefit of the auto and oil corporations. City governments bought the old, worn-out lines at far above their real worth, floating city bonds and bank loans to pay for them — usually from the same owners, the banks. High interest rates on these purchases are still being paid, and city governments put over fare increases that private companies could not have gotten away with that easily. This kind of swindle has made people skeptical of public ownership in general.

Similar "nationalizations" took place in some European countries under Social-Democratic regimes. "Sick" industries, needing large infusions of capital investments for technological renovation, were nationalized. When these industries were restored to "health" — at public expense — and when a new government came into office, the industries were returned to private hands again. The same charade could happen here, despite the irrational fears aroused by the very word "nationalization."

But the public ownership of the energy industry would be another matter. It is not a "sick" industry, but the most profitable. If taken over under some form of democratic control, that is, with labor and consumer organizations represented on management boards, it could immediately reduce the price of oil and electricity and still leave a large balance to help the government budget.

"If the oil companies are so poor that they can no longer drill new wells without pricing gasoline out of sight," noted Frank Rosen, general vice-president of the United Electrical Workers, "then it is time to put them out of business. Nationalize this vital industry and let it serve the interests of the people. It is *our* national resources that these companies are taking out of the ground."

Even a partial nationalization of this important industry would have an electrifying effect on its private sector. "Short of nationalization," points out Rosen, "a TVA in the oil industry could be created. Once a government-owned company became a yardstick for comparing production costs with private companies and began drilling new oil to sell to the public, we would all be amazed to see how quickly the private oil industry would resume drilling for new oil."[8]

## The Public Utilities

The public ownership of the telephone and electric utility companies is urgently needed. These companies operate as public utilities under local or state franchise which give them a monopoly over electric and telephone services. It is this government-given monopoly which guarantees them a constant rate of profit — the greater the cost of production, the greater the profit. In this way the public is shamelessly mulcted with complete government connivance through state and local public "power authorities."

A great movement to make public utilities public property is long overdue. Such a movement has already begun in a number of cities, spurred by the aroused anger of senior citizens' and other consumer organizations. But it lacks the active participation and support of the labor movement.

Another factor holding back organized labor's support for nationalization is the fear that such government take-overs will hurt trade unionism. This fear arose in a period when government employees lacked the right to organize or strike. But much has changed in the last decade. Public employee unions have grown most rapidly of all, and hundreds of thousands of government employees have been on strike in nearly every state.

There is another side to this question. The nationalization of the energy or other industries will not come without a change in the political climate in the country and a new alignment of political forces. The government of the City of New York, for example, which in the summer of 1975, broke union contracts and imposed a wage freeze on city employees, is not going to challenge the power of the private utilities over the city. Nor will a White House and Congress that permit the oil magnates to fleece the public, and chose a member of the Rockefeller family oil empire to be the nation's vice-president, do anything to take over this most lucrative of industries. For this, major political change is necessary. This does not require that the demand for nationalization await such change, for it is an issue around which consciousness of the need for change can develop.

## Breaking From the Money Parties

The American labor movement, we have noted, lacks a mass political instrument of its own. A lack of class-consciousness and a winner-take-all electoral system have led to the formation of a two-party system in which both parties are hodge-podge coalitions of diverse and often conflicting class, social and sectional interests. The single objective is to win the prize of government and to share in its booty. The principle that holds these coalitions together is a lack of principle. Policy statements are meant to catch votes and to indicate a middle-of-the-road consensus. "Radical" politics are therefore ruled out. Whenever there is a pull in that direction, a temporary split occurs for the given election. When the election is over, and especially if the maverick candidate or ticket goes down to defeat, the tendency to horse-trade principles for the sake of another election victory is strengthened once again.

One reason this has worked is that the conflicts that arose were amenable to compromise and could be contained in the established two-party political structure. Exceptions were usually short-lived, the sharpness of the issue eroding with time. Only in the national crisis over slavery did the two-party system of Whigs and Democrats crumble, and the new Republican Party of Lincoln arise. In the thirties, a regrouping took place in which the workers, Black people, Chicanos, poor farmers and lower-income middle-class groups, threw their support to the New Deal. The upsurge of the period was successfully kept within the two-party orbit, although the mass base of each party was greatly altered. The outbreak of World War II halted the process of political change, blunting the sharp edge of former differences.

In the period ahead, with conditions of sharpening class struggle, the issues of conflict will be more fundamental and less amenable to compromise. The ruling class will continue to make concessions to popular pressure, but these will no longer suffice to patch up a widening class cleavage. The need to make radical changes in economic and political power relationships will grow as the crisis of the system deepens. Issues such as the nationalization of the oil and utility industries will help make clear the nature of the cleaveage and the need for a new, antimonopoly kind of politics.

The failure of organized labor to move toward a new party of its own arises from the stifling grip of a conservative leadership and from the existence of continued illusions as to the Democratic Party. There is also fear that the formation of a new mass-based electoral party would split a liberal-labor alliance, strengthen the worst racist and anti-labor forces and jeopardize gains. This fear is prevalent also in a section of the Black peoples' movement, which does not want to lose the gains made through the election of hundreds of local, state and national Black officials.

This fear cannot be ignored. The problem is how to begin to break with the two parties of big business while preventing the extreme Right from taking power. The answer is not to be found in tagging after the liberals and giving carte blanche support to candidates selected by them. In this respect, something can be learned from the tactics of the extreme Right. George Wallace has his own independent party organization and at the same time remains a force to be reckoned with in the Democratic Party. By existing as an independent political force, with ballot status in many states, he is capable of exercising immense influence on the policies and candidates of both major parties, each of which seeks the Wallace votes. This is far different from the anemic role played by labor leaders and the professional reformers within the Democratic Party.

In its early years, the CIO sought to become an independent political force. It built its own tightly knit political apparatus, and in New York State established an independent political party, the American Labor Party (ALP). The ALP worked with Democrats to defeat Rightist candidates, but also formed alliances to defeat Tammany Hall in New York City. It helped initiate the movement which elected Fiorello LaGuardia as Mayor, Vito Marcantonio as ALP Congressman; and it created a climate in which two Communist leaders, Peter V. Cacchione of Brooklyn and Benjamin J. Davis of Harlem were elected to the City Council. The ALP supported the Roosevelt New Deal, but also exerted independent pressure upon it. Had the cold war not intervened, the ALP could have become the New York State base for a new national political party of progressive labor and its allies.

The possibility of a new political realignment and a new peoples' party will grow in the period ahead. It should be worked for openly and boldly, utilizing every opportunity for coming forward with independent politics. Will Parry, president of the Washington-Alaska Conference, Association of Western Pulp and Paper Workers, believes that the starting point is the running of independent labor candidates:

> I think the starting point is with the best sons and daughters of our movement, the labor movement, being advanced to run for office on the union's program, not the Democratic Party's program. What the hell is that program? Whatever the individual Democrat wants to make it, right? Lets get men and women to run on our program. Sure they can run as Democrats. That's the way the Black people are doing it. They're electing Blacks on a program that's responsive to the needs of their Black people. They've got a substantial, meaningful, gutty power base in the Congress of the U.S. and the mighty labor movement has not got it.[9]

The running of independent labor candidates on their own programs would represent a step forward, although their running on the Democratic Party line increases the danger of their being sucked into the swamp of Democratic Party politics. A saying frequently repeated by Arnold Miller needs to be remembered: "We have only one political party in the country — the Money Party. And it has two branches — the Republican branch and the Democratic branch."

When this truth is fully understood in the labor movement, a new day in American politics will not be far off.

Many other new and vexing problems face the labor movement. We have previously discussed the problems arising from the conglomerates and multinational corporations. Without an increased workers' unity that crosses union lines, coordinated bargaining and coordinated action are impossible. Great unity is also essential if the job of organizing the unorganized is to move forward. Without such unity, new opportunities to greatly enlarge the labor movement will be lost.

New conditions of struggle also put old tactics to the test and bring forth new ones. In a number of recent labor struggles, especially that of the farm workers, the consumer boycott support movement has been of great importance. The same was true in the militant strike of the Farah pants-workers. And when the Rheingold Brewery Plant in Brooklyn, New York, was shut down without notice by the Pepsico Company the workers refused to accept the shutdown and occupied the plant, and the union threatened Pepsico with an organized labor boycott of all its products. Where plants are to be shut down, or where workers cannot withstand a long strike or fear scabs taking their jobs, the old and effective sit-in tactics of the mid-thirties may reappear on a wider scale.

One of the most important issues that will arise again and again is the right of workers to strike over shop grievances. In France and Italy, for example, "the freedom to strike belongs to a political tradition; it is seen as a human right, comparable to the freedom of speech or the freedom of association." It is guaranteed by the constitution. In both countries, a strike is "not a breach of contract, but merely its suspension." And in Italy, the lockout is not an equivalent right; its use can be a breach of contract.[10]

Unions will also find an increasing need to intervene in company production and investment policies, refusing to concede these to "company prerogatives." Corporations are social institutions, operating under government license. What they do, what they produce, where and on what they invest their capital, are not matters that affect them alone. These are social questions affecting society. It is not a matter of indifference to workers or the public that the General Electric plant in Schenectady, New York, for example, is one of the main polluters of the Hudson River. Nor is it a private company matter that GM, Ford and Chrysler continue to build new model cars every year, at higher and higher prices, when the market for cars is declining, and cluttered streets and highways have become hazardous to human life. Under these circumstances, the auto union has every right to demand that some plants in the industry be converted to the production of road and rail vehicles for mass public transportation. And when unions begin to lead this kind of a fight, they will earn the respect, affection and allegiance of millions of people, for they will be speaking for them, too, and for the nation as a whole.

## The Organized Left

Basic change in the labor movement will not come of itself. Worsening workers' conditions will produce new upsurge, but this alone will not ensure a basic change in labor's over-all policy and leadership. Mass consciousness of what is wrong and how to correct it is needed. Much depends therefore on the state of the organized Left — its program, tactics, and ability to relate to, work with, and influence the thinking and action of workers.

It was the existence of a well-organized Left, mainly associated with the Communist Party, which made possible the great advance of the thirties. Under the leadership of William Z. Foster, the Trade Union Educational League (TUEL) was formed in the early twenties. It set out to educate workers to the need for industrial unions, exposed class-collaboration policies, urged the formation of a labor party, and sought to unify workers in the fight for union democracy. Later, the TUEL was replaced by the Trade Union Unity League as a center organizing workers into independent industrial unions where established unions refused to do this.

Today, once again, the responsibility of class-conscious workers is immense. The present crisis in the labor movement dates from the expulsions of the fifties, when "much of the effective and democratic leadership in the labor movement was either ousted or muzzled."[11] More than two decades have passed since then, but the losses suffered have not yet been fully made up.

A new generation has entered industry and begun to fight. Rank-and-file movements have mushroomed. A national paper that reports on the rank-and-file scene, *Labor Today,* now exists, as does a center for Trade Union Action and Democracy. A new race consciousness among minority workers is now linking up with a growing class awareness. There has also been the great awakening of women and the formation of Black and women's movements within organized labor to help reinforce and energize it. The young generation is bringing a new spirit of militancy into shops and unions, which, when united with the greater experience of older workers, has a tremendous rejuvenating power.

Of greatest importance is the emergence of the Communist Party from the long period of political repression. No other organization in American history has been so persecuted for such a long period of time. But the Communist Party is rapidly replenishing its ranks with young militants, many of them trade unionists. The Young Workers Liberation League is also making important headway, bringing minority and white youth together on a common class outlook. The Communist Party, despite errors made, has stood its ground, never giving way to the anti-Communist witch hunt, or departing from its basic Marxist philosophy and its confidence in the American working class as the decisive force for ultimate social change. It has consistently fought racism in the ranks of the workers and in public life generally, recognizing that Black-white unity is the touchstone for the attainment of working-class unity in the United States.

Progressive change in the labor movement will be a process. In some respects it will be harder to attain than in the thirties. The main job then was to organize the unorganized, and the new unions this brought into being were more democratic and responsive to workers' needs. But now the main job is to transform existing unions, not to form new ones. This is more difficult, requiring great tenacity and flexibility and, above all, the ability of class-conscious and Left-minded workers to unite with those who may disagree with them on ideological questions but who also want progressive labor change.

## Left and Center Unity

The effort to organize the mass-production industries in the thirties led to a coalition of Left and Center forces. Without this unity the job would not have been done. A simliar type of unity is needed again to infuse new hope and vitality into the labor movement. This can come only from the bottom up. But this does not exclude unity with labor leaders as well. When there is an absence of rank-and-file pressure and an organized Left presence, conservative influences predominate. Even sections of leadership that could be moved in a more progressive direction succumb to right-wing intimidation. Lewis, Murray and Hillman would not have undertaken the drive to organize the mass production industries, had Communists and other left-wing workers not shown the way. Nor would they have formed an alliance with the Left, temporary and unequal though it was, if they had not recognized the Left as possessing capable, energetic and influential workers' leaders.

Thus the existence of an ever growing Left is a precondition for attaining and maintaining a broader unity of all honest and progressive workers. But this is only possible if the Left works in a nonsectarian way, constantly seeking to forge the broadest unity.

This requires recognition of the existence of different ideological and political trends. The very nature of trade unions, as collectives of *all* workers in a given trade or industry, regardless of their race, nationality, sex, religion, or ideological-political affinities or affiliations, means that differences over many questions are quite natural and must be encompassed within the framework of an over-all trade union discipline and unity. Only one demand is essential — that each member respect the viewpoint of others and agree to support any decision the union makes in its struggle with the employers.

Union democracy presupposes the existence of both a class struggle and a class-partnership trend within the movement. Neither of these can be exorcised by decree. They arise from the contradictory conditions of struggle under capitalism, which includes periods of sharp clash as well as those of temporary lull. Conditions should be created in which these two ideological trends can compete for the support of the membership, and present their different analyses and policies to be voted up or down. Because of past practices and existing constitutional bars, this requires the elimination of all restrictions on the rights of Communists to belong, to be active, and to be elected to union office.

## Socialism for America

The deepening crisis of the world capitalist system and the trend toward lowered living standards in the United States, are tearing away the cultivated postwar illusions that "advanced capitalism" is free of economic tailspins, that it has learned to flatten the economic cycle, and that it is capable of improving the material conditions and quality of life of the people. Under these conditions, the ideas of scientific socialism are bound to win ever greater adherents.

Already there is a great questioning of the system. No longer is the "American way of life" seen as sacrosanct and superior. A new generation has also grown up without the same irrational fears and prejudices. The Vietnam trauma has taught many that U.S. imperialism is not the peace dove it pretends to be, but a war-hawk intent on preventing other peoples from deciding their own destinies. And it is becoming evident to many that the capitalist social system is decaying and that socialism represents that which is new and rising in the world.

Socialism is not yet a mass issue among American workers. But it will become such, for there is no other basic answer to the crisis of our time. As long as the great productive forces of society remain in private hands, for private profit, the crisis cannot end. It will grow increasingly worse. Recently a newspaper columnist made the observation that what America fears the most — socialism — may be its only salvation. The merit of this statement is that it places the question of socialism for public discussion.

It is less important at this moment to get full ideological agreement on how socialism is to be attained and what forms it will take — though these are extremely important questions — than to legitimize a discussion about socialism.

Such a discussion must be won inside the labor movement as well, if long-term goals are to be established. This has been impossible because blatant, blind anticommunism has held reign so long. There are a number of reasons for the virulence with which the labor hierarchy reacts to the question of socialism and/or communism. In the first place, it is a backhanded recognition that socialist ideas find their natural soil in workers' conditions of life and struggle. The bureaucracy seeks to expurgate this "menace" before it sinks roots and rapidly spreads. Anticommunism is also a tactical device by which to confuse and divide workers, branding every rank-and-file movement as "communistic."

There is still another reason why anticommunism is more malignant in the United States than elsewhere, even though the movement for socialism in this country is relatively weaker. From its very inception, the Soviet Union has been viewed as the polar extreme of the United States, the socialist countermagnet to U.S. capitalism in world power and influence. It is this challenge to American capitalism, inherent in the very existence and rapid growth of the Soviet Union which explains the irrationality of the attacks upon it. So all-pervasive is this anti-Sovietism that it even takes on a "Left" twist. One can be the reddest of revolutionaries — in rhetoric — and still be accepted by the Establishment as quite respectable, so long as this is accompanied by anti-Sovietism.

But the truth about the socialist countries cannot be indefinitely hidden. With socialist Cuba only 90 miles away, and given world peace, detente and trade, more people will realize that despite great hardships, weaknesses and mistakes, and a hostile capitalist world, the socialist countries have given their people a sense of security and well-being that we, in the richest land in the world, have never approached and are moving further away from every day.

Socialism, when it comes to the United States, will not be a duplicate of socialism anywhere else in the world. It will learn from both the successes and mistakes of other countries, and it will be a socialism as different as is our level of economic development, history, culture and tradition.

NEW Labor winds are blowing. Every indication is that events will propel workers toward greater militancy, unity and class consciousness. A new labor radicalism is on the horizon.

*The greatest hope of American labor is in the rank-and-file membership, the men and women who pay the dues and who maintain the unity and solidarity at the bench, the lathe, and the assembly line. When a little more experience has taught them a few more facts of life, they will decide they have had enough. The leaders who have forgotten their origin and mission will be swept aside. Their places will be taken by younger and more militant leaders. . . . Rest assured, this new and younger leadership is already in the making. We may not yet have heard their names, but to doubt that these future leaders exist is to doubt the whole of American labor history.*

Wyndham Mortimer, from his
autobiography, *Organize!*

# REFERENCE NOTES

## INTRODUCTION
1. Alvin H. Hansen, *The Postwar Economy* (W.W. Norton, Inc., N.Y., 1964), p. 24.
2. Daniel Bell, *The End of Ideology* (The Free Press, 1960).
3. Erich Fromm, *Marx's Concept of Man* (Ungar, New York 1961). Also see Dirk J. Struik, Introduction to *The Economic and Philosophical Manuscripts of 1844* (International Publishers, New York, 1964)
4. S.M. Miller, *Labor History,* Winter. 1966.
5. Caroline B. Herron, (*New York Times,* June 3. 1973,
6. Daniel Bell, op. cit., 2nd revised edition (Collier Books, N.Y., 1962) p. 365.
7. C. Wright Mills, *The Marxists* (Dell Publishers, N.Y., 1962), pp. 108-9.
8. Herbert Marcuse, *One Dimensional Man* (Beacon Press, Boston, 1967), p. 109.
9. Karl Marx and Frederick Engels, *The Holy Family, Collected Works* Vol. 4 (International Publishers, New York, 1975), p. 37.
10. Karl Marx and Frederick Engels, *Selected Correspondence* (International Publishers, New York, 1935), p. 115, p. 469.
11. Carl Farris, National Labor Coordinator of the Southern Christian Leadership Conference (*Labor Today,* August-September, 1972).
12. *American Magazine,* June, 1948.
13. *The Challenge of Automation* (Public Affairs Press, Washington, D.C., 1955).
14. Frank Rosen, President District 11, United Electrical Workers, *Notes on U.S. Economy* (mimeographed paper, 1975).
15. James O'Connor, "The Expanding Role of the State" *Capitalist System,* (Prentice-Hall. Englewood Cliffs, N.J., 1972), p. 193.

## CHAPTER 1
1. *Historical Statistics of the United States 1789-1945,* U.S. Department of Commerce, Bureau of the Census, Washington, D.C., Government Printing Office, 1949, p. 65, Table #D 62-76.

2. Ibid.
3. Ibid.
4. *Statistical Abstract of the United States*, U.S. Department of Commerce, Bureau of the Census, Washington, D.C., Government Printing Office, 1972, p. 219, Table #346.
5. *Historical Statistics*, op. cit., p. 72, Table D 218-223.
6. *Manpower Report of the President*, Washington, D.C., Government Printing Office, 1972, p. 228 and *Statistical Abstract*, 1975, p. 360.
7. *Statistical Abstract of the United States*, U.S. Dept. of Commerce, Bureau of the Census, Washington, D.C . Government Printing Office, p. 223.
8. *Statistical Abstract of the United States*, 1972, op. cit., p. 584 and *Statistical Abstract of the United States*, 1975. p 360.
9. Ibid, p. 584.
10. *Statistical Abstract of the United States*, 1939, p. 19.
11. *Statistical Abstract of the United States*, 1972, op. cit., pp. 26, 29.
12. *Statistical Abstract of the United States*, 1975, p. 628.
13. Ibid., p. 612.
14. *New York Times*, April 19, 1974.
15. *Statistical Abstract of the United States* 1972, op. cit., p. 230.
16. *Statistical Abstract of the United States*, 1956, p. 499 and *Statistical Abstract of the United States*, 1972, op. cit., p. 525.
17. *Statistical Abstract of the United States*, 1972, op. cit., p. 105.
18. Andrew Levison, *The Working Class Majority* (Coward McCann & Geoghegan, Inc., N.Y., 1974).
19. Ibid., p. 229.
20. *Bureau of Labor Statistics Handbook of Methods*, U.S. Dept. of Labor, Washington, D.C., Bulletin 711, p. 5, note
21. Karl Marx, *Theories of Surplus Value*, Part I (Foreign Languages Publishing House, Moscow), p. 399.
22. Michael Reich, "The Evolution of the United States Labor Force," in *The Capitalist System*, op. cit., p. 180.
23. Eva Mueller, *Technological Advance in an Expanding Economy* (Univ. of Michigan Press, 1969), p. 27.
24. Ben B. Seligman, *Forward to a Notorious Victory – Man in the Age of Automation* (The Free Press, N.Y. 1966), p. 333.
25. Arnold R. Weber, "Collective Bargaining and the Challenge of Technological Change," in *Industrial Relations: Challenges and Responses*, Edited John H. Crispo (Univ. of Toronto Press, Toronto, Canada, 1966), p. 76.
26. Ibid., p. 77.
27. B. Seligman, op. cit., p. 155.
28. Ibid., p. 191.
29. Ibid., p. 193.
30. William D. Smith, "Gas Stations: A Way of Life Changing," *New York Times*, May 27, 1973.
31. Vincent Lombardi and Andrew J. Grimes, "A Primer for a Theory of White-Collar Unionization," *Monthly Labor Review*, May, 1967.
32. Theodore V. Purcell, *Blue-Collar Workers – Patterns of Dual Allegiance in Industry* (Howard Univ. Press, Cambridge, Mass., 1960), pp. 158-9, 161.
33. J. B.S. Hardman, at 3rd Annual Meeting of Industrial Relations Research Assoc., pp. 153-4.
34. Peter Mattiesen, *Sal Si Puedes – Cesar Chavez and the New American Revolution* (Dell Publishers, N.Y., 1969), p. 20.

35  S.M. Miller and Frank Riessman, *Social Class and Social Policy* (Basic Books, N.Y., 1969), p. 70.
36. Kenneth B. Clark, *Dark Ghetto* (Harper and Row Publishers, New York, 1965), p. 36.
37. Russell B. Nixon, "New Labor Force Entrants," *Encyclopedia of Social Work*, pp. 2-3.

## CHAPTER 2

1   John T. Dunlop, "Structural Changes in American Labor Movement," in *Labor and Trade Unionism*, Walter Galenson and Seymour M. Lipset, editors (John Wiley and Sons., N.Y., 1960), p. 113.
2.  Virgil Jordan at Annual Convention Investment Bankers Association of America, Hollywood, Florida, Dec. 10, 1940.
3.  Vernon K. Dibble, "The Garrison Society," *New University Thought* Special Issue, 1966-67.
4.  Joseph G. Rayback, *A History of American Labor* (MacMillan & Co., N.Y., 1959), p. 389.
5.  Richard O. Boyer and Herbert M. Morais, *Labor's Untold Story* (Cameron Associates, N.Y., 1955), p. 343.
6.  Ibid., p. 344.
7.  Harry H. Milles and Emily Clark Brown, *From the Wagner Act to Taft-Hartley* (Univ. of Chicago Press, Chicago, 1950), p. 30
8.  Rayback, op. cit., p. 389.
9.  Milles-Brown, op. cit., pp. 306-8.
10. *Economic Handbook* (Thomas & Crowell & Co., N.Y., 1957), p. 84.
11. Rayback, op. cit., p. 390.
12. Milles-Brown, op. cit., p. 313.
13. Rayback, op. cit., p. 390.
14. *Handbook of Labor Statistics*, 1974, U.S. Dept of Labor, pp. 241-3. Also, National Center for Educational Statistics, HEW, the *New York Times*, December 10, 1975.
15. James R. Schlesinger, "Market Structure, Union Power and Inflation," in *Labor and Trade Unionism*, op. cit., p. 166.
16. *Statistical Abstract of the United States*, 1975, op. cit., p. 355.
17. Ibid., p. 166.
18. John Kenneth Galbraith, *The New Industrial State* (Houghton Mifflin Co., Boston 1967), p. 205.
19. Ibid., p. 181.
20. Milles-Brown, op cit., p. 313.
21. Rayback, op. cit., p. 392.
22. Milles-Brown, op. cit., p. 470.
23. Ibid., p. 404.
24. Ibid., p. 545.
25. Ibid., p. 548.
26. Boyer-Morais, op. cit., p. 345.
27. Ronald Radosh, *American Labor and United States Foreign Policy* (Random House, N.Y., 1970), pp. 21-26.
28. *New York Herald Tribune*, January 29, 1950.
29. Paul F. Douglass, *Six Upon the World* (Little, Brown & Co., Boston, 1954).
30. Henry Lee Moon, *Balance of Power: The Negro Vote* (Doubleday & Co., N.Y., 1948).
31. Wilson Record, *The Negro and the Communist Party* (Univ. of North Carolina Press, Chapel Hill, 1951).
32. Paul Jacobs, *Labor Looks at Labor, Some members of the United Auto Workers*

*Undertake a Self-Examination,* Center for the Study of Democratic Institutions, the Fund for the Republic, 1963, pp.13-14.

## CHAPTER 3

1. Len De Caux, *Labor Radical* (Beacon Press, Boston, 1970), p. 475.
2. F.S. O'Brien, *Labor History,* Spring, 1968. Also see John J. Abt, "The Cold War, the Supreme Court and Political Liberty in the United States, ' in *Review of Contemporary Law,* publication of International Association of Democratic Lawyers.
3. *U.S. News and World Report,* cited Boyer-Morais, op. cit., p. 239.
4. F.S. O'Brien, op. cit.
5. *New York Times,* June 24, 1941.
6. James R. Prickett, "The Ambiguities of Anti-Communism," in *Autocracy and Insurgency in Organized Labor,* Edited by Burton Hall (Transaction Books, New Brunswick, N.J., 1972), p. 246.
7. See Ronald Radosh, "Corporate Ideology of American Labor," in *For A New America,* Editors, James Weinstein and David W. Eakins (Random House, N.Y., 1970), pp. 125-151.
8. Ibid., p. 151.
9. Gus Hall, *Political Affairs,* September 1949.
10. Vernon H. Jensen, *Strife on the Waterfront: The Port of New York* (Cornell Univ. Press, Ithaca, N.Y., 1974), p. 212.
11. Karl Marx, *The Eighteenth Brumaire of Louis Bonaparte,* Selected Works, Vol. II, (International Publishers, N.Y. 1936), p. 319.

## CHAPTER 4

1. Karl Marx, *Capital,* Vol I (International Publishers, New York, 1967), p. 409.
2. *Statistical Abstract,* 1975, op. cit, p. 729.
3. Karl Marx, "Address to the General Council of the International Working Men's Association," 1865, published as *Value, Price and Profit,* and contained in *Selected Works,* Vol I (International Publishers, New York, 1936), p. 334.
4. Kenneth Larson, *The Workers* (Bantam Books, N.Y., 1972), p. 7.
5. Vera C. Perrella, "Women and the Labor Force," *Monthly Labor Review,* Feb., 1968.
6. *Handbook of Labor Statistics,* 1975, U.S. Dept. of Labor, p. 101 and Geoffrey H. Moore and Janice N. Hedges, "Trends in Labor and Leisure," *Monthly Labor Review,* Feb., 1971.
7. Vera C. Perrella, "Moonlighters: Their Motivations and Characteristics," *Monthly Labor Review,* August, 1970.
8. A. Gramsci, *Prison Notebooks* (International Publishers, New York, 1971), p. 303.
9. Bennett Kremen, "No Pride in this Dust," *The World of the Blue-Collar Worker,* Editor Irving Howe (Quadrangle Books, N.Y., 1972), p. 16.
10. *Daily World,* Dec. 28, 1971.
11. Dan Berman, "Health and Safety on the Job," *Health Right News,* March, 1972.
12. Patricia and Brendon Sexton, *Blue Collars and Hard Hats* (Random House, N.Y. 1971), p. 104.
13. BLS Bulletin "Work Injuries in the United States," as reprinted in the *United States Handbook of Facts and Statistics,* 1964-5 (Fairfield Publishers, Stanford, Conn., 1965), p. 246.
14. Edgar Weinberg, "Reducing Skill Shortages in Construction," *Monthly Labor Review,* Feb., 1969.
15. *Daily World,* July 31, 1973.
16. Moore and Hedges, op. cit.

17. Benneth Kremen, "Lordstown — Searching for a Better Way of Work," *New York Times*, Sept. 9, 1973.

18. Ibid.

19. Gramsci, op. cit., p. 303.

20. Keith Sward, *The Legend of Henry Ford* (Rinehart Co., N.Y., 1948), pp. 48-9.

21. William R. Bailey and Albert E. Schwenk, "Wage Differentials Among Manufacturing Establishments," *Monthly Labor Review*, May, 1971.

22. *Manpower Report of the President*, 1972, U.S. Dept. of Labor, p. 271.

23. Karl Marx, *Capital*, op. cit., p. 537.

24. Arthur Rose, "Wage Differentials in the Building Trades," *Monthly Labor Review*, Oct., 1969.

25. Ibid, p. 369 and Harry Ober, "Occupational Wage Differentials," *Monthly Labor Review*, July, 1965.

26. Everett M. Kassalow, *Trade Unions and Industrial Relations: An International Comparison* (Random House, N.Y., 1969), pp. 238-9.

27. Norman Birnbaum, *The Crisis of Industrial Society* (Oxford Univ. Press, 1969), p. 33.

28. James R. Bright, "Automation and Wage Determination," *Industrial Relations: Challenges and Responses*, Edited John H. Crispo (Univ. of Toronto Press, 1966), p. 59.

## CHAPTER 5

1. Frederick Engels, *The Condition of the Working Class of England*, 1844 (Stanford Univ. Press, 1958), pp. 88-89.

2. Robert Tilove, *Challenges to Collective Bargaining*, Lloyd Ulman, Editor (Prentice-Hall, Englewood, N.J., 1967), pp. 45-6.

3. *U.S. Riot Commission Report* (Bantam Books, N.Y., 1968), p. 258.

4. *Statistical Abstract*, 1972, op. cit., p. 228-9.

5. Phyllis Groom, "Prices in Poor Neighborhoods," *Monthly Labor Review*, October, 1966.

6. Gilbert Burck, "The Ever Expanding Pension Balloon," *Fortune*, October, 1971.

7. Ewan Clague, Balraj Palli and Leo Kramer, *The Ageing Worker and the Union* (Praeger, NY. 1971), p. 5.

8. *New York Times*, August 26, 1973.

9. *Comparative Survey of Major Collective Bargaining Agreements*, Industrial Union Dept., AFL-CIO, Washington, D.C., May, 1971.

10. Gilbert Burck, op. cit.

11. Robert W. Dunn, "The Welfare Offensive," in J.B.S. Hardman, *American Labor Dynamics* (Harcourt Brace Jovanovich, New York, 1938), p. 218.

12. Robert Tilove, "Pensions, Health and Welfare Plans," in *Challenge to Collective Bargaining*, op. cit, p. 56.

13. From an interview with a community organizer, July 25, 1973.

14. Irving M. Levine, "A Strategy for White Ethnic America," quoted in Andrew M. Greeley, *Why Can't They Be Like Us?* Institute of Human Relations Press, 1969, p. 64.

15. John H.M. Laslett, *Labor and the Left* (Basic Books, N.Y., 1970), p. 99.

16. Isaac H. Hourwich, *Immigration and Labor*, first published in 1912, (AMS Press, N.Y., 1972), p. 321.

17. John H.M. Laslett, op. cit, p. 117.

18. Moses Rischin, "The Jewish Labor Movement in America," *Labor History*, Fall, 1963., p. 233.

19. Ibid., p. 233 and p. 241.

20. Isaac H. Hourwich, op. cit., p. 455.

## CHAPTER 6

1. Joseph M. Bloch, "The Strike and Discontent," *Monthly Labor Review*, June, 1963.
2. *Handbook of Labor Statistics*, 1970, U.S. Department of Labor, p. 285.
3. *Economic Report on Corporate Mergers*, Hearing before Senate Subcommittee on Antitrust and Monopoly, U.S. Printing Office, Wash., D.C., 1969, p. 212.
4. Ibid., p. 37.
5. Richard Barber, *The American Corporation – Its Power, Its Money, Its Politics* (E.P. Dutton & Co., N.Y., 1970), p. 45.
6. Willard F. Mueller, "Conglomerate Mergers," in *Collective Bargaining Today*, Proceedings of Collective Bargaining Forum, Bureau of National Affairs, Washington, D.C., 1970, pp. 105-6.
7. *Fortune*, Feb. 1969, p. 80.
8. Senate Subcommittee Report, op. cit., p. 458.
9. Mueller, op. cit., pp. 112-13.
10. Otis F. Brubaker, "An Appraisal of Unions," *Collective Bargaining Today*, op. cit., p. 124.
11. *Magazine of Wall Street*, April 29, 1967, quoted by Senate Subcommittee Report, op. cit., p. 513.
12. Gilbert Burck, "The Merger Movement Rides High," *Fortune*, February, 1969.
13. Mueller, op. cit., p. 110.
14. Jennings, op. cit., p. 274.
15. Arnold R. Weber, "Collective Bargaining and the Challenge of Technological Change," in *Industrial Relations; Challenge and Responses*, op. cit., p. 77.
16. *New York Times*, July 2, 1973.
17. Weber, op. cit., pp. 77-8.
18. Ibid., p. 78.
19. Barber, op. cit., p. 251.
20. *Statistical Abstract*, 1956, p. 889, also *Statistical Abstract*, 1972, p. 767.
21. Ibid.
22. Barber, op. cit., pp. 256-7.
23. Ibid., p.252.
24. *Statistical Abstract*, 1972, op. cit., p. 785.
25. Ibid., p. 700.
26. Paul Jennings, op. cit., p. 275.
27. UN Monthly Bulletin of Statistics, *National Yearbook Organization*, Quarterly Bulletin, Yearbook, 1966-70.
28. Harry Weiss, "The Multinational Corporation and Its Impact on Collective Bargaining," in *Collective Bargaining Today*, op. cit., p. 300.
29. Nathaniel Goldfinger, director of research, AFL-CIO, *New York Times*, March 3, 1973.
30. Weiss, op. cit., p.299.
31. William C. Shelton, "The Changing Attitude of U.S. Labor Unions Toward World Trade," *Monthly Labor Review*, May, 1970.
32. Steve Babson, "The Multinational Corporation and Labor," *The Review of Radical Political Economists*, Spring, 1973.
33. *Daily World*, December 6, 1972.
34. *Daily World*, March 21, 1973.
35. *How Foreign is "Foreign" Competition*, UE Publication, 1971, N.Y.
36. *The Machinist*, publication of the IA of M, June, 1975.
37. *Labor Relations Reporter*,
38. *The Machinist*, op. cit., June, 1975.

## CHAPTER 7

1. Donald N. Michael, *Cybernetics the Silent Conquest,* (Center for the Study of American Society, Santa Barbara, Calif., 1962.)
2. Norbert Wiener, *The Human Use of Human Beings* (Doubleday Anchor Books, Garden City, N.Y., 1950), p. 160-2.
3. Statement of Ad Hoc Committee for Triple Revolution, *New York Times,* March 23, 1964.
4. "Labor Management Policy Commission Report on Automation," *Monthly Labor Review,* Feb., 1962.
5. Ibid.
6. Ben B. Seligman, op. cit., p. 333.
7. *New York Times Magazine,* Jan. 10, 1965.
8. James R. Bright, "Automation and Wage Determination," *Industrial Relations: Challenge and Responses,* op. cit., p. 47.
9. *Facts and Statistics,* 1964-5, op. cit., U.S. Dept. of Commerce, p.219.
10. Robert L. Stern, "Reasons for Nonparticipation in the Labor Force," *Monthly Labor Review* July, 1967.
11. *Statistical Abstract,* 1972, op. cit., p. 259.
12 *Handbook of Labor Statistics 1974,* U.S. Dept. of Labor, p. 158 and *Handbook of Labor Statistics, 1975,* U.S. Dept. of Labor, p. 184.
13 Seligman, op. cit., p. 341.
14. Victor Perlo, *The Unstable Economy* (International Publishers, New York, 1973), p. 62.
15. *Handbook of Labor Statistics,* op. cit., footnote, p. 158.
16. *News* bulletin, U.S. Dept. of Labor, June 11, 1974.
17. Rose N. Zeisel, "Technology and Labor in the Textile Industry," *Monthly Labor Review,* Feb., 1968.
18. *Labor Looks at Automation,* AFL-CIO Publ., Washington, D.C., p. 3.
19. Seligman, op. cit., p.133, p. 154.
20. Arthur S. Herman, "Manpower Implications of Computer Control of Manufacturing," *Monthly Labor Review,* Oct., 1970.
21. Thomas E. Mullaney, "The Productivity Challenge," *Business Section, New York Times,* Sunday, Oct., 7, 1974.
22. *Report to National Commission on Productivity,* Sept., 1972.
23. Arnold R. Weber, "Collective Bargaining and the Challenge of Technological Change," *Industrial Relations: Challenge and Responses,* op. cit., p. 80.
24. *Hammond Lockout Facts,* Strike paper, Nov., 1973.
25. Quoted by *Grapic Arts Worker,* published by members of the Communist Party in the New York graphic art unions, Dec., 1974.
26. Seligman, op. cit., p. 243.
27. Letter of Kurt E. Volk, Jr., President, Master Printers of America.
28. "A Common Strategy for Dockers," *Peoples World,* Nov. 16, 1974.
29. *Hammond Lockout Facts,* op. cit.
30. Charles P. Larrowe, *Harry Bridges, The Rise and Fall of Radical Labor in the U.S.,* (Lawrence Hill and Co., 1972), p. 354.
31. Seligman, op. cit., p. 246.
32. ILWU full page ad in *New York Times,* March 13, 1972.
33. Joe Higgins, "The Struggle of the New York Printers," *Political Affairs,* August, 1974.
34. Interview with author in May, 1965.
35. Seligman, op. cit., p. 248.
36. "Some Words From the Docks," *Peoples World,* Nov. 30, 1974.

37. Higgins, op. cit.
38. Seligman, op. cit., p. 355.

CHAPTER 8

1. Barber, op. cit., pp. 188-9.
2. *Statistical Abstract*, 1974, p. 373.
3. *Statistical Abstract*, 1974, p. 227, and *Statistical Abstract*, 1939, p. 184.
4. Commerce Clearing House, State Tax Guide, June, 1975.
5. See Victor Perlo, *The Unstable Economy*, (International Publishers, N.Y., 1973), pp. 38-45.
6. *Statistical Abstract of the United States*, 1975, op. cit., pp. 548-9 and Barber, op. cit., pp. 133-7.
7. Benjamin Aaron, "Labor Relations Law," *Challenges to Collective Bargaining*, op. cit., p. 113.
8. Douglas V. Brown, "Legalisms in U.S. Industrial Relations," *Monthly Labor Review*, March, 1971.
9. *Handbook of Labor Statistics 1970*, U.S. Dept. of Labor, op. cit., pp. 361-2, and Douglass V. Brown, *Monthly Labor Review*, March, 1971, and *Labor Relations Year Book*, Washington, D.C., B.N.A., 1974.
10. Brown, op. cit.
11. George W. Brooks, "The Security of Worker Institutions," *Monthly Labor Review*, June, 1963.
12. Jack Barbash, *Labor's Grass Roots* (Harper & Bros., N.Y., 1961), p. 133.
13. James J. Matles and James Higgins, *Them and Us* (Prentice-Hall Inc., Englewood Cliffs, N.J.), 1974, p. 198.
14. Jack Barbash, op. cit. p. 133.
15. Brooks, op. cit.
16. Brooks, op. cit.
17. James Youngdahl, "An Exchange: Law and the Unions," *Autocracy and Insurgency in Organized Labor*, Burton Hall, Editor (Transaction Books, New Brunswick, N.J., 1972), p. 128.
18. Burton Hall, "Law, Democracy and the Unions," ibid., p. 111.
19. Ibid., p. 116.
20. McFarland, op. cit., p. 408.
21. Richard Hofstadter, *The American Political Tradition: And the Men Who Made It* (Alfred A. Knopf, New York, 1948), p. 338.


CHAPTER 9

1. Matthew Josephson, *Sidney Hillman, Statesman of American Labor* (Doubleday, N.Y., 1952).
2. Sidney Lens, *The Crisis of American Labor* (Sagamore Press, N.Y., 1959).
3. Selig Perlman, *The Theory of the Labor Movement*, first printing 1928 (August M. Kelley, N.Y., 1968), p. 156-8.
4. Jack Barbash, op. cit., p. 207.
5. Charles P. Larrowe, *Harry Bridges, The Rise and Fall of Radical Labor in the U.S.*, op. cit., pp. 117-18.
6. Ibid., p. 360.
7. Gus Tyler, *The Labor Revolution* (Viking Press, N.Y., 1967), pp. 4-5.
8. George Morris, *Rebellion in the Unions* (New Outlook Publs., N.Y., 1971), pp. 102-3, and UAW Administrative Letter, Feb. 8, 1967, p. 4.
9. *Colliers*, October 27, 1951.
10. William Serrin, *The Company and the Union* (Alfred Knopf, N.Y., 1973).

11. Ibid., p. 147.
12. Ibid., p. 148.
13. Ibid., p. 149.
14. Ibid., p. 151.
15. Ibid., p. 152.
16. Ibid., p. 150.
17. Saul Alinsky, *John L. Lewis, An Unauthorized Biography* (Putnam, N.Y., 1949).

CHAPTER 10

1. Brit Humes, *Death and the Mines: Rebellion and Murder in the UMW* (Grossman Publishers, N.Y., 1971), p. 16.
2. Ibid., pp. 43, 62.
3. Ibid., p. 44.
4. Ibid., p. 48.
5. Henry Spira, "Rebel Voices in the NMU," in *Autocracy and Insurgency in Organized Labor*, Burton Hall, Editor, (Transaction Books, New Brunswick, N.J., 1972), pp. 47-50.
6. *New York Times*, March 10, 1973.
7. Henry Spira, op. cit., p. 55.
8. James Morrissey, "Curran Dictatorship Under Fire," in *Autocracy and Insurgency in Organized Labor*, op. cit., p. 58.
9. Henry Spira, "Rule and Ruin in the NMU," in *Autocracy and Insurgency in Organized Labor*, ibid., pp. 65-66.
10. James Morrissey, op. cit., p. 55.
11. Herbert Hill, "The ILGWU Today: The Decay of a Labor Union," in *Autocracy and Insurgency in Organized Labor*, ibid., p. 152.
12. Dorothy Rabinowitz, "The Case of the ILGWU," in *The World of the Blue Collar Worker*, Irving Howe, Editor (Quadrangle Books, N.Y. 1972).
13. Jack Barbash, *Labor's Grass Roots* (Harper & Bros., N.Y., 1961), p. 27.
14. F.S. O'Brien, "The 'Communist Dominated' Unions in the United States Since 1950," *Labor History*, Spring 1968, pp. 190-1.
15. UAW Constitution, Article VI, Section 2, a.
16. Ibid., Article X, Section 8.
17. H.W. Benson, "Apathy and Other Axioms," in *The World of the Blue Collar Worker*, op. cit., p. 219.
18. Len De Caux, "UE: Democratic Unionism at Work," in *World Magazine*, April 27, 1974.
19. Charles P. Larrowe, op. cit., *Harry Bridges – The Rise and Fall of Radical Labor in the U.S.*, op. cit., pp. 380-81; also ILWU Constitution.

CHAPTER 11

1. See Ralph and Estelle James, *Hoffa and the Teamsters, A Study of Union Power* (D. Van Nostrand Co., Inc., Princeton, N.J., 1965).
2. I.L.A. Constitution.
3. United Steelworkers Constitution.
4. Charles Craypo, "The National Union Convention As an Internal Appeal Tribunal," *Industrial and Labor Relations Review*, July, 1969, p. 493.
5. Ibid., p. 506.
6. G.D.H. Cole, *An Introduction to Trade Unions* (Allen and Unwin, London, 1955) pp. 61-2.
7  James Matles, op. cit., p. 12.

8. Robert Tilove, "Pension, Health and Welfare Plans," in *Challenges to Collective Bargaining*, op. cit., pp. 56-57.
9. Gilbert Burck, *Fortune*, October, 1971.
10. Robert Tilove, op. cit., p. 56.

CHAPTER 12
1. Jack Barbash, op. cit., p. 189.
2. Ibid., p. 45.,
3. From Minutes of the General Executive Board, Hotel and Restaurant Employees and Bartenders International, Palm Springs, California, February 24-March 4, 1975. In *Catering Industry Employee*, June, 1975.
4. E. Robert Livernash, in *Trade Union Government and Collective Bargaining*, op. cit., p. 249.
5. Barbash, op. cit., p. 71.
6. Ibid., p. 119.

CHAPTER 13
1. John Galbraith, *The New Industrial Society*, op. cit., pp. 268, 278-9.
2. Richard A. Lester, *As Unions Mature* (Princeton Univ. Press, N.J., 1958), pp. 17, 26.
3. Milton R. Konvitz, "Labor Management, Labor Organization and Labor Establishment," in *Trade Union Government and Collective Bargaining* (Praeger Press, N.Y., 1970), p. 14.
4. Stanley Aronowitz, *False Promises* (McGraw-Hill, N.Y., 1973), p. 262.
5. Jack Barbash, *Labor's Grass Roots*, op. cit., p. 201.
6. Stanley H. Ruttenberg, "The Union Member Speaks," in *Blue-Collar Workers* (McGraw-Hill, N.Y., 1971), p. 157.
7. George Brooks, "The Security of Workers' Organizations," *Monthly Labor Review*, June, 1963.
8. H.W. Benson, "Apathy and Other Axioms," in *The World of the Blue-Collar Worker*, p. 217.
9. Aronowitz, op. cit., pp. 56-58.
10. Aronowitz, ibid., p. 255.
11. E. Wight Bakee, *Mutual Survival* (Archon Books, Hamden, Conn., 1966), pp. 6-8.
12. Ibid., pp. 6-8.
13. Ibid., pp. 87-88.
14. Ibid., pp. 16-17.
15. Selig Perlman, *The Theory of the Labor Movement*, 1928 (Augustus M. Kelley, N.Y., 1968 edition), p. 156.
16. Karl Marx, "Wage Labor and Capital," *Selected Works*, Vol. I (International Publishers, New York, 1936), pp. 336-7.
17. V.I. Lenin, "Guerilla Warfare," *Collected Works*, Vol. II (Foreign Languages Publishing House, Moscow, 1962), p. 221.
18. Karl Marx, "Value, Price and Profit," *Selected Works*, Vol. I (International Publishers, New York, 1936), p. 337.
19. Ibid., p. 337.
20. Aronowitz, op. cit., p. 441.

CHAPTER 14
1. Richard Barber, op. cit., p. 120; Andrew Hacker, *The End of the American Era* (Atheneum, N.Y., 1970), p. 75; Daniel Bell, *The Coming of the Post Industrial Society*

(Basic Books, N.Y., 1973); also Bell, "The Measurement of Knowledge and Technology," in *Indicators of Social Change*, (Russell Sage Foundation, N.Y., 1968), p. 159.

2. James R. Bright, "Automation and Wage Determination," *Industrial Relations: Challenges and Responses*, op. cit., pp. 23-46.
3. Derek C. Bok and John T. Dunlop, op. cit., p. 44.
4. William Z. Foster, *The Great Steel Strike and Its Lessons* (B.W. Huebsch, N.Y., 1920), p. 62.
5. *A Decade of Organizing – An Expanded Look at NLRB Elections*, Industrial Union Department, Research Section, AFL-CIO, Richard Prosten, Director, August, 1973.
6. Daniel Bell, in *Labor and Trade Unionism*, op. cit., p. 89.
7. Irving Bernstein, "The Growth of American Unions: 1945-60," *Labor History*, Spring, 1961.
8. Interview with Silvia Boba, International Department, Italian General Confederation of Labor (CGIL), Feb., 1973.
9. James J. Matles and James Higgins, *Them and Us – Struggles of a Rank-and-File Union* (Prentice-Hall, Englewood Cliffs, N.J., 1974), p. 71.
10. Irving Bernstein, op. cit.
11. *Statistical Abstract*, 1972, op. cit., p. 241; also National Directory of National Unions and Employees Assocs., 1973, Department of Labor, Washington, D.C., 1974.
12. *The Southern Patriot*, Sept., 1973.
13. Frank J. Donner, *UE News*, March 24, 1975.
14. *Southern Patriot*, Sept., 1973.
15. *Southern Patriot*, Nov., 1974.
16. William Z. Foster, *American Trade Unionism*, (International Publishers, New York, 1947), p. 36.
17 James J. Matles and James Higgins, op. cit., pp. 161-2.
18. Seymour Lipset, "The Political Process in Trade Unions — A Theoretical Statement," in *Labor and Trade Unionism*, op. cit., p. 232.

## CHAPTER 15

1. Speech before National Conference Industrial Board, January, 1958.
2. *Labor Today*, February, 1974.
3. *Daily World*, December 4, 1973.
4. Sanford Cohen, *Labor in the U.S.* (C.E. Merrill Books, Columbus, Ohio, 1960), pp. 449-50.
5. *New York Times*, October 2, 1968.
6. Vernon H. Jensen, op. cit., p. 387.
7. Ibid., p. 391; also *New York Times*, November 6, 1968.
8. Vernon H. Jensen, ibid., pp. 395, 400.
9 Henry Spira, "Rule and Ruin in the NMU," in *Autocracy and Insurgency in Organized Labor*, op. cit., p. 67.
10. Peter Mattiessen, op cit., p. 280.
11. Jack Barbash, in *Trade Union Government and Collective Bargaining*, op cit., p. 41.
12. Ibid., p. 52.
13. Phillip Taft, "Rank and File Unrest in Historic Perspective," in *Trade Union Government and Collective Bargaining*, ibid., p. 101.

## CHAPTER 16

1. Charles McCarry, *Citizen Nader* (Saturday Review Press, N.Y., 1972), p. 241.
2. Ibid., pp. 248-9.
3. Brit Humes, op. cit., p. 70.

4. *New York Times,* May 7, 1972.
5. Charles McCarry, op. cit., p. 255.
6. Ibid., p. 256.
7. *New York Times,* May 7, 1972.
8. Brit Humes, op. cit., p. 170.
9. Ibid., p. 174.
10. Ibid., p. 111.
11. Ibid., p. 112.
12. Ibid., pp. 122-24.
13. Ibid., p. 134.
14. Ibid., p. 138.
15. Art Shields, "The Miners Did It," *Political Affairs,* April, 1974.
16. Brit Humes, op. cit., p. 70.
17. *Labor Today,* November, 1972, and *New York Times,* May 29, 1972.
18. *Labor Today,* January, 1974.
19. *Daily World,* January, 29, 1972.
20. *Labor Today,* April, 1973.
21. Ibid.
22. *Labor Today,* January, 1975.
23. Ibid.
24. *Labor Today,* September, 1974.
25. *Daily World,* February 17, 1973.
26. *Labor Today,* April, 1973.

## CHAPTER 17

1. James J. Matles, *The Young Worker Challenges the Union Establishment,* pamphlet published by United Electrical Workers, N.Y.
2. *Detroit Free Press,* Aug. 20, 1970.
3. Bennett Kremen, "No Pride in this Dust," in *The World of the Blue Collar Worker,* op. cit., p. 17.
4. *1966 Convention Proceedings,* United Steel Workers of America.
5. *Aliquippa Steelworker,* August, 1967, quoted by Jack Barbash, "The Causes of Rank and File Unrest," in *Trade Union Government and Collective Bargaining,* op. cit.
6. Quoted by Bennett Kremen, op. cit., pp. 16-17.
7. Ibid., p. 20.
8. Vera C. Parrella, "Young Workers and their Earnings," in *Monthly Labor Review,* July, 1971.
9. Quoted by Kremen, op. cit., p. 21.
10. Ibid., p. 19.
11. Excerpts from young worker interviews, National Consultation on Young Worker Alienation, American Jewish Committee, Dec. 15, 1972.
12. Kremen, op. cit., p. 19.
13. Jack Barbash, op. cit., p. 48.
14. Ewan Clague, Balraj Palla and Leo Kramer, *The Aging Worker* (Praeger Publishers, N.Y., 1971), pp. 10-13.
15. Ibid., p. 14.
16. William K. Stevens, *New York Times,* March 19, 1975.
17. Ewan Clague, op. cit., p. 10 and *Handbook of Labor Statistics, 1974,* U.S. Department of Labor, p. 36.
18. Ibid., p. 17.
19. *The Multiple Hazards of Age and Race,* Survey of the Special Committee on Aging, U.S. Senate, Government Printing Office, 1971, p. 6.

20. Ralph Nader and Kate Blackwell, *You and Your Pension* (Grossman Publishers, N.Y., 1973), p. 16.
21. Ibid., p. 16.
22. Ibid., p. 21.
23. Hearings, Sub-Committee on Labor, U.S. Senate, 1968.
24. Ralph Nader, op. cit., p. 7.
26. Ibid., p. 9.
26. Ibid., p. 50.
27. Ibid., p. 3.
28. Edmund Faltermayer, "A Steeper Climb Up Pension Mountain," *Fortune*, Jan., 1975.
29. *New York Times*, Sept. 3, 1974.
30. Faltermayer, op. cit.
31. Ibid.
32. Ibid.


CHAPTER 18
1. Foner, op. cit., p. 395.
2. Ibid., pp. 398-9.
3. Ibid., p. 405.
4. Foster, op. cit., pp. 351-2.
5. James Allen, *Reconstruction–The Battle for Democracy* (International Publishers, New.York., 1937), pp. 163-4; also Foster, p. 352.
6. V. I. Lenin, *Imperialism, Collected Works*, Vol. 22 (Progress Publishers., Moscow, 1964), p. 283.
7. Martin Openheimer, "The Sub-Proletariat: Dark Skins and Dirty Work," *The Insurgent Sociologist*, Winter, 1974.
8. Victor Perlo, "Economic Conditions of Black Workers," *Political Affairs*, November, 1973.
9. *Dollars and Sense*, Nov., 1974.
10. Victor Perlo, *Economics of Racism* (International Publishers, New York, 1975) p. 53.
11. Richard Child Hill, "Unionization and Racial Income Inequality in the Metropolis," *American Sociological Review*, August, 1974.
12. Perlo, op. cit.
13. *Wall Street Journal*, March 5, 1974.
14. Herbert Hill, "Racism and Organized Labor," *New School Bulletin*, Feb. 8, 1971.
15. *Rank and File Report*, of the National Steelworkers Rank and File Committee, Nov.-Dec., 1973.
16. *Daily World*, April 18, 1974.
17. *Rank and File Report*, June, 1974.
18. *New York Times*, Jan. 29, 1975.
19. Ibid.
20. *Rank and File Report*, Nov.-Dec., 1973.
21. *New York Times*, Nov. 10, 1974.
22. *New York Times*, Feb. 11, 1973.
23. *New York Times*, June 24, 1973.
24. Herbert Hill, op. cit.
25. *Daily World*, July 27, 1974.
26. Thomas Dennis, *Political Affairs*, June, 1973.
27. Pat Walters, "Workers, Black and White in Mississippi," in *The World of the Blue Collar Worker*, op. cit., p. 38.

28. William Lucy, "The Black Partners," *The Nation*, Sept. 7, 1974.
29. Ibid.
30. *Daily World*, May 9, 1974.
31. Ibid.

CHAPTER 19

1. K. Marx and F. Engels, *Selected Correspondence* , op. cit., p. 255; also P. Foner, *History of the Labor Movement in the United States*, Vol. 1 (International Publishers, New York, 1947) p. 385.
2. Margie Albert, "Something New in the Womens' Movement," *New York Times*, Dec. 12, 1973.
3. *New York Times*, March 25, 1974.
4. *World Magazine*, Dec. 15, 1973.
5. BLS, *Handbook of Labor Statistics*.
6. Ibid.
7. Judith B. Agassi, "Women Who Work in Factories," in *The World of the Blue-Collar Worker*, op. cit., pp. 241-2.
8. Donald J. McNulty, "Differentials in Pay Between Men and Women Workers," *Monthly Labor Review*, Dec., 1967.
9. U.S. Congress, Joint Economic Committee, *Economic Problems of Women*, 93rd Congress, 1st session, July, 1973.
10. A. J. Jaffee and Joseph Froomkin, *Technology and Jobs–Automation in Perspective* (Praeger, N.Y., 1968), p. 103.
11. Ibid., p. 105.
12. BLS, *Handbook of Labor Statistics*
13. *New York Times*, July 29, 1973.
14. Helen H. Lamale, "Workers' Wealth and Family Living Standards," *Monthly Labor Review*, June, 1973.
15. Janice Neipert Hedges and Jeanne K. Barnett, "Working Women and the Division of Household Tasks," *Monthly Labor Review*, April, 1972.
16. From an unpublished paper of Arthur Kinoy, 1974.
17. Margaret I. Miller and Helene Linker, "Equal Rights Amendment Campaigns in California and Utah," *Society*, May-June, 1974.
18. Myra Wolfgang, "Young Women Who Work," An interview in *The World of the Blue-Collar Worker*, op. cit., pp. 28-29.
19. Margaret Miller and Helene Linker, op. cit.
20. *U.S. News & World Report*, Nov., 1972.
21. Directory of National Unions and Employees Associations, 1971, U.S. Dept. of Labor.
22. Virginia A. Bergquist, "Women's Participation in Labor Organizations," *Monthly Labor Review*, October, 1974.
23. *The Nation*, Feb. 23, 1974.

CHAPTER 20

1. Eugene Varga, *Politico-Economic Problems of Capitalism*, (Progress Publishers, Moscow, 1968), pp. 130-31.
2. Marx and Engels, *Selected Correspondence*, (International Publishers, N.Y. 1935), pp. 115-16.
3. Ibid., p. 399.
4. Varga, op. cit., p. 134.
5. Quoted by Robert A. Brady, *Organization, Automation and Society*, (Univ. of Calif. Press, Berkeley, 1963), pp. 39-40.

6. Kassalow, op. cit., pp. 130, 133.
7. Ibid., p. 133.
8. *Handbook of Labor Statistics,* 1974, U.S. Dept. of Labor, p. 289.
9. Kassalow, op. cit., p. 243.
10. "Worldwide Developments in Social Security, 1967-69," *Monthly Labor Review,* October, 1970.
11. Janet L. Norwood, "Wages in Japan and the United States," *Monthly Labor Review,* April, 1967.
12. *Statistical Abstract,* 1972, op. cit., p. 812.
13. *Handbook of Labor Statistics,* 1974, p. 416.
14. Wolfgang Abendroth, *A Short History of the European Working Class* (Monthly Review Press, N.Y., 1972), pp. 185, 194-5.
15. *Labour Legislation in the USSR* (Novosti Press, Moscow, 1972), pp. 42, 77, 78, 85.
16. Hisashi Kawada and Ryuji Komatsu, "Post War Labor Developments in Japan," in *The International Labor Movement in Transition,* edited by Adolph Sturmthal and James G. Scoville (Univ. of Illinois Press, Chicago, 1973), pp. 125-36.
17. Peter Losche, "Stages in the Evolution of the German Labor Movement," in *The International Labor Movement in Transition,* ibid., pp. 113-16.
18. Frederick Engels in *Selected Correspondence of Marx and Engels,* op. cit., p. 336.
19. Quoted by Daniel L. Horowitz, *The Italian Labor Movement* (Harvard Univ. Press, Cambridge, Mass., 1963).
20. *The Trade Union Situation in the USSR,* Report of a Mission of the International Labor Office, Geneva, Switzerland, 1960, p. 80.
21. Ibid., p. 72.
22. Ibid., p. 78.
23. Charles Lipton, "Canadian Unionism," in *Capitalism and the National Question in Canada,* edited by Gary Teeple (Univ. of Toronto Press, Toronto and Buffalo, 1972), p. 110.
24. Ibid., p. 110.
25. Ibid., p. 111.
26. Based on figures in *Statistical Abstract* 1975, pp. 729, 831.
27. Richard J. Lidin, *San Juan Star,* March 30, 1975.
28. Ibid.
29. Ibid.


CHAPTER 21
1. Harold L. Wilensky, "Class, Class Consciousness and American Workers," in *Labor in a Changing America,* edited by William Haber (Basic Books, N.Y., 1966), p. 17.
2. Ibid., p. 19.
3. F. Zweig, *The Worker in an Affluent Society* (Free Press of Glencoe, N.Y., 1961), p. 135.
4. Stephan Thernstrom, "Class and Mobility in a 19th Century City," in Reinhard Bendix and S. M. Lipset, Editors, *Class, Status and Power,* 2nd Edition, N.Y., (Free Press of Glencoe, N.Y., 1966), pp. 602-15.
5. Selig Perlman, op. cit., p. 242.
6. Ibid., pp. 7-8, p. 246.
7. Kassalow, op. cit., p. 85.
8. Ibid., p. 85.
9. Perlman, op. cit., pp. 163-65.
10. Ibid., p. 211.
11. Michael Harrington, "Old Working Class, New Working Class," in *The World of the*

   *Blue-Collar Worker,* op. cit., pp. 152-3.
12. Norman Birnbaum, *The Crisis of Industrial Society* (Oxford University Press, N.Y., 1969), pp. 66-68.
13. F. Zweig, op. cit., p. 206.
14. Wilensky, op. cit., p. 40.
15. Ibid., pp. 36-37.
16. *Statistical Abstract,* 1975, p. 520.
17. Joseph Bensman and Bernard Rosenberg, "Mass Media and Mass Culture," in *America As a Mass Society* (Free Press of Glencoe, N.Y., 1963), p. 171.
18. Ibid., pp. 170-71.
19. *Statistical Abstract,* 1975, op. cit., p. 521.

## CHAPTER 22
 1. *New York Times,* Feb. 16, 1975.
 2. *Labor Today,* July-August, 1972.
 3. *Labor Today,* May, 1975.
 4. *Labor Today,* Jan., 1974.
 5. Ernest DeMaio, "A Program to Put America Back to Work," *Labor Today,* September, 1975.
 6. *Labor Today,* Sept., 1974.
 7. Harry Bridges, *The Dispatcher,* Jan., 1974.
 8. *Labor Today,* May, 1975.
 9. *Labor Today,* Dec., 1974.
10. Eric Jacobs, *European Trade Unionism* (Holmes & Meier Publishers, Inc., N.Y., 1973), p. 50.
11. Carl Farris, op. cit.

# ABBREVIATIONS

| | |
|---|---|
| ACW | Amalgamated Clothing Workers |
| AFL | American Federation of Labor |
| AFL-CIO | American Federation of Labor and Congress of Industrial Organizations |
| AFSCME | American Federation of State, County and Municipal Employees |
| ALA | Alliance for Labor Action |
| ALP | American Labor Party of New York |
| AMCU | Amalgamated Meat Cutters |
| BLA | Black Lung Association |
| BLS | Bureau of Labor Statistics |
| CBTU | Coalition of Black Trade Unionists |
| CGIL | Italian General Confederation of Labor |
| CGT | General Confederation of Labor, France |
| CIO | Congress of Industrial Organizations |
| CLUW | Coalition of Labor Union Women |
| COLA | Cost of Living Adjustment |
| CNTU | Confederation of National Trade Unions, Canadian |
| CUT | United Confederation of Labor, Chile |
| DWU | Distributive Workers, Independent |
| ERA | Equal Rights Amendment |
| FGE | Federation of Government Employees |
| HM & RE | Hotel, Motel and Restaurant Employees |
| IA of M | International Association of Machinists |
| IB of B | International Brotherhood of Boilermakers |
| IB of P | International Brotherhood of Painters |
| IBT | International Brotherhood of Teamsters |
| ICFTU | International Confederation of Free Trade Unions |
| ILA | International Longshoremen's Association, AFL-CIO |
| ILGWU | International Ladies Garment Workers Union |
| ILWU | International Longshoremen's and Warehousemen's Union, Independent |
| IMF | International Metalworkers Federation |

| | |
|---|---|
| ITU | International Typographical Union |
| IUE | International Union of Electrical Workers |
| IWW | Industrial Workers of the World |
| LNPL | Labor's Non-Partisan League |
| MFD | Miners for Democracy |
| NAACP | National Association for the Advancement of Colored People |
| NALC | Negro American Labor Committee |
| NCLU | National Colored Labor Union |
| NHU | National Union of Hospital and Health Care Employees, also known as 1199 |
| NLRB | National Labor Relations Board |
| NLU | National Labor Union |
| NMU | National Maritime Union |
| PAC | Political Action Committees |
| PUSH | People United To Save Humanity |
| RAFT | Rank and File Team, Steelworkers Union |
| RWDSU | Retail, Wholesale and Department Store Union |
| SACB | Subversive Activities Control Board |
| SEU | Service Employees Union |
| SIU | Seamen's International Union |
| SUB | Supplementary Unemployment Benefits |
| SRFC | Steelworkers National Rank and File Caucus |
| TUAD | Trade Union Action and Democracy |
| TUEL | Trade Union Educational League |
| TUUL | Trade Union Unity League |
| UAW | United Auto Workers |
| UE | United Electrical Workers, Independent |
| UFT | United Federation of Teachers |
| UFW | United Farm Workers |
| UMWA | United Mine Workers of America |
| USA | United Steelworkers of America |
| USW | United Shoe Workers |
| UTWA | United Textile Workers of America |
| WFTU | World Federation of Trade Unions |

# INDEX

## OTHER BOOKS BY GIL GREEN

The Enemy Forgotten (1956)

Revolution Cuban Style (1970)

The New Radicalism (1971)

Portugal's Revolution (1976)